AF778817

PUNISHMENT

in Australian Society

Other titles in the Australian Retrospectives series

Daryl Adair and Wray Vamplew
Sport in Australian History

Philip Bell
Implicated: The United States in Australia

Graeme Davison
The Unforgiving Minute: How Australia learned to tell the time

James Jupp
Immigration

Beverley Kingston
Basket, Bag and Trolley: A history of shopping in Australia

Andrew Moore
The Right Road? A history of right-wing politics in Australia

Graeme Osborne and Glen Lewis
Communication Traditions in 20th-century Australia

Roger C. Thompson
Religion in Australia: A history

AUSTRALIAN RETROSPECTIVES

PUNISHMENT

in Australian Society

Mark Finnane

Melbourne

OXFORD UNIVERSITY PRESS

Oxford Auckland New York

OXFORD UNIVERSITY PRESS AUSTRALIA

Oxford New York
Athens Auckland Bangkok Bombay
Calcutta Cape Town Dar es Salaam Delhi
Florence Hong Kong Istanbul Karachi
Kuala Lumpur Madras Madrid Melbourne
Mexico City Nairobi Paris Port Moresby
Singapore Taipei Tokyo Toronto

and associated companies in
Berlin Ibadan

OXFORD is a trade mark of Oxford University Press

© Mark Finnane 1997
First published 1997

This book is copyright. Apart from any fair dealing for the purposes of private study, research, criticism or review as permitted under the Copyright Act, no part may be reproduced, stored in a retrieval system, or transmitted, in any form or by any means, electronic, mechanical, photocopying, recording or otherwise, without prior written permission. Enquiries to be made to Oxford University Press.

Copying for educational purposes
Where copies of part or the whole of the book are made under Part VB of the Copyright Act, the law requires that prescribed procedures be followed. For information, contact the Copyright Agency Limited.

National Library of Australia
Cataloguing-in-Publication data:

Finnane, Mark
Punishment in Australian society.

Bibliography.
ISBN 0 19 553732 7.

1. Punishment — Australia — History. 2. Correctional institutions — Australia. 3. Criminal justice, Administration of — Australia. 4. Criminology — Australia — Social aspects. I. Title. (Series: Australian retrospectives).

364.994

Edited by Lucy Davison
Text design by Steve Randles
Cover design by Anitra Blackford
Cover photograph supplied by International Photographic Library
Typeset by Desktop Concepts P/L, Melbourne
Printed through Bookpac Production Services, Singapore
Published by Oxford University Press,
253 Normanby Road, South Melbourne, Australia

Series Foreword

In this series we have invited authors to examine formative issues in our national history in a style accessible to non-specialists. A number of authors have responded enthusiastically to this project, welcoming the opportunity it provides to address major questions in a brisk and intelligently speculative manner. No book in this series is designed to be the last word on its subject. By treating major themes over an extended period, Australian Retrospectives brings a historical perspective to bear on matters of vital concern to Australians in the 1990s. James Jupp's study of immigration proved an excellent starting point. Immigration has been at or near the centre of Australia's white history for two hundred years. There followed Roger and Phillip Bell's *Implicated: The US in Australia*, Graeme Davison's *The Unforgiving Minute*, Beverley Kingston's *Basket, Bag and Trolley*, Roger C. Thompson's *Religion in Australia*, Andrew Moore's *The Right Road?* and Graeme Osborne and Glen Lewis's *Communication Traditions* in *20th Century Australia*, and Daryl Adair and Wray Vampley's *Sport in Australian History*.

In the latest book in the series, Mark Finnane provides a new reading of the role of crime and punishment in Australian history. He offers a lucid review of the convict period and the historiographical debates it has generated, but goes on to argue that an obsession with the convicts has produced an unbalanced history. Since crime and its management have continued throughout our history, it is time to develop a new historiography for post-convict Australia. In mapping this new territory, Finnane combines a sophisticated grasp of theory with a detailed knowledge of the empirical base of his study, its archival sources, and research possibilities.

Australian Retrospectives is an important publishing initiative. We have a talented pool of authors to draw from and a nation of readers demanding intellectual nourishment. We hope to honour their intelligent interest in Australia at a time when the nation is calling for new ideas and new ways of communicating them.

David Walker
Centre for Australian Studies
Deakin University

For Ingrid, Anna and Julia

Contents

Acknowledgments

This book is the outcome of a number of years of academic as well as more practical involvement in the study and organisation of punishment. More than a decade ago, a Brisbane lawyer, Tony Woodyatt, brought to fruition a long period of planning for the establishment of an unusual community legal service: a service specifically for prisoners. The foundation of the Prisoners Legal Service (Qld) Inc. entailed the organisation of a management committee, on which I was fortunate to serve for a number of years, learning more than I could in any library about some of the realities faced by prisoners. My first debt, then, is to Tony and to the other practitioners and community workers associated with this organisation, which remains Australia's only independent community legal service for prisoners.

Research for this book has been facilitated by two Australian Research Council small grants (1991–93), as well as by the Faculty of Humanities at Griffith University (1993–96). Christina Scott did the major work of gathering official materials, including annual reports, parliamentary papers, and media data. Deborah Edwards in Sydney, Andrew Gill in Perth, and Iris Petrass in Melbourne have all assisted in archival research in those places. Other assistance has been contributed by Bronwyn Hammond, Margaret De Nooyer, Pamela Murray, and Ros Kidd. I have benefited enormously from the professional contributions of all these people. As this range of assistance will suggest, a good deal of data-collection lies behind the brief treatment of the subject offered in this book, and further articles of a more detailed kind are planned. The intellectual debts of this work are recorded in the footnotes, but I have especially valued over recent years the stimulus provide by historical work on Australia, New Zealand, and Canada by Stephen Garton, John Pratt, and Carolyn Strange, as well as many discussions with David Moore on some of the conflicts involved in changing criminal justice systems. Regrettably the writing of this book concluded before the publication of John Ramsland's official history of corrective services in New South Wales.

Once again I have to thank Oxford University Press and Jill Lane for their commitment to publishing this work, and David Walker for its inclusion in the Australian Retrospectives Series. Lucy Davison at Oxford has been an expert editor, refining my prose and checking my referencing. At Griffith University, Margaret De Nooyer has been an indispensable assistant in the final stages of writing, proofing, and indexing. The responsibility for what appears here of course remains mine.

Harper Collins Publishers have kindly granted permission to reprint an extract from Les Newcombe's *Inside Out* (Angus & Robertson, Sydney, 1979, pp. 69–70). An extract from the Royal Commission into Aboriginal Deaths in Custody, *Report of the Inquiry into the Death of the Young Man who Died at Wujal Wujal on 29 March 1987* (AGPS, Canberra, 1991, sec. 1.8) is reproduced with the permission of the Commonwealth of Australia.

A period of study leave granted by the University and the patience of my family has made possible the completion of this book. I thank Maureen once again for her generous support for my work, and I dedicate the book to our children — Ingrid, Anna, and Julia —who are growing up in a time of revived fervour for imprisonment. I hope this book helps to foster an understanding of the complex history of the subject and, most importantly, helps to build an informed debate in Australia about the choices that must always be made about punishment.

Mark Finnane
Brisbane
March 1997

INTRODUCTION

European settlement in Australia began with the convicts, and that experience has dominated conceptions of the Australian past and images of Australian identity. Yet punishment did not disappear 'after the convicts' but developed along new lines, only tangentially related to the experiences of transportation. As in so much of Australian history, a question remains: how did the gold rushes and the great mid-century free migrations, which coincided with colonial self-government, affect colonial institutions, culture, and social relations? The object of this book is to turn attention away from the seemingly inexhaustible vein of convict history to the little-explored later history of punishment.

Botany Bay, as Jeremy Bentham highlighted in a famous pamphlet in 1802, was an experiment in punishment that, almost from its beginning, had to contend with the imagined benefits of a new kind of prison.[1] The cessation of transportation to Australia was only secured once the penitentiary had been put in place. From the 1830s, the future of punishment in the colonies, as elsewhere, seemed to lie in the promise of reform through the prison. As colonial self-government developed, so did its institutions. Among these were the prisons, gaols, and police lock-ups. Especially in New South Wales and Victoria, there was an enormous investment in a carceral archipelago, some of whose buildings remain standing and in use. Not many material traces of the convict penal system survived a process of forgetting, as colonists sought to distance themselves from a shameful past. In the imagination, however, the convict past was more immanent, and was possibly influential in shaping some choices about punishment.

1 J. B. Hirst, *Convict Society and its Enemies: A History of Early New South Wales*, Allen & Unwin, Sydney, 1983, ch. 1.

The story of punishment after the convict period is part of a history of transformation that is international in its dimensions. Part of the interest of this story is the very active debates over penal policy and prison practice that have been evident through the generations since 1850. Just as it has been shown recently that the lessons of Botany Bay were vital in French debates over the choice between the prison and transportation,[2] so in Australia, there was a dialogue with expertise abroad, not just at 'Home' in Great Britain and Ireland, but in France, Italy, and the USA especially. There is a local story to tell about punishment, but the prison and other penalties of modern punishment are also part of a self-conscious international movement in the government of populations and social groups. We cannot write the history of punishment while remaining ignorant of practice and innovation internationally; but neither should we presume that policy and practice elsewhere are the only guides to the realities of national and more local stories.

In this context, the story of punishment in Australia as a settler society has a particular poignancy. The original dispossession of the indigenous people of this country was caused by a penal experiment: colonisation through the exile of convicted criminals. Institutions of punishment did not, however, discontinue their role in dispossession at that point. As the most intensive inquiry in Australian history into the contexts and functions of punishment, the Royal Commission into Aboriginal Deaths in Custody was more than an ironic commentary on the bicentenary of settlement: it was also a lesson on the cultural meanings and functions of punishment. The subsequent difficulties experienced in implementing its recommendations are a lesson in the limits and failures of punishment as a response to offending in its many guises. The history of punishment as part of a history of dispossession is but one of the justifications for this book, but an important one given the national and international dimensions of the current situation with regard to the imprisonment of Aborigines and Torres Strait Islanders.[3]

2 C. Forster, *France and Botany Bay*, Melbourne University Press, Melbourne, 1996.

3 See C. Cunneen & D. McDonald, *Keeping Aboriginal and Torres Strait Islander People out of Custody: An Evaluation of the Implementation of the Recommendations of the Royal Commission in Aboriginal Deaths in Custody*, Aboriginal and Torres Strait Islander Commission, Canberra, 1997; R. Harding, R. Broadhurst, A. Ferrante, & N. Loh, *Aboriginal Contact with the Criminal Justice System and the Impact of the Royal Commission into Aboriginal Deaths in Custody*, The Hawkins Press, Sydney, 1995; J. Purdy, 'Postcolonialism: The Emperor's New Clothes', *Social and Legal Studies*, vol. 5, no. 3, 1996, pp. 405–26.

A further objective is to highlight the differentiations within punishment, especially in the development of prisons and other forms of custody. Such differentiation is part of the story of changing penal strategies over time, evident in the design and custodial practice of reformatories for women, and for juveniles. More is known at this stage about the incarceration of juveniles than of women, whose custody was little examined between the 1830s and the 1980s. The writing of a comprehensive history of punishment would, of course, go beyond the formal institutions of State custody to look at a variety of other practices. The history of changing attitudes to corporal punishment offers such possibilities. It is an archetypal instance of the differentiation of punishment, of the tendency to divide the means and objects of punishing in ways that speak of deep cultural and emotional anxieties, inhibitions, and desires.

It goes without saying that the history of punishment is a profoundly political business. The story is one of political choices from beginning to end, whether in the decision to found a penal settlement, to execute a death sentence, to remit prisoners' sentences for good behaviour, or to prohibit imprisonment for the offence of public drunkenness. But it is also political at another level: in the organisation of resistance within a prison to abusive authority, or in the organisation outside a prison of a movement to reform the objectives and institutions of custody. Through studying the political history of punishment, we understand both the possibilities and the limits of change in prisons and the criminal-justice system.[4]

This is a short book, covering episodes and practices in a number of jurisdictions and over a long period of time. It does not pretend to be comprehensive, but rather aims to stimulate further inquiry and, especially, to inform contemporary debates on punishment with some historical perspective. Its focus is above all on the prison, but it begins and ends with different kinds of penalty: exile through transportation at one end; the aspirations of 'community justice' at the other. As part of a perennial discourse about punishment, it does not seek to stand outside and judge social institutions that are offensive to some, or most, of us at some time or other. Rather, it aims to encourage inquiry and debate about why we choose to punish, what we get out of it, and what

4 For an excellent discussion of the politics of justice, see C. Strange, 'Introduction', in Strange (ed.), *Qualities of Mercy: Justice, Punishment and Discretion*, UBC Press, Vancouver, 1996.

limits we seek to place on punishment. In this task the presumption of this book is that the choices we make, the satisfaction we get, and the limits we desire are not ones that we are wholly in control of, since we are the products of histories that we understand only partially.

1

BEFORE THE PENITENTIARY

Australians do not need to be reminded that their nation-state's origins were an experiment in punishment. Before the penitentiary there was transportation, and depending on one's perspective, Botany Bay was either the apotheosis of transportation or a lesson on what to avoid. New South Wales might easily have foundered as a settlement during its first couple of decades; attempts to establish penal settlements were usually hazardous operations, with relatively short lives. The relative success of the penal-colony experiment in Australia helps to explain Australian historians' preoccupation with this early history of the uses of punishment — a history that is of international significance. No history of punishment in Australia after the convict era can proceed without acknowledging the significance of this experiment in penal systems.

Something of this subject's importance as a national story can be learnt if we compare the sustained attention it has received in Australia with the treatment of convicts in North American historiography. Before Botany Bay there had been more than half a century of transatlantic trade in convicts from the British Isles to the American colonies.[1] The trade was a substantial one — perhaps totalling some 50 000 transports from 1718 to 1775. Its significance as a penalty in the justice systems of England and Ireland (it was less used in Scotland) was notable. At mid-century some three-quarters of non-capital convictions in England resulted in transportation, declining somewhat over the decade prior to the outbreak of the American rebellion.[2]

1 The subject has been of only minor significance in American historiography, the best study being A. R. Ekirch, *Bound for America: The Transportation of British Convicts to the Colonies, 1718–1775*, Clarendon Press, Oxford, 1987.

2 Ekirch, *Bound for America*, ch. 1; J. Beattie, *Crime and the Courts in England 1660–1800*, Clarendon Press, Oxford, 1986, p. 548.

Punishment in the American colonies was primarily organised through the indenture of transported convicts to private masters. In some areas, convicts provided the foundations of the colonial workforce. Transportation to the American colonies was privatised from beginning to end: merchants tendered for the right to transport a human cargo of convicts to their new stations in the colonies. There they marketed the use of convict labour to private masters. 'In short', notes Roger Ekirch, 'commercial, not penal, priorities guided the flow of convicts to America. Government authorities, wedded as they were to the immediate task of expelling criminals from British shores, happily granted merchants free rein over other phases of transportation'.[3] Although there is substantial evidence that it was difficult to secure the loyalties of such compulsory servants (for instance, the absconding of convicts, sometimes to return across the Atlantic to the United Kingdom, was widespread), Ekirch concludes that the behaviour of the convicts, once landed, was considerably better than colonial fears of their criminal pasts might have suggested. A new land and new social conditions, combined perhaps with less opportunity for crime (in the non-urban settings in which many convicts found themselves), produced the kind of rehabilitation that was also to be experienced in Australia.[4]

In spite of the interest of this story, American historians (other than the specialists) tend to ignore it. Hence, notwithstanding its broad sweep and depth of research, Lawrence Friedman's recent general history of *Crime and Punishment in American History* (1993) contains not a single reference to the fact that colonial America was also a dumping ground for convicts.[5] Transportation appears, therefore, to be less a part of the USA's national history than it is an excrescence of its colonial pre-history — one that belongs more to the history of Great Britain and Ireland than of post-Revolutionary America.

By contrast, transportation has been a major theme of Australian history since the 1920s.[6] Once considered a deservedly forgotten period of colonial history — the memories of which, if stirred, would revive the 'con-

3 Ekirch, *Bound for America*, p. 119.

4 Ekirch, esp. ch. 6.

5 L. M. Friedman, *Crime and Punishment in American History*, Basic Books, New York, 1993.

6 For the historiography, see S. Garton, 'The Convict Origins Debate: Historians and the Problem of the "Criminal Class"', *Australian and New Zealand Journal of Criminology*, vol. 24, no. 2, 1991, pp. 66–82; and B. Dyster, 'Convicts', *Labour History*, no. 67, November 1994, pp. 74–83.

vict taint' — the subject developed into a central preoccupation. The dominant questions, however, have been strongly informed not as much by considerations in the history of punishment as by issues of national identity and moral worth.

One stream considers the question 'Who were the convicts?' and delivers answers that are informed by varying degrees of theoretical, methodological, and political rigour. For some, such as George Arnold Wood in the 1920s, the convicts were essentially victims of a harsh social order who prospered as a result of the better opportunities afforded by the new colonies.[7] For others, such as Manning Clark and Lloyd Robson in the 1950s, who counted samples of the convict shipping indents, they were offenders whose criminal behaviour flourished in the slums of Great Britain and the rural chaos of Ireland.[8] Robson notes that the causes of crime were complex, while nevertheless drawing attention to the phenomena of repeat offenders whose criminal behaviour was encouraged by the concentrations of poverty in the major cities of the British Isles; transported to a different environment, their behaviour tended to improve.[9] Women convicts were poorly regarded in this revisionist literature, with Robson in particular concluding that, at best, they 'were an indifferent batch of settlers', while drawing attention to the views of contemporaries on their moral degradation and rebelliousness.[10] It was a judgment that persisted, even after being turned on its head by Anne Summers in her iconoclastic feminist history *Damned Whores and God's Police*.[11] From a different angle, most commentators sought to recognise the particularity of the 'political prisoners',

7 G. A. Wood, 'Convicts', *Journal of the Royal Australian Historical Society*, vol. 8, no. 4, 1922, pp. 177–208.

8 C. M. H. Clark, 'The Origins of the Convicts Transported to Eastern Australia, 1787–1852', *Historical Studies*, Part 1, vol. 7, no. 26, May 1956, pp. 121–35; Part 2, vol. 7, no. 27, November 1956, pp. 315–27; L. Robson, *The Convict Settlers of Australia: An Enquiry into the Origin and Character of the Convicts Transported to New South Wales and Van Diemen's Land 1787–1852*, Melbourne University Press, Melbourne, 1965.

9 Robson, *Convict Settlers*, pp. 51, 157.

10 Robson, *Convict Settlers*, pp. 85, 76–7.

11 A. Summers, *Damned Whores and God's Police: The Colonization of Women in Australia*, Penguin Books, Melbourne, 1975. On the image of women convicts in Summers's and later texts, see the critiques in M. Sturma, 'Eye of the Beholder: The Stereotype of Women Convicts, 1788–1852', *Labour History*, no. 34, May 1978, pp. 3–10; D. Oxley, 'Gendered Images and Realities', *Australian and New Zealand Journal of Criminology*, vol. 24, no. 2, July 1991, pp. 83–98; Oxley, *Convict Maids: The Forced Migration of Women to Australia*, Cambridge University Press, Melbourne, 1996, ch. 8; and S. Garton, 'The Convict Origins Debate', pp. 73–4.

especially the Irish after 1798 and the agricultural labourers who participated in the Swing riots of the 1820s and 1830s. Most notably, George Rudé idealises this history, developing the distinction that he and Eric Hobsbawm draw between political protest and ordinary crime.[12]

The character of the convicts was one preoccupation. What role they played in the establishment of a new society was another. This has been the more influential theme of recent years, during which a number of important studies have emerged. In *Convict Society and its Enemies*, John Hirst argues that transportation was more a means of forging a new settler society than it was simply a senseless and repressive form of punishment. Critics — free settlers and emancipists in the colonies and, in Great Britain and Ireland lobbyists who advocated the penitentiary or opposed slavery — brought the system to an end, either because it conflicted with their desire for a free society or failed to match their expectations of a penal system.[13] Other historians have outlined the way in which convicts were active participants in the legal and social relations that characterised this colonial society — notably the peculiar conditions of a penal colony conditioned access of convicts to legal and property rights that they certainly did not possess in the United Kingdom, or later in prisons.[14]

If convicts possessed an unusual degree of access to the courts, they also laboured in ways that would be unknown to those later sentenced to terms of penal servitude. In *Convict Workers*, Stephen Nicholas and his colleagues tackle the 'convict origins' and the 'convict society' debates to suggest that the convicts were primarily workers, both in their social origin and their contribution to the foundation of a new society.[15] Developing a similar methodology to discuss transported women, Deborah Oxley has also described their contribution as workers, but with a gendered inflection. Mirroring

12 G. Rudé, *Protest and Punishment: The Story of the Social and Political Protesters Transported to Australia, 1788–1868*, Clarendon Press, Oxford, 1978; E. J. Hobsbawm & G. Rudé, *Captain Swing*, Lawrence & Wishart, London, 1969.

13 Hirst, *Convict Society and its Enemies*. See also the debate between Hirst and D. J. Neal in Neal, 'Free Society, Penal Colony, Slave Society, Prison?' *Historical Studies*, no. 89, October 1987, pp. 497–518, and Hirst, 'Or None of the Above: A Reply', *Historical Studies*, no. 89, October 1987, pp. 519–24.

14 D. J. Neal, *The Rule of Law in a Penal Colony: Law and Power in Early New South Wales*, Cambridge University Press, Melbourne, 1991; P. J. Byrne, *Criminal Law and Colonial Subject: New South Wales, 1810–1830*, Cambridge University Press, Melbourne, 1993; B. Kercher, *An Unruly Child: A History of Law in Australia*, Allen & Unwin, Sydney, 1995.

15 S. Nicholas (ed.), *Convict Workers: Re-interpreting Australia's Past*, Cambridge University Press, Melbourne, 1988.

Ekirch's approach to the American transportees, these historians seek to characterise transportation as an experience of compulsory migration — indeed, Oxley's sub-title is *The Forced Migration of Women to Australia.*[16] These historians imply that the random selectivity of the criminal-justice system should not be allowed to disguise the fact that this historical phenomenon shared a major characteristic with the international political economy of the eighteenth and nineteenth centuries: large scale migration of labour and populations. This does not mean that their account ignores the ways in which transportation was also punishment. Indeed, they discuss the possible economic functionality of particular types of punishment, such as flogging, which they suggest varied in use according to factors of both input (labour skill) and output (product refinement).[17] We will return to flogging and its role in punishment in Chapter 4.

Hence historians have paid substantial attention to the history of transportation in Australia, though not always in the way that someone approaching the subject from the point of view of the history of punishment would. The particularity of this perspective is indicative of a more general theme in recent debates about punishment. David Garland has emphasised the significance of punishment as an element of cultural history: one cannot understand punishment and its evolution without understanding changing sensibilities; and one cannot understand a culture without taking account of the role of punishment in its social order and formation.[18] This approach suggests that the stories we tell about punishment, the ones available to a particular culture, have a role to play in distinguishing the elements of that culture — the things that influence the formation of individuals and institutions.

If both approaches are valid, then the particular preoccupation of Australian writers and historians with the convict origins of their settler society has its point, shaping and reshaping matters of national identity at the same time as it influences debates about particular forms of punishment. Did the rapid decline in the use of corporal punishment in Australian

16 Compare Ekirch's assertion that, 'Next to African slaves, [transported felons] constituted the largest body of immigrants ever compelled to go to America' (*Bound for America*, p. 2); Oxley, *Convict Maids*.

17 See R. Evans & W. Thorpe, 'Power, Punishment and Penal Labour: Convict Workers and Moreton Bay', *Australian Historical Studies*, no. 98, 1992, pp. 90–111, which argues that the quantitative method of *Convict Workers* fails to account for the documentary evidence of systemic abuse of power in some places, such as Moreton Bay.

18 D. Garland, *Punishment and Modern Society*, Clarendon Press, Oxford, 1990, chs 9, 11.

penality in the late nineteenth century spring from a desire to avoid association with what had become an emblem of the convict past? Possibly so. In any case, in reviewing the history of transportation to Australia as punishment, one has to keep in mind the constant relation of this theme to other dimensions of a national history.

One of those other dimensions, very importantly, is the matter of the colonies' place in the Empire — a place that was, at once, dependent and initiating. The efficacy of transportation, the modes of administering convicts in a new settler society, the sharp light that colonial experience often threw on rationales for punishment — all these factors played an active role in reshaping the conditions of punishment in Great Britain, Ireland, and beyond. For the experience of establishing an Australian penal colony, and the interpretation of this experience, also played a crucial role in debates about punishment in Europe, and especially in France, which debated the efficacy of penal colonies as a solution to the crime problem for many decades before embarking on a late experiment of its own.[19] Botany Bay was an experiment, and was debated as such for over half a century. Did it justify the claims of the defenders of transportation or did its history add to the case for the penitentiary? The answers to that question affected the subsequent history of punishment not only in Australia, but in many other countries as well.

TRANSPORTATION AS PENALTY

If we examine the availability of transportation as a penalty in British (and Irish) criminal justice, we will see that the incidence of its use went through a series of rises and falls between the British *Transportation Act* of 1718 and the effective cessation of transportation in the later nineteenth century, first in Western Australia in 1868 and then in Gibraltar in 1875. Transportation to the American colonies became the standard sentence for non-capital or remitted capital offences by the middle of the eighteenth century. But prior to the cessation of transportation to America in 1775, there was already a decline in its use. John Beattie suggests that this decline was a result of policy. As was the case in Australia fifty years later, governments and the judiciary were concerned that transportation was less a

19 See Forster, *France and Botany Bay*; and P. O'Brien, *The Promise of Punishment*, Princeton University Press, Princeton, NJ, 1982 on the French penal colonies in New Caledonia and French Guiana.

punishment than an opportunity for those so sentenced. The contradiction at the heart of a system that transported criminals to a colony was that, in the end, their punishment became a means for the convicts to establish themselves in a new life, their passage having been afforded by the government and sentencing authorities.

Beattie's study of sentencing in Surrey shows the very significant impact of transportation as an option from the 1720s to the middle of the century. For non-capital felonies, it became the preferred mode of punishment. In addition, it had become an important means of administering mercy, with about a third of death sentences being commuted by pardon and subsequent transportation after the 1720s. But its uses varied in accordance with the broader context of sentencing decisions, such as the state of the country — whether it was at peace or at war. Its unavailability in Surrey for a decade after 1775 corresponded with an increased use of hanging.[20]

The establishment of a penal colony at Botany Bay enabled the revival of transportation as a penalty. During the heyday of transportation to New South Wales, from 1811 to 1836, transportation was the sentence in more than a third of all cases being tried at assizes and sessions courts in England. By the 1840s, by which time transportation to New South Wales had ceased and most were landed in Van Diemen's Land, the sentence accounted for only about one in five penalties awarded to those convicted.

The proportion of those sentenced to transportation who were actually transported remained limited until the infrastructure of the penal colonies in Australia was established, enabling the convicts' effective accommodation and use. In the three decades following 1818, there was a high likelihood (better than 60 per cent) that those sentenced to transportation would be sent to Australia.[21] At the same time, the development of imprisonment as a sentencing option saw a gradual decline in the use of transportation. As a new mode of punishment — the penitentiary — became dominant in the 1840s, the proportion of convicted felons who were sentenced to transportation dropped to less than one in five. This transition was aided not only by the increasing preference for imprisonment, but also by the growing reluctance of the Australian colonies to accept convicts.[22] By the 1830s the demand for transported labour, once essential in meeting the infrastructural needs of a penal colony, was

20 Beattie, *Crime and the Courts*, pp. 514, 532–3, Table 10.1.
21 A. G. L. Shaw, *Convicts and the Colonies*, Melbourne University Press, Melbourne, 1977 (1966), p. 150.
22 Nicholas (ed.), *Convict Workers*, p. 37.

declining, as new schemes of colonisation proved increasingly capable of meeting Imperial requirements. Principle and pragmatism vied for recognition in both Imperial and colonial decisions on transportation. Hence in 1849, at a time when one group of colonists in Sydney were vigorously resisting the off-loading of a shipment of convicts, another group at Fremantle in Western Australia were calling for convicts, who were needed to sustain the labour needs of the still struggling colony. The result was that a further 10 000 convicts were transported there during the following two decades.[23]

As a punishment, transportation possessed features that were attractive to government and sentencers alike. It provided, most obviously, an alternative to the death penalty, during a period when an alternative was sought. In removing large numbers of offenders from local communities, it acted as a safety valve in societies under significant pressure from expanding populations. The sending of convicts to places as remote as Botany Bay was seen to be, at least initially, a weighty deterrent: the terrors that transportation promised of an uncertain voyage, and of an indeterminate fate in what was regarded as an inhospitable land, made it a transparently attractive penal option.

Transportation, however, was not mere removal of the unwanted and dangerous. Its punishment rationale was articulated according to Imperial objectives. While historians have debated at length whether the settlement at Botany Bay was selected in order to address the pressing problem of overcrowded hulks or to secure strategic advantage in the South Seas, the answer matters little in retrospect.[24] In the larger context of the expansion of Europe, the transportation of large numbers of convicts to Australia was made possible by the reality of Empire and contributed to its consolidation. In this context, the penal purposes of transportation to Australia were never clearly separated from the Imperial issues of governance and authority in a new colony. The colony was penal — but the contradiction between setting aside a place for punishment and the promise of a new society in the Antipodes was never far from the surface in the subsequent debates over just how severe a punishment transportation was.

23 P. Statham, 'Why Convicts I: An Economic Analysis of Colonial Attitudes to the Introduction of Convicts', *Studies in Western Australian History*, vol. 4, December 1981, pp. 1–10.

24 The debate is reviewed at length in G. Martin (ed.), *The Botany Bay Debate*, University of Queensland Press, St Lucia, 1974; it is more recently the subject of revisionist studies by A. Frost in *Botany Bay Mirages*, Melbourne University Press, Melbourne, 1994.

This tension was present at each critical stage in the history of transportation to the Australian colonies. How penal were the penal colonies? The issue was the focus of numerous reviews of the transportation system, especially that conducted in New South Wales itself by Commissioner Bigge from 1819 to 1821. Bigge was charged with the task of examining the efficiency and effectiveness of the penal colonies as a gaol, as well as considering the state of the colony itself.[25] Over the previous three decades, some 25 000 convicts had been transported, most to New South Wales. Their fortunes after arrival in the colony of New South Wales varied, but broadly two patterns of placement had developed under Governor Macquarie (1810–21). The majority of convicts were assigned to private masters under a system that created an essential underlay for the establishment of local agricultural and pastoral industries. Initially there were few private masters available — excepting the members of the armed forces who had accompanied the convicts. Land grants to officers of the New South Wales Corps in the 1790s contributed to a demand for convict labour to support the expanding agricultural economy and helped found some of the largest early colonial fortunes. A trickle of free settlers and, especially under Macquarie, an increasing number of emancipated convicts with land grants expanded the pool of private employers looking for convict servants.[26]

During the time of their convict servitude (typically for seven years, fourteen years, or life, which Macquarie regulated after 1813 to mean 15 years), the transports might serve under a number of masters. There was a market in convict labour, and employers were free to return unsatisfactory workers and take out others. But the convicts themselves also had freedoms in this context. Typically, labour hours were not fixed, but linked to task completion. This task work left a period of time each day and on weekends when convicts might be free to work for their own profit. Enterprising ones did just that; but others used the time in more hedonistic pursuits, satisfying a prodigious thirst for spirits being chief among them. In the urban areas, of course, the problems of controlling such a degree of licence were visible and provoked demands for stricter regulation of convict life.

Such were the opportunities afforded these convicts that, after thirty years of settlement, there were complaints within the colony and in London that

25 J. Ritchie, *Punishment and Profit*, Heinemann, Melbourne, 1970, pp. 64–5.
26 J. Ritchie, *Lachlan Macquarie: A Biography*, Melbourne University Press, Melbourne, 1986, pp. 126–9.

the convict system was no longer a means of punishment. Instead, it allowed convicts to attain a level of wealth and ease that was quite unavailable to people of such a class in Great Britain or Ireland. The penal functions of the colony were brought into conflict with the realities of its economic growth, to which the convicts were contributing, and from which many benefited. After the expiry of their sentences, emancipated convicts could become recipients of land grants, which many turned to advantage. The enthusiasm that contemporary Australians have for discovering and demonstrating their convict heritage is testimony to the colonial reality: convicts sent to the colonies for punishment might be released into circumstances that enabled them to attain a footing in the world — a footing that their location in Great Britain or Ireland had denied them.

During Macquarie's time, however, the pool of private employers was limited. Between 1810 and 1815, only about sixty free settlers a year arrived in New South Wales, compared with about 700 convicts annually. After 1815 the number of convicts increased to over 2000 a year, and by 1821 over 40 per cent of the colony was of convict status. One consequence was the high level of employment of transported convicts on public works.[27] By 1819, male convicts working on public works in Sydney, who had previously resided in private accommodation around the town, were housed in special barracks at Hyde Park in Sydney. The establishment of the barracks was necessary to provide a greater degree of labour discipline among those constructing the buildings and roads of the growing metropolis. The barracks, in which the convicts were housed at night, also solved the problem of convicts being at large after their work was completed. Encouraging the convicts to enter the barracks and stay there, after two decades of finding their own quarters, was itself a challenge; Macquarie met the challenge by throwing a party at the opening of the barracks for all convicts who chose to reside there.[28] Concern about the prevalence of cohabitation and prostitution among female convicts at Parramatta led to the construction of a new barracks for women after 1818, known as the Female Factory. Simultaneously a place for moral protection and punishment, it continued a tradition of institutional con-

27 B. Dyster, 'Public Employment and Assignment to Private Masters, 1788–1821', in Nicholas (ed.), *Convict Workers*, pp. 127–53.

28 On the party, see Hirst, *Convict Society*, p. 42; on the design of the barracks, see J. S. Kerr, *Out of Sight, Out of Mind (Australia's Places of Confinement, 1788–1988)*, S. H. Ervin Gallery, National Trust of Australia (NSW), Sydney, 1988, pp. 24–5.

finement for women that went back to Governor King's establishment of an earlier female prison in 1804.[29]

Macquarie's view was that the colony was a place of settlement, in which a large labour force of convicts provided a key resource for development. It was a view that Bigge contested, and vigorously. The relative freedoms of the convicts under the systems of assignment and government service allowed too much licence to those who were supposed to have been undergoing a severe punishment. There was uncertainty about what transportation actually meant once the convict had arrived in New South Wales. This was a threat to the integrity of the British criminal-justice system itself. And the living conditions of many convicts were better than those of the lowest class of labourers. In a telling example cited by Hirst, the convicts on farms west of Sydney refused maize and other substitutes for their preferred wheaten bread, while their masters subsisted on the inferior diet in order to increase surplus produce for sale on the market.[30]

Bigge's recommendations were aimed at reinstituting certainty of punishment and reducing the living standards of convicts. Henceforth the convicts were to be subject to a strict regimen of control. The mere removal of the convict from Great Britain or Ireland was no longer in itself the penalty of transportation; rather the circumstances of bondage in Australia were to be such that no one could regard transportation as a free ticket to a better life in the colonies.[31]

By itself, however, such a system would only have produced an introverted and ultimately unproductive economy, oriented primarily to the maintenance of the penal system itself. With the erosion of a punishment rationale for transportation by the middle of the century, such a system would have been doomed to obscurity. Early hopes that New South Wales would provide the British Navy with the resources for a significant outfitting base in the Pacific collapsed in the face of scarce and poor-quality resources (flax and timber at Norfolk Island proving inadequate). In recommending a turn in colonial administration towards a more rigorous penal regime, Bigge was also mindful of the productive potential of penal

29 J. S. Kerr, *Design for Convicts*, Library for Australian History, Sydney, 1984, pp. 42–3; A. Salt, *These Outcast Women: The Parramatta Female Factory, 1821–1848*, Hale & Iremonger, Sydney, 1984, p. 85.

30 Hirst, *Convict Society*, p. 49.

31 Ritchie, *Punishment and Profit*, p. 218.

labour. Convict servants, having served a term of punishment in labour gangs, were to be made available to free settlers.

Transportation without the visible punishment of hard labour was not punishment enough. For the next two decades, convict labour was organised in order to maintain the colony's penal character. The hardest convicts were confined to remote penal settlements. The less reliable were condemned to lengthy service in the government-run penal labour gangs, whose task was the building of roads, bridges, and ports, providing the infrastructure for a growing economy. A substantial proportion of convicts were thus employed in government service or subject to secondary punishment in specifically designed penal settlements.

The private economy, however, benefited equally from the reorganised convict system. Under the system of assignment, convicts were indentured to free settlers, whose powers over the use of their labour were considerable. The system of assignment was to become the focus of severe criticism in 1837–38, as evangelical critics and others active in the anti-slavery campaigns turned their attention to forced labour in the Australian penal colonies. History belongs to the victors: this criticism moulded the subsequent history and reputation of the convict system. Equating convictism with slavery, the Molesworth Committee on Transportation in 1838 asserted that the system of assignment delivered convicts into private hands, rendering them vulnerable to abuses of power incompatible with a free society, or with certainty and justice in punishment.[32] The recommendations of the Committee coincided with an emerging debate in New South Wales itself: the development of a free, self-governing colony was incompatible, it was said, with its continuing use as a dumping ground for convicts from Great Britain. Yet the Committee's depiction of New South Wales as a place of brutal punishment was not warmly greeted, being regarded as the outcome of prejudice that failed to recognise the realities of the penal colony.[33]

In the United Kingdom itself, the penitentiary was now emerging as the favoured means of punishment — a punishment linked to reform of the incarcerated prisoner through subjection to a regime of silence, dissocia-

32 United Kingdom, Parliament, *Report from Select Committee on Transportation (1837–38)* (Molesworth Committee), British Parliamentary Papers (hereafter BPP), London, 1837–38, p. xxii.

33 J. Ritchie, 'Towards Ending an Unclean Thing: The Molesworth Committee and the Abolition of Transportation to New South Wales, 1837–40', *Historical Studies*, vol. 17, no. 67, October 1976, pp. 144–64; Shaw, *Convicts and the Colonies*, pp. 273–4.

34 M. Ignatieff, *A Just Measure of Pain: The Penitentiary in the Industrial Revolution, 1750–1850*, Penguin Books, London, 1989; R. Evans, *The Fabrication of Virtue: English Prison Architecture, 1750–1840*, Cambridge University Press, Cambridge, 1982.

tion from the social world of crime and offending, and contemplation of one's faults.[34] But other concerns about the uses of transportation were also evident. Since the late eighteenth century, moves towards criminal law reform had been increasingly focused on securing greater certainty in punishment together with some mitigation of the code's severity, principally with respect to the use of capital punishment. The result was that, by the 1820s, there was a reduction in the number of capital offences, and a decade later, Lord John Russell, as Home Secretary, determined to revise the criminal law in ways that would also limit the use of transportation as a sentence.[35]

By 1840 the conjunction of an emerging program of prison-building in the United Kingdom, together with opposition to transportation as an uncertain punishment and colonial stirring against it, ended transportation to New South Wales. Colonial resistance quickly entrenched itself: attempts to land convicts at Sydney in 1849 were rendered impossible by local protest. In later years, up until the cessation of transportation to Tasmania in 1853 and Western Australia in 1868, transportation continued under circumstances of growing colonial indifference to the labour that had earlier been indispensable. As David Meredith concludes, the economic and penal objectives, which had always contradicted each other to some extent, had become quite opposed.[36] The growth of free immigration from the 1830s provided a more reliable and less costly means of supplying labour, while the punishment rhetoric that had been used to justify transportation as a penalty had shifted its focus towards the prison.

The end of transportation was associated with a consolidation of the State's modes of punishment. The prison as the archetypal institution of punishment had become unequivocally a State institution by the mid-nineteenth century. Ironically, this development coincided with the 'privatisation' of punishment, in the sense that it became less visible to the public. The functions of the prison were linked to a range of other institutions of social governance (schools, asylums, hospitals, poorhouses, and medical inspection), most of which were, in the Anglo-American world, strongly public in their management and regulation. Transportation, on the other hand, while possessing a State rationale in the eighteenth century, had been especially joined to private interests — through the shipping companies' interest in their human cargoes and the need for labour in the American colonies. Both State and private interests exercised a powerful influence over the role of transportation

35 Ritchie, 'Towards Ending an Unclean Thing', pp. 158–62.
36 D. Meredith, 'Full circle? Contemporary Views on Transportation', in Nicholas (ed.), *Convict Workers*, pp. 14–24.

in the colonial economies of Australia. But private interest in the system always relied on the convict system's capacity to resolve a labour-scarcity problem. For private employers, punishment was useful to the extent that it extracted labour. For State interests, on the other hand, punishment was more complex in its functions: economic in relation to its use of labour in the foundation of a new colony, symbolic in its exemplary role as a deterrent, and transformative in its rehabilitative function. In a penal colony, the State's interest was equally evident in the governor's 'ownership' of the convict's labour, which became an important factor in the debates over the autocratic nature of early government in New South Wales.[37]

By the 1830s, State interests also increasingly expected that predictability in punishment would be an element of the rule of law — hence the powerful theme of the Molesworth Committee's report in 1837–38, which described the arbitrary character of assignment to private service as a symptom of the 'lottery of punishment' epitomising the convict system.[38] Although Molesworth himself wanted the total abolition of transportation, his Committee sought a modified form instead, recommending the formation of penal establishments of the penitentiary kind at Port Arthur and Norfolk Island, which would be remote from free settlements. As the modes of punishment and their purposes became the focus of State policy in the mid-nineteenth century, a rationale for mass transportation became increasingly difficult to defend. Its links to colonisation projects became the focus of subsequent consideration, dominating the policy considerations underlying the transportation of convicts to Western Australia in the 1850s and 1860s. When a Commons Select Committee concluded in 1861 that the system of transportation of convicts to Bermuda and Gibraltar for labour on public works, prior to eventual discharge back in Great Britain, had 'nothing in common with transportation properly so called', they were drawing attention to the Imperial interest both in the removal of offenders from home, and in the contribution that convicts made to colonisation abroad.[39] Punishment by

37 See United Kingdom, *Report from Select Committee on Transportation (1837–38)*, pp. iv–v on the provisions of the Transportation Act, 5 Geo. 4, c. 84; see also A. Atkinson, 'The Free-Born Englishman Transported: Convict Rights as a Measure of Eighteenth-Century Empire', *Past & Present*, no. 144, August 1994, pp. 88–115, which discusses this legal provision as a mark of the difference between convict status in the American colonies before about 1750 and the status of convicts in Australia.

38 United Kingdom, *Report from Select Committee on Transportation (1837–38)*, pp. xx–xxi.

39 United Kingdom, Parliament, *Report from Select Committee on Transportation*, BPP, London, 1861, vol. 13, p. iv. On the multitude of penal objectives served by transportation, see especially S. Devereaux, 'In Place of Death: Transportation Penal Practices and the English State, 1770–1830', in Strange (ed.), *Qualities of Mercy*.

this time was a matter of State interest, calculable in terms of a matrix of Imperial and colonial concerns, from which private profit was largely excluded.

WHO WERE THE CONVICTS?

Historical debates about the origins of the convicts have been a major preoccupation of Australian historians of transportation. This historiography has been informed by changing ideas about Australian identity and nationhood, but it has also significantly reflected theoretical developments in criminology and associated disciplines. Changing historical method, however, has helped refine the picture of what kind of people were transported, while debate about their antecedents and social character has continued much as it began. With the notable exception of work influenced most by economic history, debate about convict origins still swings between vindication and condemnation.[40]

The statistics on the convicts are reasonably clear. There were approximately 160 000 transported from 1787 to 1868. The bulk of these, were shipped in the 1820s and 1830s. The great majority, predictably, were male. But the colonisation rationale determined that, wherever possible, women convicts would be chosen, to assist the reproductive potential of the transported population. About 25 000 of the total were women. The convicts were also a young and able-bodied population, and it was this factor that made their colonising role especially profitable. Compared with typical free immigrant populations, convicts were more likely to be concentrated in the age cohorts that were most able to work.[41] This did not mean, of course, that they were inevitably suited to the work with which they were charged.

About half the convicts (78 000) were landed in New South Wales, some 66 500 in Van Diemen's Land, and nearly 10 000 in Western Australia, which succeeded the other colonies as the destination during the 1850s and 1860s. Smaller numbers were landed directly at penal stations on Norfolk Island, and at Moreton Bay and Port Phillip during the declining years of transportation to the eastern mainland colonies (1836–51).

40 See Rudé, *Protest and Punishment*; Garton, 'The Convict Origins Debate', pp. 74–7; Nicholas (ed.), *Convict Workers*; Oxley, *Convict Maids*; R. Hughes, *The Fatal Shore: A History of Transportation of Convicts to Australia 1787–1868*, Collins Harvill, London, 1987.

41 Nicholas (ed.), *Convict Workers*, pp. 47–51.

Where did they come from? The research of many scholars has enabled us to describe the (mainly) British and Irish origins of the convicts in considerable detail.[42] The convict population consisted disproportionately of those tried in England — especially in London and the south-east, who made up nearly one-third of all convicts sent to Australia. Irish convicts (or rather those tried in Ireland, for there were also Irish convicts who had been tried in England, having migrated there) made up nearly one-quarter of the total. The smaller numbers of Scots transported to Australia have been attributed to the different criminal law and penal code of Scotland. During this period, Scotland had a relatively less punitive penal code, and consequently, those who were eventually sentenced to transportation were both fewer and convicted of more serious offences than those sentenced in England and Ireland.

Other social characteristics of the convicts have been mapped. They were more likely to have been city-dwellers — either by birth or subsequent migration — before being convicted. Disproportionately, of course, they were male, but the extent of the disproportion varied more than can plausibly be explained by variations in the rate of original offending. Hence, in the early decades about one-quarter of those transported were women, but in the 1820s and 1830s the proportion was one-eighth. The most recent research concludes that the reasons for the variation cannot be confidently determined as too little is known about the factors influencing both the rates of sentence and the decisions to transport particular convicts.[43] By the end of transportation to Australia, changing penal policy, as well as completely altered colonial conditions (free migrants now providing the population base for colonial development), meant that only males were sent to Western Australia.

The shifting composition of the convict population is illustrated equally well by another Western Australian phenomenon: few Irish were transported to Western Australia after an initial shipment in 1853 because Irish

42 The following summary draws especially on S. Nicholas & P. R. Shergold, 'The Convict Period', in J. Jupp (ed.), *The Australian People: An Encyclopedia of the Nation, its People and their Origins*, Angus & Robertson, Sydney, 1988. This is the most recent overview of the demography of the convicts, which was developed earlier in Shaw, *Convicts and the Colonies*, and Robson, *Convict Settlers*.

43 Oxley, *Convict Maids*, p. 60; on the women convicts, see also P. Grimshaw, M. Lake, A. McGrath, & M. Quartly, *Creating a Nation: 1788–1990*, McPhee Gribble, Melbourne, 1994, ch. 1; P. Robinson, *The Women of Botany Bay*, Macquarie University, Sydney, 1988; B. Smith, *A Cargo of Women: Susannah Watson and the Convicts of the Princess Royal*, 2nd edn., Sun Australia, Sydney, 1992; K. Alford, 'Convicts and Immigrant Women Before 1851', in Jupp (ed.), *Australian People*, pp. 43–7.

prisons were at the forefront of a penal innovation. The marks system, which involved progression through a series of stages of reform, diminished the call for transportation as a sentence. When Irish convicts did come to Western Australia, it was mainly as 'State prisoners': the Fenian rebels whose arrival in 1867 aroused such alarm that the use of the colony as a penal settlement came to a speedy end.[44]

Recent research has conclusively demonstrated the quality of the transported population in terms of its labour skills and value: in contrast to the voluntary immigrant population in the nineteenth century (which included those who were too young or too old for the manual workforce), the forced migration of the convicts delivered to Australia a useful labour force of substantial numbers. The transportees were youthful and offered a range of work skills. The government turned this resource to good use, as those familiar with the colonial architecture of New South Wales and Tasmania can attest. Quality Georgian architecture, designed by convicts and built by convicts, was just one part of what the punishment complex in Australia achieved. Another was an extensive system of roads and port facilities. Forced labour was essential to the development of a colonial infrastructure — but it was forced labour extracted from a relatively skilled workforce, which in many cases turned the circumstance of punishment to ultimate private advantage.

For many historians of the convict system in Australia, the evidence of the convict records is transparent. The crimes recorded in the convictions of these felons have an immediate social meaning: they become an index of personal worth measured against a cultural norm of non-offending behaviour. The vagaries of a criminal-justice system that is notoriously unreliable in comprehensively detecting all offending behaviour tend to be overlooked by the historians who seek a message for Australian history in the records of the convicts. Hence, the history of transportation has become less a history of crime and its punishment than one of the moral worth of those so selected by the system for shipping to Botany Bay.

An alternative view of who the convicts were assesses them against their recorded history subsequent to their arrival in the colonies. Here the story is one of considerable interest for historians of penality because, for a considerable proportion of convicts, transportation became a means of establishing new and occasionally very prosperous roots in a new land. Transportation was a determinate sentence. Some might fall foul of the conditions of their

44 See G. C. Bolton, 'The Fenians Are Coming, The Fenians Are Coming', in *Studies in Western Australian History*, vol. 4, December 1981, pp. 62–7.

punishment and be sentenced anew to a further period in one of the places of 'exile within exile', the places of secondary punishment: Port Arthur, Norfolk Island, Moreton Bay, and elsewhere. But in most cases, serving one's time eventually led to release on licence or to pardon — some, in the early decades, even receiving land grants with which to establish themselves. Other released convicts took on roles in the urban workforce. The relative success of many convicts could be regarded as confirmation of the arguments both for and against transportation. For those principally interested in a mode of punishment that would reform, the evidence of convict success in a new society was proof enough of their original virtue; for opponents of transportation, the emancipist story in Australia was a sign that exile was not terrible enough to deter the criminals at home from offending. Such different readings of the same evidence were as common in French debates about the relative merits of transportation and the penitentiary as they were in the debates that raged in England and the colonies.[45]

For those with artisan's skills or business acumen, the opportunities kept growing. After only three decades in New South Wales, the prosperity and influence of the 'emancipists' were of such significance that they inspired officials to take a new look at the effectiveness of transportation as punishment. Even after a significant hardening of official attitudes against emancipists in the 1820s, their longer term success in the colony was assured by their growing numbers and the prominence of some of their most active representatives. The ranks of those who turned the opportunities afforded by growing wealth in the colonial economy to good account included many emancipated women. The subsequent lives of these women gave the lie to the attacks on their characters to be found in much of the correspondence and observations of those who had been in authority over them in the early decades. For one recent historian of these women's lives in the penal colonies, their fates suggested less the gloominess of Robert Hughes' 'fatal shore' than the attainment of a 'second chance'.[46]

45 Forster, *France and Botany Bay*.

46 B. Smith, *A Cargo of Women*, p. 174. The debate on this point is reviewed in M. Aveling, 'Bending the Bars: Convict Women and the State', in K. Saunders & R. Evans (eds), *Gender Relations in Australia*, Harcourt Brace Jovanovich, Sydney, 1992; L. Ryan, 'From Stridency to Silence: The Policing of Convict Women, 1803–1853', in D. Kirkby (ed.), *Sex, Power and Justice: Historical Perspectives on Law in Australia*, Oxford University Press, Melbourne, 1995; and Oxley, *Convict Maids*. See also a cautionary tale of the losers in R. P. Davis, 'Victims or Initiators? Three Irish Women Convicts of Van Diemen's Land', in B. Reece (ed.), *Irish Convict Lives*, Crossing Press, Sydney, 1994.

The social distinctions marked out by the terms 'exclusive' and 'emancipist' helped define one of the earliest domains of political debate in the colony of New South Wales. Around the conflict between these terms was shaped the colonial political culture, notably one that focused strongly on the law as a means of seeking remedy against one's accusers or abusers, and on legal institutions as a means of asserting freedom in an autocratic political State.[47]

There remain, however, those who were less fortunate in this system. Their stories have preoccupied the myth-makers of Australian history, linking the uncertainties of a convict life to systemic abuses that became the object of liberal and radical critiques, both in the colonies and in the United Kingdom, by the 1840s. The archetypal convict in these accounts is Rufus Dawes, the hero of Marcus Clarke's 1870s novel, *For the Term of his Natural Life*.[48] Transported for life for a crime that he did not commit, Dawes becomes a victim of the system, as his struggles against the abuse of power (even against 'Power' in general) drive him further and further into the extremities of the penal archipelago. As we will see later, such a story about the dark side of the convict system has had a material impact on later debates about punishment, although perhaps less so than one might expect in a country that has worked and reworked the convict past in fiction and film narratives.[49] This theme, romanticised and lurid as it might have become in literary representations of the convict system, recalls us nevertheless to the questions of transportation *as* punishment, and the punishments of transportation.

THE PUNISHMENTS OF TRANSPORTATION

Transportation was, in itself, punishment: the punishment of exile. But associated with it were other punishments, calculated to ensure that transportation acted as a deterrent. We have already seen that the history

47 Neal, *The Rule of Law*; Hirst, *Convict Society*; Byrne, *Criminal Law and Colonial Subject*; Atkinson, 'The Free-Born Englishman Transported'; M. Sturma, *Vice in a Vicious Society: Crime and Convicts in Mid-Nineteenth-Century New South Wales*, University of Queensland Press, St Lucia, 1983; Kercher, *An Unruly Child*.

48 M. Clarke, *For the Term of his Natural Life*, University of Queensland Press, St Lucia, 1976 (1874).

49 See especially, G. Turner, *National Fictions*, Allen & Unwin, Sydney, 1986; L. Hergenhan, *Unnatural Lives*, University of Queensland Press, St Lucia, 1993; B. Hodge & V. Mishra, *Dark Side of the Dream*, Allen & Unwin, Sydney, 1990.

of convict labour in Australia, under government or on private assignment, was bedevilled by recurrent debates about its standing in relation to the punitive functions of the penalty. One's standing as a convict, however, was marked especially by the powers that employers possessed in extracting labour. Service for the government rendered one immediately vulnerable to a range of punishments that included flogging and extensions to sentences, to be served in one of the penal settlements. Assignment to private employers frequently involved service in places beyond the easy reach of magisterial justice (although in some cases the employers themselves were the local justices), which could nevertheless still be invoked to reinforce private admonishments. In recent years, historians of the system have shown the extent to which this system of labour-control must be interpreted in the light of convicts' capacities to develop their own subversive, informal resistance to this regime of formal and informal control.[50]

Apart from the starvation years — in which conditions in Sydney were difficult for all, regardless of status — the condition of being a convict was in many ways superior to that in which much of the British and Irish population found themselves. Food was of better quality, and there was more of it. Housing varied enormously, but a good proportion of the convicts before 1820 were not housed in institutions; if they were on farms, their living conditions in the early years of establishing a property were rarely very different from those of their masters.

What distinguished convicts' status especially was their vulnerability to corporal punishment, and in the first three decades, women as well as men could be, and were, whipped.[51] The subject has been one of continuing controversy in the debates about punishment, both at the time and more recently. In recent years the debate about the use of flogging in the penal settlements has been vigorous, a symptom in itself of the strong emotions that attach to the subject of punishment.

There is much evidence that there was a high incidence of flogging at different times and places in the penal colonies. Unlike the American colonies, flogging in Australia was not a punishment that could be given indiscriminately by a private master; it was a legal punishment that resulted from hearing a charge against the convict defendant. Its use was consis-

50 For example, A. Atkinson, 'Four Patterns of Convict Protest', *Labour History*, no. 37, November 1979, pp. 28–51.

51 See Ryan, 'From stridency to silence', p. 72, for an account of the whipping of a woman 'at the cart's tail' in Hobart in 1806.

tent with its continuing role as a punishment in the armed services, though Greg Dening suggests that avoiding its too frequent use was a mark of a naval captains' capacity to govern authoritatively, even in the eighteenth century.[52] That is to say, even before the evangelical campaigns against flogging that characterised the early and mid-nineteenth century, changing sensibilities had affected some in the services in ways that suggest changing norms in relation to the means of governing subordinates.[53] The very routinisation of flogging as a punishment in Australia, its statistical enumeration in the 1820s and 1830s, which forms the basis of our evidence for and against the system today, was another symptom of the changing field of punishment — it was a further reminder of the State-controlled, even bureaucratised, character of transportation to Australia, distinguishing it from the more privatised mode of the earlier transatlantic trade in convicts.

For Hirst, flogging was part of the system of labour discipline. Its incidence, he suggests, must be judged against the contemporary reality of its use in other social contexts, and as the other side of a system of labour discipline that also contained many incentives and rewards. Above all, he adds, freedom (in New South Wales, this prison without walls) and flogging were inseparable. Without the discipline of a closed institution, what other punishments were available? And the labour rationale of flogging was its compatibility with an early return to work. Flogging, suggests Hirst, was not directly related to work and did not even seriously impede the relations of master and servant — hence the example of a Sydney merchant who had his convict labourer flogged and then re-employed him as a fencing contractor.[54]

Contradicting this position to some extent, it has been suggested that flogging, in fact, had a very specific function in relation to work. Nicholas has argued that there was a rational calculus of flogging that governed its use discriminately. The volume of flogging was impressive, but its incidence

52 G. Dening, *Mr Bligh's Bad Language*, Cambridge University Press, Cambridge, 1992, pp. 142–7, on 'Some Cliometrics of Violence'.

53 M. C. Glenn, 'The Naval Reform Campaign against Flogging: A Case Study in Changing Attitudes toward Corporal Punishment, 1830–1850', *American Quarterly*, vol. 35, Fall 1983, pp. 408–15; J. Dinwiddy, 'The Early Nineteenth-Century Campaign against Flogging in the Army', *English Historical Review*, vol. 97, 1982, pp. 308–31; L. Radzinowicz & R. G. Hood, *The Emergence of Penal Policy in Victorian and Edwardian England*, Clarendon Press, Oxford, 1990, ch. 21, 'The Mentality of the Cat and the Birch'.

54 Hirst, *Convict Society*, pp. 62–4, 68–9.

varied greatly depending on the time and place. Flogging was imposed most frequently on the unskilled labourers in government work gangs, fear of physical punishment being a factor in extracting the maximum amount of brute physical strength and effort on road-building and other such arduous tasks. By contrast, Nicholas suggests that there was little use of flogging against skilled artisans, whose performance would have been severely affected by the physical afflictions that accompanied a flogging.

The discussion in these terms is scarcely palatable today, when a different sensibility, moulded by two centuries of critique of corporal punishment, is part of our disposition. Indeed, it was true even at the time that reports from the colonies of the extent to which flogging was used were regarded by some as proof of the system's failure — hence, Alexis de Tocqueville, writing for a French audience in 1836, wondered how it could be that 'in a nation in the van of civilisation, men are made to submit to treatment worthy of savage countries and barbarous times?'.[55] Therefore, discussion of flogging (which has come to be regarded as a barbaric punishment in Western cultures) in terms of probabilities and calculations, rather than in terms of an empathetic response to the plight of the flogged, is abhorrent to many. In reaction to Nicholas's thesis, Ray Evans and Bill Thorpe have robustly contested the approach to flogging in terms of a calculus of pain. Their evidence in response, however, draws on the experience of Moreton Bay, one of the secondary penal settlements to which reoffending convicts were sent, associated in its early years with the exploits of a notoriously brutal commander, Patrick Logan.[56]

Concern about flogging beset discussions of convict society in the 1830s. Attacks on the convict system commonly invoked the spectacle of a brutal flogging as a symbol of all that was archaic and despotic in the system. A result was numerous administrative inquiries about the incidence of flogging and an increasing determination to limit its use. The debate arguably moulded a colonial aversion to its use, which saw its decline as a judicial punishment much earlier than in England.[57]

Beyond the punishments associated with labour (whether direct or indirect), there were also the punishments necessary for addressing offences

55 As quoted in Forster, *France and Botany Bay*, p. 111.

56 See Nicholas (ed.), *Convict Workers*, pp. 180–3, on the 'frequency of flogging'; R. Evans & W. Thorpe, 'Power, Punishment and Penal Labour', pp. 90–111.

57 See the comparative tables on the use of corporal punishment in numerous countries of the Empire/Commonwealth in Departmental Committee on Corporal Punishment (Cadogan Committee), *Report*, His Majesty's Stationery Office, London, 1938, discussed in Chapter 4.

committed within the penal colony itself. During the early decades of both New South Wales and Van Diemen's Land, capital punishment was considered an indispensable instrument of order. Macquarie, a humane governor, whose sympathies with the convicts were criticised, was nevertheless not averse to the frequent display of hanging as a punishment: an average of eleven a year during his period as governor made hanging a relatively more frequent occurrence in the colony than it was in England at this time. More extreme was the example of Governor Arthur in Tasmania, where the rate of hanging in the 1820s was intense, reaching a total of 182 executions in the first four and a half years of Arthur's regime.[58] The punishment of colonial offences was not restricted to flogging and hanging. More expense, and in many ways greater notoriety, arose from the establishment of the special penal settlements — the extension of isolated pockets of punishment out into the Australian continent and its surrounding seas. The history and management of these settlements drew on the models of the penitentiary developing at the same time in the United Kingdom and North America. And in particular respects, the history of these settlements and its connotations influenced metropolitan considerations of appropriate punishment regimes of the future, if not always with positive results.

We can see this dialectic at play, on the one hand, in the architecture of new prisons in the waning years of the transportation era — at Port Arthur (Tasmania) and Fremantle (Western Australia) — and, on the other, in the experiments and policy recommendations of Norfolk Island's governor of the 1840s, Alexander Maconochie. Taking the first example, the Port Arthur Penitentiary — built between 1848 and 1852 — was one of a number of early Australian prison sites that replicated the ideas of prison architects in England. Its chapel, for example, was constructed on the same principle as the well-known chapel at Pentonville, which was designed to prevent prisoners communicating with each other: they were led into place wearing their hooded masks and then locked into place in separate cubicles. The design functioned to make the entire assembly of prisoners visible, individually, to the warders, but to prevent communication between them.[59]

58 Ritchie, *Lachlan Macquarie*, p. 130; L. Robson, *A History of Tasmania*, vol. 1, Oxford University Press, Melbourne, 1983, pp. 147–8: the settler population of Tasmania in 1825 was 13 604. See also R. P. Davis, *The Tasmanian Gallows: A Study of Capital Punishment*, Cat & Fiddle Press, Hobart, 1974.

59 M. Weidenhofer, *Port Arthur: A Place of Misery*, Oxford University Press, Melbourne, 1981, pp. 80–1; Evans, *Fabrication of Virtue*, pp. 361–7.

Such replication was not a matter of mere imitation, of course: there were direct links between 'Home' and the colonies, and Joshua Jebb (the Surveyor General of Prisons and architect of the Pentonville Model Prison and especially of its solitary cell) was consulted in the planning of this and other colonial prisons, just as he was required to be in the case of any new institution in England. Moreover, the prisons in Australia were very frequently designed and administered by the Royal Engineers, preserving a measure of architectural and administrative influence that demonstrates the importance of a military ethos in the formation of the Australian penal colonies. The constraints of distance did limit consultation, however, and local factors could subtly change the architecture imported from England. James Kerr, historian of prison architecture in Australia, has documented the way in which designs were adapted in Western Australia at the new Fremantle Convict Depot in order to substitute limestone masonry for Jebb's preferred corrugated iron cell walls. At the same time, much of the gaol fabric, the doors, and iron railings for the galleries were imported from England, as was the case in other colonial prison constructions before the 1860s.[60]

Another interplay of metropolis and colony in the moulding of nineteenth-century punishment was evident in the career of Alexander Maconochie. He was one of the many administrators of the transportation era whose career illustrates the serendipity of British Imperial administration. While secretary to the Governor of Van Diemen's Land in the late 1830s, Maconochie developed a keen interest in prison discipline. The result was a series of pamphlets, letters, and proposals to government concerning what he called the 'marks system' of prison discipline. As his biographer notes, this term was not the one preferred by Maconochie, who originally conceived of it as the 'social system' of prison discipline. 'Social' it was, in its attention to how a convicted criminal might be reformed through an administrative design that ordered the prisoner's life into a series of stages, each marked by accumulation of merit through the completion of tasks and other signs of improved conduct. His proposals earned him the post of governor of Norfolk Island for the years 1840–44. There he confronted the problem of converting theory into practice, and met with many of the obstacles faced by other prison reformers, including resistance from those with vested interests, such as warders, and the inevitable difficulties associated with

60 Kerr, *Out of Sight, Out of Mind*, pp. 64–7.

the expense of a program that favoured non-physical punishments. However, the rhetoric of reforming the prisoner, the emphasis on non-physical means of reformation, and the 'progressive', staged character of the marks system itself were influential in shaping international debates about penal policy in the second half of the century. According to some later observers, Maconochie's ideas had a significant impact on some major post-1850 programs, including the development of Crofton's system of staged release and the later evolution of the indefinite sentence. Maconochie focused on the reformation of the prisoner, and saw this as the essence of a penal policy that would prevent crime rather than merely punish it. Writing in 1958, the Australian jurist and biographer of Maconochie, John Barry, identified an adaptation of this focus in the 1870 Declaration of Penological Principles by the American National Prison Association.[61] More recently it has been suggested that Maconochie can be seen as part of a lineage connecting the penitentiary and the reformatory.[62]

We can see, then, that the field of British penality during the transportation era was truly global in its reach. English-speaking penality is perhaps the more accurate representation in view of the obvious interplay of ideas and practices across the Atlantic and to the Antipodes. Transportation was an integral part of sentencing policy in Great Britain and Ireland during the first half of the nineteenth century. Its administration constituted a laboratory in which ideas of punishment could be advanced and tested — many of them soon abandoned. The astonishing fact about the later history of transportation to Australia is just how much expense was risked with so little return. While the spate of penitentiary-building in the United Kingdom and the USA from the 1830s onwards delivered a major infrastructure of punishment, which lasted well into the twentieth century, the monuments to penal folly in Van Diemen's Land and on Norfolk Island had much shorter histories. Their failure, however, is part of the history of penal policy during the transportation era, constituting a constant background noise during the decades in which the penitentiary idea took physical shape.

61 J. V. W. Barry, *Alexander Maconochie of Norfolk Island*, Oxford University Press, Melbourne, 1958, pp. 231–2.

62 W. G. Waite, 'From Penitentiary to Reformatory: Alexander Maconochie, Walter Crofton, Zebulon Brockway, and the Road to Prison Reform — New South Wales, Ireland, and Elmira, New York, 1840–70', *Criminal Justice History*, vol. 12, 1991, pp. 85–105.

TRANSPORTATION OR THE PRISON?

The penal colony at Botany Bay had barely begun when its opponents commenced their campaign against transportation and in favour of the prison. Bentham's 1802 pamphlet expressed the choice starkly: 'Panopticon versus New South Wales'.[63] Hirst's argument that the historiography of Australian convict society has been shaped by the anti-transportation movement's triumph might be extended more generally to histories of the rise of the prison. The revisionist history of the prison in Great Britain has tended to be indifferent to the phenomenon of mass transportation during the post-Napoleonic period. Consequently the recent history of the prison has been a little too whiggish. Because, since the mid-nineteenth century, the prison has become the dominant mode of punishment of serious crime, the history of its alternatives has been less visible to those writing the history of British punishment. Hence, in the widely read history of the rise of the penitentiary by Michael Ignatieff, transportation is a barely noticed feature of the penal landscape, having virtually no presence at all between its re-establishment in 1787 and its cessation in eastern Australia in 1853.[64]

Does this mean that transportation was irrelevant to the consideration of the proper modes of punishment over these seven decades? Hardly. From the contentious history of Bentham's (entrepreneurial) opposition to the experiment of Botany Bay, through the numerous select committees and departmental inquiries into the effectiveness of transportation, down to the Molesworth Committee in 1837–38, and beyond it to the select committees on secondary punishment in 1856 and on prison discipline in 1863, transportation was consistently one of the choices offered to sentencers and law-makers. The deterrent value of transportation, its effectiveness as a reform agent, and its changing meanings in an age of mass migration were critical matters, preoccupying Imperial governing elites as much as, if not more than, those in the colonies. If, as suggested by many critics, transportation was not punishment enough, then the history of its shortcomings constitutes a key point in debates about punishment and the policies regulating it in early nineteenth-century Great Britain and Ireland. Rather than being regarded as just a dead end in the evolution of punishment, transportation might be reassessed from this point of view as actively contributing to the formation of new possibilities of punishment. Such a perspective challenges the view that the rising tide of imprisonment,

63 See especially Hirst, *Convict Society*, ch. 1.
64 Ignatieff, *A Just Measure of Pain*, pp. 91–3, 200–4.

as opposed to transportation, was inevitable — a perspective implicit in Ignatieff's history, as well as in the magisterial study of crime and sentencing in eighteenth-century England by John Beattie.[65] A reading of French debates about the penitentiary versus transportation compels us to re-evaluate such a perspective — to remember that there was an era when some doubted the prison's suitability for the job mapped out for it by John Howard, Bentham, and others. 'It is only with the advantage of hindsight', concludes Pieter Spierenburg, the Dutch historian of early modern punishment, 'that we can call [transportation] an "old-fashioned" type of punishment'.[66]

Australian historians have made up for the neglect, it is true, but they more often seek to explain the riddles of a national history formed out of a convict past. Hence, the debate about transportation in colonial and post-colonial history has been preoccupied with the characteristics of the convict population and its fate in exile. Less attention has been paid to what is, from the standpoint of the history of punishment, the more fundamental questions: In what ways was transportation punishment? And how was it managed to carry out punishment objectives? As this overview has shown, transportation to Australia was a diverse punishment. This conclusion is not just a reflection of the historian's conventional predilection for complexity and the partiality of any truth. Transportation to Australia, in fact, lasted for a long period of time, during which British penal policy changed dramatically. In 1787 convicts embarked for a place unsettled by Europeans. By the 1830s those who reoffended might be lodged in penal institutions, at Norfolk Island or Port Arthur, whose regimes of discipline and punishment were inextricably tied to contemporary practices in Great Britain, Ireland, and North America. The majority were engaged in the work of bonded labour, whether in government labour gangs or in private service. Their rights were circumscribed, but the variable conditions of colonial settler society provided opportunities for the assertion of rights and of personal desires, which confinement in a penitentiary never allowed.

65 Beattie, *Crime and the Courts*, p. 601.

66 P. Spierenburg, *The Prison Experience: Disciplinary Institutions and their Inmates in Early Modern Europe*, Rutgers University Press, New Brunswick, 1991, p. 276; compare with Forster, *France and Botany Bay*. In Germany too there was sufficient interest in transportation for it to be the subject of a major history of the punishment, including a long treatment of the history of the penal colony in New South Wales; see F. Von Holtzendorff, *Die Deportation als Strafmitteln in alter und neuer zeit und die Verbrecher colonien der Engländer and Franzosen*, Verlag von Johann Ambrosius Barth, Leipzig, 1859; S. Nicholas & P. Shergold, 'Transportation as Global Migration', in Nicholas (ed.), *Convict Workers*, p. 36.

Their time served, convicts turned themselves into small-property owners or more commonly joined the large class of emancipated labourers. Many became the parents of the first generation of European settlers in the new land. Before the gold rushes changed the demography of European Australia dramatically in the 1850s, the colonial population was dominated by emancipists and their children.

By 1848–49, while colonists in the eastern colonies were forcibly resisting the landing of transports, some in Western Australia were calling for their introduction to what had been Australia's first 'free enterprise colony'.[67] When their wishes were met by a British government still experimenting with the possibilities of removing convicts, a transportation regime in the western colony was set up, to be governed by a class of penal administrators who were well attuned to the mid-century trend towards a strict regimen. Only male transports arrived in Western Australia. They were administered first by Captain Henderson, who later returned to Great Britain to join the ranks of prison commissioners and eventually became head of the Metropolitan Police, supervising convicts on tickets of leave in a system that had strong links with earlier colonial experiments in supervision. Succeeding him in Western Australia was Lieut. Edmund Du Cane, whose subsequent British administrative career was devoted to maintaining the strictest rigour in prisons regulation under a system in which punishment was a deterrent and governed by the principle of less eligibility.[68] In this way the circle of punishment was completed, the colonial administration of transportation becoming a training ground for the refinement of punishment in British prisons.

67 Statham, 'Why Convicts', p. 1.

68 See A. Hasluck, *Unwilling Emigrants*, Fremantle Arts Centre Press, Fremantle, 1991 (1959); A. Hasluck, *Royal Engineer: A Life of Sir Edmund Du Cane*, Angus & Robertson, Sydney, 1973.

2

The Carceral System

The convict period overlapped with self-government in the Australian colonies, but convictism's impact on punishment was rarely direct. This may appear odd in a culture that, in its available myths, is almost defined by the spectre of imprisonment.[1] In many ways, the tenor of debate, policy, and practice was influenced as much by a desire to avoid aspects of the convict experience in the foundation of Australia as it was by the imitation of penal strategies in other countries. The convict system left little usable fabric of punishment, although there were visible remnants, which preserved the memory of an unwanted history and awaited a more nostalgic age that would seek to reconstruct them as part of a national cultural heritage.

When Anthony Trollope visited Australia in 1871–72, he sensed the strong colonial desire to put distance between the convict era and that of the self-governing colonies. Pondering the possible future uses of the massive and expensive infrastructure at Port Arthur, Trollope was forced to concede that it was unlikely that it might serve in future as a convict depot for all of the Australian colonies. The Tasmanians would not take the convicts anyway 'because they fear the contamination of the stain attached to the name of a convict colony'. Furthermore, the other colonies desired self-sufficiency and would not wish to transport their convicts: Queensland had its St Helena, 'New South Wales is proud of Darlinghurst; and Victoria very proud indeed of Pentridge; — so proud, that were Tasmania annexed to Victoria . . . she would not even then condescend to send her convicts to Port Arthur'.[2]

1 See especially Turner, *National Fictions*, ch. 3.
2 A. Trollope, *Australia*, ed. P. D. Edwards & R. B. Joyce, University of Queensland Press, St Lucia, 1967 (1873), pp. 517–18; on the convict stain as a theme in Tasmania's later colonial history, see H. Reynolds, 'That Hated Stain: The Aftermath of Transportation in Tasmania', *Historical Studies*, no. 53, 1969, pp. 19–31.

The colonies had replaced one set of penal institutions with another. The loss of Imperial convicts did not mean a loss of inmates for prisons, which were being built as part of the necessary public infrastructure of the self-governing colonies, especially from the 1850s. In the following pages, we examine some of the major themes of what is in Australia a largely unknown history. First, it will be necessary to consider the array of penal measures and the populations subject to them in the years after convictism. Second, we look at some of the discourses and practices of punishment in these decades, and the relation between colonial and other jurisdictions in changing penal strategies. Finally, the architecture of custody is a major theme in the nineteenth century, intimately linked to the development of a 'penal discipline', the rationale for the system of imprisonment.

THE PATTERNS OF PUNISHMENT

Prisons are the dominant image of nineteenth-century punishment, but how important were they in the spectrum of punishment in the post-convict era? Since so much of the subsequent period (from the 1880s) was spent searching for measures to reduce imprisonment, some calculation of the prison's significance as a penalty is vital to understanding later changes.

The introduction in 1853 of the sentence of 'penal servitude', which replaced transportation, was a change in sentencing that affected the colonies as much as it did the United Kingdom, although the precise meanings and objectives of the sentence remained subject to some doubt.[3] In contrast to the long sentences of bondage that had characterised transportation, the sentence of penal servitude was initially shorter. In the colonies, the patterns of sentencing are somewhat obscured by the lack of consistent statistics before the 1870s. We can take a snapshot of the penal options in that decade, a period midway between self-government, with its accompanying flush of institution-building, and the end of the century, by which time reform of sentencing options and penal strategies was assisting a general reduction in the uses of the prison.

For those offenders convicted and sentenced to a lengthy term of imprisonment, the destination was one of the handful of penitentiaries or 'penal establishments' that were scattered through the colonies by the 1870s. In Victoria in 1874, the largest institution of punishment was Pentridge. It

3 C. Emsley, *Crime and Society in England 1750–1900*, 2nd edn, Longman, London, 1996, pp. 276–7.

received 305 prisoners from other gaols during the year and regularly housed nearly 600, although some prisoners still served their time on the prison hulk *Sacramento* or at the Williamstown convict depot, notorious as the location of the murder of its commandant, John Price, in 1857.[4] In addition to these three institutions, there were nine other gaols throughout the colony, including the capital's main receiving house, the Melbourne Gaol, through which over 5000 prisoners passed during 1874. Most of those in prison at any one time were already convicted (only 66 of the 1614 prisoners still there at the end of the year were on remand).[5]

Not surprisingly, in view of the great differences in offending between men and women, there were significant variations in the sentencing patterns of the two sexes. 'Prisons' were mostly male institutions; the Victorian penal institutions so named by the 1870s were classified as exclusively male, after the women had been removed from Pentridge. While women were incarcerated in significant numbers — over 27 per cent of new sentences in 1874 — their terms of imprisonment were relatively short. The result was that just over 16 per cent of prisoners in Victoria in the 1870s were women, most of them held at Melbourne Gaol.[6] Most women were incarcerated for minor offences, especially on police charges of vagrancy arising out of their involvement in prostitution,[7] although convictions for larceny were common enough in cases involving women offenders. Male imprisonment, on the other hand, resulted from conviction for a great spectrum of violent and non-violent offences.

A central difference between women and men in their experience of imprisonment arose from the less serious nature of charges against women. Women who ended up in prison very rarely served more than two years in any one sentence period. In the 1870s, however, about 40 per cent of

4 J. Barry, *The Life and Death of John Price: A Study of the Exercise of Naked Power*, Melbourne University Press, Melbourne, 1964.

5 The data for Victorian imprisonment in 1874 are from *Statistics of the Colony of Victoria, 1874*, Government Printer, Melbourne, 1875.

6 These differences are commonly noted in other jurisdictions. See, for example, L. Zedner, *Women, Crime and Custody in Victorian England*, Clarendon Press, Oxford, 1991, pp. 134–5, for roughly similar figures in local prisons in England and Wales. In Ireland, however, women made up 30–40 per cent of committals to local and convict prisons in the later nineteenth century — see M. Luddy, *Women and Philanthropy in Nineteenth-Century Ireland*, Cambridge University Press, Cambridge, 1995, pp. 149–51

7 On women and vagrancy in Melbourne, see S. Davies, '"Ragged, Dirty . . . Infamous and Obscene": The "Vagrant" in Late-Nineteenth-Century Melbourne', in D. Philips & S. Davies (eds), *A Nation of Rogues? Crime, Law and Punishment in Colonial Australia*, Melbourne University Press, Melbourne, 1994.

males sentenced in the Victorian courts were sentenced for periods longer than two years, most of them with hard labour on the roads or public works. Was this apparently harsh sentencing pattern for males peculiar to Victoria, where one of the colony's sternest criminal court justices, Redmond Barry, was notorious for the severity of his sentencing?[8] Possibly not: comparable sentence lengths were being awarded in New Zealand at the same time.[9]

We can see just how severe such sentencing was by comparing change in sentence length over the subsequent decades. As Table 2.1 shows, the change in sentencing patterns in the higher Victorian courts between 1870 and 1900 was little short of dramatic. There was an undeniable shift in the modal length of sentence from two–four years to less than twelve months. The declining popularity of the death penalty was also evident: ten such sentences were passed on males in 1870 but only three in 1900 (a decline evident in other jurisdictions as well). In fact, by 1900 the sentencing of males more closely mirrored the modal length of sentence awarded to women throughout this period — that is, less than twelve months.

Table 2.1 Sentencing of males convicted on indictable charges in Victoria, 1870–1900

Sentence	*% of total sentences*			
	*1870**	*1880*	*1890*	*1900*
Death	2.20	1.32	0.66	0.87
10–14 years	1.29	0.53	0.83	1.45
7–10 years	2.58	1.32	1.49	1.74
4–7 years	18.42	10.85	7.43	3.19
2–4 years	32.23	38.36	19.47	12.17
> 12 months	19.71	25.40	26.24	8.99
6–12 months	14.55	6.08	23.10	35.36
1–6 months	7.00	10.05	16.67	21.74
< 1 month	0.74	0.79	1.32	3.19
Fined	0.74	2.65	0.83	0.29
Other	0.92	2.65	1.98	11.01
Total number	535.00	378.00	606.00	345.00

* Data for 1870 collapses two sentence types: penal servitude less than 4 years and imprisonment greater than 2 years.

Source: Statistics of the Colony of Victoria (for relevant years).

8 A. Galbally, *Redmond Barry*, Melbourne University Press, Melbourne, 1995, pp. 108–9, 185–6. See also ch. 4 below.

9 See J. Pratt, *Punishment in a Perfect Society: The New Zealand Penal System, 1840–1939*, Victoria University Press, Wellington, 1992, p. 128, who nevertheless suggests that the data implies an absence of lengthy sentences in this period.

This transformation in the punishment of more serious offences replicated a trend in the lower courts. An examination of the summary court jurisdiction in Victoria (Table 2.2) shows reductions in prison sentences between 1880 and 1900, and a continuation of the use of the fine (which increased markedly in the sentencing of women).

Table 2.2 Sentences in summary courts, Victoria, 1880–1900

Sentence	*% of male sentences*		*% of female sentences*	
	1880	*1900*	*1880*	*1900*
2 years	0.21	0.05	0.00	0.03
1–2 years	1.52	0.73	2.62	1.48
6–12 months	2.46	1.25	4.76	2.65
4 months	0.26	0.04	0.24	0.17
3 months	6.40	3.26	9.14	2.59
2–3 months	1.84	0.57	1.23	1.81
1–2 months	6.57	4.66	8.50	5.88
15–30 days	0.12	0.34	0.26	0.20
8–15 days	3.84	4.20	5.82	5.88
<7 days	27.55	36.60	35.63	34.51
Fined	41.35	41.82	19.90	28.99
Bail	2.12	0.84	1.79	0.59
Industrial school	3.09	3.49	5.47	10.54
Lunatic asylum	1.96	1.67	4.50	4.15
Other	0.70	0.45	0.15	0.53
Total number	12549	14797	3402	3587

Source: Statistics of the Colony of Victoria (for relevant years).

Given the larger numbers being processed through the lower courts, these changes represented a significant reduction in incarceration. For example, the drop in numbers of women being sentenced to three months in prison (from 9.1 to 2.6 per cent) represented a reduction in the number of individuals incarcerated from 311 to 93. Later we will have occasion to examine some of the associated changes in penality that occurred around the turn of the century. But it is evident from this data that a change of some magnitude was occurring in the adjudication of the criminal courts.

Evidence from other colonies suggests that these reductions were not replicated in all jurisdictions. Table 2.3, which compares sentencing disposals in New South Wales in 1880 and 1900, shows little change in the overall numbers being imprisoned directly from the magistrates court.

Aside from the fine's dominance as a mode of punishment at this time, the striking feature of this data is the volume of incarceration arising from fine default. Most people entering custody for punishment were, in fact,

Table 2.3 Summary Court punishments by type of offence, New South Wales, 1880–1900

Sentence	*Type of offence*							
	1880				*1900*			
	Total against (%)	*Offences against the person (%)*	*Offences property (%)*	*Other (%)*	*Total (%)*	*Offences against the person (%)*	*Offences against property (%)*	*Other (%)*
Fine	57.60	64.82	45.47	57.68	53.58	60.82	30.88	54.98
Prison (fine default)	30.81	16.97	16.19	34.35	35.98	22.15	20.89	37.77
Prison	7.00	6.62	31.31	4.69	7.25	14.51	45.79	3.97
Bound over	1.08	5.38	2.13	0.33	0.51	2.00	2.10	0.32
Other	3.51	6.21	4.90	2.96	2.68	0.51	0.34	2.95
Total number	42205	5151	3286	33768	48102	4473	3666	39963

Source: Statistical Register of NSW

there as a result of inability or unwillingness to pay a fine. Legislation allowing part payment of fines before or during imprisonment was later to decrease the rate of imprisonment for fine default,[10] although fine-default imprisonment remains a significant cause of incarceration today.

A further lesson to be gained from the data is the relative seriousness with which property crimes were treated in the summary courts, compared with offences against the person. One might think that this trend was an artefact of the jurisdictional boundaries, since serious offences against the person — those likely to receive prison sentences — were more commonly the prerogative of the higher courts. Magistrates faced with assaults involving personal injury were perhaps more likely to commit those cases to a higher court if they considered the evidence justified it. Yet the New South Wales evidence in this period suggests that a slightly higher proportion of property offences were committed to trial in a higher court; hence, if imprisonment is taken as the criterion by which, culturally, an offence's severity is measured, it would appear that property crime was treated with greater gravity. An offence's seriousness and its relation to the mode of punishment is a subject demanding further longitudinal historical research. For the moment, we can conclude this brief survey of punishment patterns in the later nineteenth century by considering the social attributes of those who were the subjects of punishment at this time.

We have already considered some Victorian evidence suggesting that women were more likely to be incarcerated than we might have expected them to be in the later nineteenth century, but that their patterns of sentencing, linked mostly to their patterns of offending, meant that they were inclined to spend less time in custody than men. Gender was not the only criterion by which the record-keepers of lock-ups and prisons differentiated inmates: they frequently compiled data on the age, birthplace and/or race, education, and occupation of those received into their institutions.

Looking at the social patterns of incarceration in the later nineteenth century, Western Australia stands apart from the other colonies in that large numbers of Aborigines were imprisoned during the course of expansion into the north. So great were the numbers of Aborigines imprisoned that one might argue that the later pattern of large-scale Aboriginal incarceration in that state was conditioned by this not so distant

10 P. Grabosky, *Sydney in Ferment*, ANU Press, Canberra, 1977, p. 117; S. Garton 'Bad or Mad? Developments in Incarceration in NSW, 1880–1920', in Sydney Labour History Group (ed.), *What Rough Beast?* Allen & Unwin, Sydney, 1982, pp. 102–3.

historical experience.[11] As early as 1840, Western Australia established the country's only prison specifically for Aborigines, at Rottnest Island. But by the 1890s the colony had a number of other institutions that were primarily 'Aboriginal' prisons. A detailed picture of Aboriginal imprisonment emerges by 1900, following two decades in which, each year, some hundreds of Aborigines were prosecuted in the summary and higher courts, as indicated by Table 2.4.

Table 2.4 Aborigines charged in Western Australian courts, 1894–1900

	1894	*1895*	*1896*	*1897*	*1898*	*1899*	*1900*
Summary convictions	430	349	370	442	417	349	374
Tried in higher court	10	11	20	16	16	13	8
Convicted in higher court	10	6	19	14	5	9	7
Total	450	366	409	472	438	371	389

Source: Western Australia Statistical Register for the Year 1900, pp. 14, 16.

The numbers charged were relatively small compared with the non-Aboriginal population (the total summary convictions in Western Australia increased from 4403 to 9925 during these gold-rush years), but the nature of the charges tended to bring long terms of imprisonment. Although special provision was made for Aboriginal prisoners at a number of sites, the main custodial centres receiving Aborigines in 1900 were in the northern parts of the colony — at Derby, Roebourne, and Wyndham — while a number still served lengthy terms at the designated reformatory at Rottnest. The Aboriginal population of Western Australian prisons and lock-ups was not wholly male — 32 females were imprisoned in 1900, along with 289 males, but this was a lower proportion than for the non-Aboriginal population in custody. The Aboriginal cohort was more juvenile, however, with some 17 per cent of sentenced Aboriginal prisoners being under the age of twenty-one, compared with 9 per cent of the whole prison population.

The particular contexts of Aboriginal imprisonment — especially its origins in the often fierce encounters between Aborigines and settlers in the

11 See Royal Commission into Aboriginal Deaths in Custody, *National Report*, AGPS, Canberra, 1991; R. Broadhurst, 'Imprisonment of the Aborigine in Western Australia, 1957–1985', in K. Hazlehurst (ed.), *Ivory Scales: Black Australians and the Law*, NSW University Press, Kensington, 1987.

Kimberley in the 1880s and 1890s — help explain the different patterns of detention. Where Aboriginal resistance had been overcome early on in most colonies by more brutal methods, the relatively late development of Western Australia and the scarcity of labour in the north-west combined to create a distinctive labour market. A sympathetic former government resident pointed out as much in 1884, urging the government to consider assisting Aborigines rather than exploiting and excluding them. Some 1800 Aborigines were estimated to be in the service of settlers between the Murchison and Fitzroy Rivers, and 'in no other part of Australia have their services been utilised to such an extent'.[12] The other side of Aboriginal integration with the process of settlement was a far higher risk of involvement with the criminal-justice system, which was playing a crucial role in establishing a social discipline through incarceration.

Table 2.5 Sentencing of Aborigines (compared with all sentencing) in Western Australia, 1900

Sentence	*All*		*Aboriginal*	
	% of male sentences	*% of female sentences*	*% of male sentences*	*% of female sentences*
Death	0.46	0.00	1.94	0.00
>10 years	0.58	0.00	1.16	0.00
5–10 years	0.52	0.00	0.39	0.00
2–5 years	2.47	0.00	3.49	0.00
1–2 years	7.53	1.65	33.33	3.33
6–12 months	10.98	5.49	13.95	3.33
3–6 months	14.78	12.64	16.28	10.00
1–3 months	32.95	35.71	18.22	26.67
7–30 days	26.68	39.56	10.47	43.33
<7 days	3.05	4.95	0.78	13.33
Total number	1739	182	258	30

Source: Western Australia Statistical Register for the Year 1900, p. 50.

The relative severity with which male Aboriginal offenders were sentenced reflects the frequency of their being charged with stock-theft and killing, as well as their continuing conflict with settlers. This was epitomised by the number of death sentences given to Aborigines in 1900 —

12 Communication of R. J. Sholl to John Forrest, in Western Australia, Parliament, *Report of a Commission . . . to Inquire into the Treatment of Aboriginal Native Prisoners of the Crown in the Colony*, Western Australia Parliamentary Papers (hereafter WAPP), Perth, 1884, p. 18. See N. Green, *The Forrest River Massacres*, Fremantle Arts Centre Press, Fremantle, 1995, for a detailed history of the settlement and policing of this region; and see ch. 4 below.

5 of the 8 death sentences passed that year were passed on Aboriginal offenders — highlighting a pattern that was far from unique in Australia.[13] But the table also shows that a third of male Aborigines in prison at this time were serving the relatively long sentence of one–two years, in contrast to the bulk of non-Aboriginal male offenders, who were more likely to be serving less than six months. In 1902 the severity of Aboriginal sentencing was reinforced by an exceptional amendment to the Criminal Code, which provided for summary jurisdiction to be exercised in the case of any 'aboriginal native' who pleaded guilty to a non-capital offence, thus allowing justices to award a sentence of up to three years imprisonment.[14] The Royal Commissioner inquiring into the condition of Aborigines in Western Australia in 1905 roundly condemned this amendment and summarised its effect: 'to secure a conviction the accused are accordingly made to plead guilty — at the muzzle of the rifle, if need be'.[15] The statistical impact of this provision — and of the police's aggressive response to continuing Aboriginal resistance to settlement in the north of the colony — became evident in the large-scale incarceration of Aborigines before the First World War.

Table 2.6 Aborigines in Western Australian Prisons, 1905–1960

	Male	*Female*	*Total*	*Percentage of prison population*
1905	216	1	217	31.82
1909	294	0	294	42.36
1915	35	1	36	12.90
1953	68	8	76	12.99
1960	82	17	99	15.64

Source: Western Australian Prisons Department, *Annual Reports.*

Since a census is most likely to count the long-term prison population, the gravity of the incarceration rate experienced by Aboriginal people during the years of early settlement in the north and north-west of Western Australia is self-evident. Table 2.6 points to a sudden decline in criminal-justice incarceration after the first decade of the century, when the 1905 legislation establishing the 'protection' system in the state began to take effect and

13 J. McGuire, Race and Capital Punishment in Australia, paper presented to the Law and History Conference, Brisbane, July 1996. See ch. 4 below for further discussion.

14 *Act to Amend the Criminal Code 1902* (WA), s. 5.

15 Western Australia, Parliament, *Report of the Royal Commission on the Condition of the Natives* (W. E. Roth, Commissioner), WAPP, Perth, 1905, 2nd Session, p. 2.

Aboriginal people were put at risk of more general forms of containment. Coincident with the start of protection were two government initiatives that dramatically affected rates of arrest and imprisonment. The establishment of the Moola Bulla government station for Aboriginal people in the Halls Creek area, combined with a stricter regulation of police arrest policy in cattle-killing cases, led to a reduction in the number of Aborigines in the northern prisons, explaining the dramatic decline in Aboriginal incarceration between 1909 and 1915.[16]

Although Aborigines were obviously imprisoned in other colonies, the official statistical data rarely record their presence. In South Australia the official register distinguished generically the 'black or coloured prisoners' but did not identify the Aboriginal component of that category, probably the majority. But there is no evidence to suggest that incarceration rates for Aboriginal people elsewhere exceeded those in Western Australia at any time after the 1880s. A peculiarly local pattern was thus established during these decades, which revived from the 1960s, becoming clearly visible in the evidence of the Royal Commission into Aboriginal Deaths in Custody after 1987.

In the later nineteenth century the different needs of other groups of prisoners were increasingly identified as policy issues, in ways that affected subsequent custodial design and discipline for such groups. The punishment of juveniles was a matter of concern for prison reformers from the 1840s. While the numbers in custody were not large, their fate loomed prominently in debates about the wisdom of allowing prisoners to associate indiscriminately. In 1870 police took nearly 1000 children under the age of fifteen into custody in Victoria; 30 per cent were female, and the majority were under ten years of age, indicating that most were subject to the operations of the *Neglected and Criminal Children's Act*, which had come into operation in 1864. The total numbers going to trial did not change a lot over the following decades; however, much attention was paid to the continuing dilemma of how to manage children and juveniles who were perceived to be in need of care or custody following their apprehension by the police.

Women offenders, whose sentencing patterns we have already noted, constituted another significant minority in custody. Their presence was increasingly a focus of attention during the nineteenth century. In contrast, however, to the convict-era history of separate incarceration in distinctive

16 P. Biskup, *Not Slaves Not Citizens*, University of Queensland Press, St Lucia, 1973, pp. 99–100; Green, *Forrest River Massacres*, pp. 72–4.

institutions (the female factories at Parramatta and Hobart), the case for women's prisons was notably slow in gaining policy priority in the post-convict colonies. Indeed, by the time the argument for special women's prisons was finally supported by money and mortar, the numbers destined for such institutions were falling dramatically, as illustrated in Table 2.7.

By the turn of the century, the numbers incarcerated for terms of imprisonment had declined in every jurisdiction, and continued to do so up until the interwar period, when they reached an all-time low. While changes in sentencing and in the use of imprisonment helped to ease the financial pressures of the previous two or three decades, they also provided an opportunity to introduce some innovations in punishment that were already in train for other reasons.

'REFORM THROUGH SUFFERING'

The dream of classical punishment — that of the eighteenth-century reformers of the European and British criminal-justice systems — was to establish a science of penality, one that would exactly measure the degree of punishment according to the seriousness of the crime. Its focus was the crime. Neoclassical punishment, however, developed in the late nineteenth century with a different scientific aspiration. Refined in the project of Cesare Lombroso's criminology, late-nineteenth-century reformers hoped to establish a science of the criminal that would reveal the secrets of offending behaviour. Between these two different, but recognisably modern, ambitions lay one hundred years of penal history. In some respects the prison was a consequence of one science and a precondition of the other: its architecture and regimes were inspired by Bentham and Howard at the end of the eighteenth century; its inmates were the raw material for criminology's studies of the criminal one hundred years later.[17]

Yet the social history of the prison is a much messier business than its links to the sciences of punishment and crime might suggest. In their dealings with prisoners — and in the management of their own emotions, desires, and disgust with the quality of life of the lower classes inhabiting the police courts and prisons — prison-reformers and administrators frequently used a language that derived not from the Enlightenment project of science but from the Judaeo-Christian mentality that still infused Western societies.

17 See D. Garland, 'The Criminal and his Science', *The British Journal of Criminology*, vol. 25, no. 2, April 1985, pp. 109–37.

Table 2.7 Daily average number of people in prison, 1870–1910

State	*1870*		*1880*		*1890*		*1900*		*1910*	
	Male	*Female*	*Male*	*Female*	*Male*	*Female*	*Male*	*Female*	*Male*	*Female*
NSW	1326	204	1759	362	2138	281	1809	187	1214	150
Victoria	1430	296	1263	316	1504	339	981	204	765	111
Qld	206	17	301	48	580	55	554	50	479	32
WA	122	0	125	8	253	12	487	21	(508)	–
SA	186	18	376	19	220	32	255	23	230	42
Tasmania	179	61	255	82	150	32	88	11	(78)	–

Source: S. Mukherjee, A. Scandia, D. Dagger, & W. Matthews, *Source Book of Australian Criminal and Social Statistics 1804–1988*, Australian Institute of Cr Canberra, 1988, section 8; and statistical registers for each jurisdiction. Some data from Mukherjee et al. has been amended or replaced to correct ca Data for WA and Tasmania in 1910 are totals of male and fe

Mi tory tar p

…chel Foucault has drawn attention to the role of this legacy in the his… of modern punishment, and an emblem of it being the image of a soli…y prisoner in a single cell, kneeling before an invisible but all-surveillant …rison governor. Others have developed similar themes, emphasising the direct transmission of architectural forms (monastic to prison cells) in early modern European prisons, and the role of evangelical and humanitarian sensibilities in the reform of early-nineteenth-century prisons. That is to say, the religious debts of the modern prison and of modern punishment go much deeper than the elementary and mostly useless attempts of the evangelical to instil the love of the Bible in the nineteenth-century prisoner. They are embedded in the whole construction of the prison system as a regime that sought to reconstruct the person of the criminal through a process of remorse and self-reflection[18] — and through something more than this.

After his return from an ultimately fruitless four years as governor of the Norfolk Island Penal Colony Alexander Maconochie took up service as governor of Birmingham prison. It was in that capacity that he gave evidence to a British parliamentary inquiry in 1850 on the subject of prison discipline. Maconochie had developed a strong aversion to contemporary modes of sentencing. The conventional 'time sentence', under which convicted criminals served a definite period of detention, encouraged idleness in the prisoner, who became preoccupied with 'cheating time' by using up the period of sentence in the way most convenient and least burdensome. Punishment of this kind, said Maconochie, was useless and counterproductive to the main purpose of punishment: to prevent crime through reform of the criminal. Punishment not linked to reform was meaningless. But what should be the principle of such punishment?

> I quite agree that the object of punishment is the prevention of crime, but I think that crime would be better prevented by reforming through penal infliction, than by penal infliction without the object of reform. I think we should prevent crime much more by sending our prisoners out made better, than by making scarecrows of them for the community. In this way, I think that reform should be the first object, reform through suffering.[19]

18 Writings on the history of the prison that have informed this chapter include M. Foucault, *Discipline and Punish: The Birth of the Prison*, Pantheon Books, New York, 1977; Spierenburg, *Prison Experience*; Ignatieff, *A Just Measure of Pain*; N. Morris & D. J. Rothman (eds), *The Oxford History of the Prison: The Practice of Punishment in Western Society*, Oxford University Press, Oxford, 1995; Zedner, *Women, Crime and Custody*; D. Garland, *Punishment and Welfare: A History of Penal Strategies*, Gower, Aldershot, UK, 1985; Pratt, *Punishment in a Perfect Society*; and Evans, *Fabrication of Virtue*.

19 United Kingdom, Parliament, *Report from the Select Committee on Prison Discipline*, qu. 7675, BPP, London, 1850, vol. 17.

'Reform through suffering' — Maconochie was not seeking to hide the meaning of imprisonment as the imposition of productive pain or, as he called it, 'penal infliction'. His language — the language of one who was regarded, at mid-century, as the embodiment of a humane and constructive penality — cannot be understood without recognising punishment's debts to centuries of Christian regard for the redemptive power of suffering.[20] In this regard, he spoke for his time — a time in which, it seemed, society was constantly searching for the most productive means of suffering, whether it be through deprivation of human company or food, or through imposition of hard and sometimes purposefully meaningless labour.

The use of the word 'suffering' is striking at this time, if only because an important theme of the reform of prisons and punishment since the eighteenth century is said to have been the decline of physical punishment. 'By the early nineteenth century', according to Pieter Spierenburg, 'British reformers simply considered the prison as synonymous with an absence of the infliction of pain'.[21] We have seen that the experience of transportation to Australia did not embody any such principle: corporal punishment was freely used as an instrument of discipline. But when Maconochie spoke of suffering, he invoked a more subtle sense of the infliction of pain: one that was slower, more internalised, and associated more clearly with the tasks before each prisoner of reflecting on one's conduct and modifying one's behaviour, not out of fear, but out of conscience. Importantly his observation that the object of prison should not be to turn out 'scarecrows' reflects the major transformation that removed the business of punishing from the public eye. Paradoxically the high age of State-directed punishment, in which private agencies had the most limited role to play, was the one in which punishment was most privatised, in which the prisoner's plight was most hidden from view. This was in striking contrast with the eighteenth-century prison, through which visitors could wander, and in which prisoners paid the gaolers for their upkeep.

At the core of nineteenth-century punishment is the development of the idea that 'separation' solves the problems of prison discipline and prisoner rehabilitation. The 1863 Lords Select Committee into Penal Discipline

20 For the Chief Justice of NSW, Sir Alfred Stephen, in 1861, imprisonment also was a 'state of suffering' from which, one hoped, released convicts would return to society with 'changed tendencies and dispositions'. See NSW, Parliament, *Report of the Select Committee on the Public Prisons in Sydney and Cumberland*, NSW Parliamentary Papers, Sydney (hereafter NSWPP), 1861, p. 165.

21 Spierenburg, *Prison Experience*, p. 280

elaborated on the dual meanings of separation: a principle that was embodied in 'construction', on the one hand, and 'system and discipline', on the other. Through architecture, suffering could be made productive; the means by which it would become so deserve attention, in part because they gave us a material heritage evident in cities and towns throughout Australia and the Western world. Through system and discipline, the possibilities of a specialised architecture could be made manifest. Without a suitable architecture, system and discipline would be severely tested; without system and discipline, the architecture was useless.

From the 1820s to the 1840s, vigorous debates in England and the USA sought the best means of breaking associations between criminals, and between the individual criminal and his past. The advocates of the 'silent system' urged the advantages of a strict regime of silence within the prison, which allowed prisoners to associate in common areas for dining, working, religious observance and exercise. The ultimately victorious advocates of the separate system postulated an ideal prison in which each prisoner was isolated in a solitary cell, serving as the place of penal labour as well as sleep. The severity of this system of lengthy isolation was acknowledged after only a few years experimentation at the Pentonville penitentiary from 1842. Thereafter, and especially through the influence of the so-called Crofton system of staged punishment — developed by Major William Crofton in the Irish prisons, adapting Maconochie's marks system from Norfolk Island — there developed a prison system in which prisoners would progress from an initial period of total separation through two more stages of limited association with other prisoners before being released back into the community as reformed citizens.

By the time of self-government in the colonies, the dominance of the separate system as the normal mode of punishment was undisputed. In the first decades of self-government, the parliaments of most colonies considered, from time to time, the various philosophies of punishment and the most desirable structure of penal institutions for their particular purposes. We can see in their considerations the powerful influence of the debates that were simultaneously taking place 'at Home'.

Hence, on the eve of the phenomenal building program that produced the core of Victoria's prison system for the next century, the Inspector-General of Penal Establishments, William Champ (appointed after a number of years managing Tasmania's convict establishment), outlined for a parliamentary inquiry in 1857 the requirements of a suitable prison regime. Separation was essential, and to obtain it he wanted to see a 'small radiating prison, something upon the principle of the establishment at Pentonville'. In such a place, he would insist that the 'very worst characters' would be subject to a system, 'practised for some time with great success in America', of total isolation for a period of time before being allowed to pursue penal labour. Drawing on a number of transatlantic reference points in the design of prison discipline, Champ thus advocated what was effectively the 'separate and silent' system: a regime of total control, in which refractory prisoners would be subject to constant surveillance:

> the walls would be thick so that no sound could penetrate. The light would be from above so that there would be no looking out at the windows. The doors would be solid, of wood, and very thick, and closing so that no sound could come through them; each man would have his bell which he would ring if he was taken ill, or wanted the warder, and the warder would be constantly walking up and down on a carpet or matting with slippers on, and in each door there would be an inspection aperture closed with plate glass . . . with a cover, and as the warder went along he would push it to one side and see what the man was doing in each cell without being observed, and the man inside could not hear the slightest sound. The men would come out one at a time to exercise; the door of each cell in turn would be opened and the occupant would be let out, he would have his cap over his face and he would go into the airing yard, and so with No. 2 and No. 3; and each man would be allowed to walk up and down for an hour.[22]

Champ's vision was as identifiable a picture of mid-Victorian penal discipline as one could obtain from any of Joshua Jebb's guides to the construction and management of prisons. The language he spoke was one also used by the Victorian parliamentarians in their 1857 Report: the four fundamental principles of penal discipline were 'centralisation' (which was economic), 'classification of prisoners' (which prevented contamination of the different classes), 'employment' (which prevented idleness) and 'uniformity of discipline' (which avoided the danger that management might be undermined by the arbitrary actions of individual officers).[23]

The debts that colonial penal systems owed to outside ideas and influences were equally evident in the considerations of the New South Wales Select Committee on Public Prisons in 1861. The establishment of this committee was an opportunity for its chair, the colony's leading young liberal, Henry Parkes, to scrutinise the philosophies and practices of punishment in New South Wales. Questioning a number of colonial dignitaries,

22 Victoria, Parliament, *Report from the Select Committee upon Penal Discipline*, Victorian Parliamentary Papers, Melbourne (hereafter VPP), 1856–7, pp. 61–6.
23 ibid, p. xi.

Parkes sought to establish the superiority of imported progressive ideas on prison discipline over current practice in the colony. His references included the English reformers Matthew Davenport Hill and Lord Brougham,[24] as well as the American Francis C. Gray. Gray's prescription of total separation at night and useful labour at day, and his proscription of severe punishments, was embraced by both Parkes and his interrogated witness, former colonial secretary Edward Deas Thomson. Thomson had visited the USA thirty-five years earlier and was aware of the early penitentiary experiments there, having visited a prison at Baltimore in which the silent system was in operation. Parkes himself was much taken with the reputation of the New York prisons of Sing Sing and Auburn, where, he told the Committee, the system 'is mainly distinguished by its industrial character, by appropriating the prison labour on economic principles . . . turning their labour to account and advantage, and bestowing among the prisoners some means of earning their living when liberated'.[25] It was not the first time the Auburn system had been publicly praised in Sydney: the Sheriff of New South Wales, John Brennan, had told an earlier committee in 1857 that he was using a modified Auburn system to regulate prison labour in Darlinghurst gaol. In that system, he explained, prison labour was deployed without regard to the classification of the prisoners, but without speaking or making signs to each other.[26]

If anything challenged the prominence of 'separation' as a nostrum for prison management in the period after the 1850s, it was the principle of prison labour. John Pratt, a historian of New Zealand punishment, has observed in the uses of outdoor labour a noteworthy difference between colonial and Imperial systems, and one that qualifies Foucault's assertion that, at this time, there was a move away from 'semio-technique' (or punishments displayed for others to learn from).[27] For the most part, outdoor

24 'Hill on Crime' was cited by Police Magistrate David Forbes in 1857 as the major source of ideas for an earlier report on prison discipline in 1855; see New South Wales, Parliament, *Report of the Select Committee on Secondary Punishment*, NSWPP, Sydney 1857, p. 16. Parkes's interest in social policy and criminal justice contributed to his mid-century liberal activism as a social reformer. In 1862 on a visit to England he attended the conference of the influential National Association for the Promotion of Social Science, hearing papers on prison discipline and reformatories, and witnessing the association's opening by the aged Lord Brougham; see A. W. Martin, *Henry Parkes*, Melbourne University Press, Melbourne, 1980, p. 191.

25 NSW, Parliament, *Report* of the Select Committee on the Public Prisons in Sydney and Cumberland, NSWPP, Sydney, 1861, pp. 151–3.

26 NSW, Parliament, *Report of the Select Committee on Secondary Punishment*, NSWPP, Sydney, 1857, pp. 2–5; see also ibid., p. 16, for the evidence of Police Magistrate David Forbes, who describes the 'American silent system' as a model for discipline in NSW gaols in the 1850s.

labour does not appear to have played an equivalent role in Australia since the convict period. The surplus of free labour in the post-gold rush-period diminished the possibility of prison outdoor labour, except in remoter areas, as in Western Australia, where Aborigines were employed on road- and rail-building, or at the special labour prison at Trial Bay in New South Wales, where convicts struggled with the tides for many years to build a breakwater, without success.

Instead, governments and administrators were preoccupied with the uses of labour within prison walls. Once again colonial opinion constantly assessed local practice against lessons learnt elsewhere. But economic constraints also played their role; in debates on the role of prison labour, there was rarely a clear distinction made between labour that relieved the State of the burden of supporting prisoners and labour that was designed to reform. Mr Wills, MLA, moved for the establishment of the Victorian Select Committee upon Penal Discipline in December 1856, observing '[t]hat the aim of a Christian state should not be so much to punish or revenge against its laws, as to encourage in the criminal the *habit of labor*, and in all cases, where practicable, return him to the world a useful member of society'.[28] However, the debates on penal discipline in that Committee, and among its witnesses, focused as much on the best means of providing a suitable infrastructure of incarceration — an infrastructure that might function profitably through the use of prison labour.

Following lengthy evidence, Parkes's 1861 Committee in New South Wales submitted its brief report. The Committee was inclined to stress the benefits of constructing a 'great central prison, with all the requisites in cellular dormitories and properly arranged workshops, to secure the reformatory treatment of the prisoners, and the economical division and profitable employment of their labour'. After recommending both 'secular instruction' and religious teaching, the Committee stressed 'that prisoners should be employed with a discriminating consideration of their capabilities, and with a strict regard to making their labour contribute to their support, and, at the same time, fitting them for an honest course in after life'.[29] But there were considerable difficulties involved in establishing a labour regime that could meet all these requirements.

27 Pratt, *Punishment in a Perfect Society*, pp. 77–83, 86–94; and J. Pratt, '"This is Not a Prison": Foucault, the Panopticon and Pentonville', *Social and Legal Studies*, vol. 2, 1993, pp. 373–95.

28 Victoria, Parliament, *Report from the Select Committee upon Penal Discipline*, VPP, Melbourne, 1856–57, p. iii.

29 NSW, Parliament, *Report of the Select Committee on the Public Prisons in Sydney and Cumberland*, NSWPP, Sydney, 1861, pp. 10–11.

By the 1860s, a constant question was whether 'hard labour' was really that hard, whether it might be used more profitably to relieve the government of some of its economic burdens, and whether it was a sufficient penality to be effective in deterring crime. The 1868 Select Committee inquiring into 'Prison Discipline' in Queensland found that the system fell short on all these criteria, and wondered whether 'the immunity from labor now enjoyed by the worst of our felon class, to a certain extent offers a premium for the commission of crime . . . Under the present system, the State is mulct in a large annual outlay for the support of prisoners in idleness; by employing them, they would be made to assist themselves, and the burdens imposed on tax-payers would be proportionately lessened'.[30] The lack of meaningful penal labour was the theme of much of the evidence given to the Queensland inquiry. Many witnesses expressed anxiety about the possibility that conditions inside prison were better than they were outside — a major breach of the political economy principle of less eligibility, which organised so much mid-Victorian social and criminal-justice policy.[31] One witness, Doctor Bell, thought the prisoners in Brisbane often got better bread than he did and gave hearsay evidence to the effect that it would be better to be in 'Sneyd's lodging house' (Sneyd was the governor of Brisbane gaol at the time) than 'going about making nothing' outside the gaol. He suggested that a remedy might be to adopt 'Yankee notions' and use prison labour productively to make articles for sale by export.[32]

The application of international experience in a colonial setting was nowhere so consciously considered as in the extensive reports of the Victorian Royal Commission on Penal and Prison Discipline (1870–2). Its recommendations on sentencing (for lengthier sentences, which would satisfy the principle of deterrence as well as enhancing the time available for individual reformation of the convict) drew authority directly from the Imperial Parliament's 1863 Royal Commission on Transportation and Penal Servitude; on juvenile delinquency and neglected children, the Victorian Commission drew from the extended debates on the boarding out of children that were being conducted in England at that time; and on prisoner management, the Crofton system, which was developed in Ireland and adapted in England, was considered. The language of political economy governed the Commission's recommendations on the uses of prison

30 Queensland, Parliament, *Report of the Select Committee on Prison Discipline*, Queensland Parliamentary Papers (hereafter QPP), Brisbane, 1868, p. 9.

31 Pratt, *Punishment in a Perfect Society*, pp. 17, 133–5; Garland, *Punishment and Welfare*, pp. 10, 17.

32 Queensland, Parliament, *Report of the Select Committee on Prison Discipline*, QPP, 1868, p. 36.

labour, summed up in the proposition that the most effective means of diminishing crime 'is by enforcing on criminals habits of systematic and unremitting industry which they will afterwards retain'. Moral reform, it was conveniently calculated, was 'proportional to profitable employment'.[33]

This Commission, however, was distinguished by its assessment of the colonial context in discussing the introduction of the Crofton system. The Commission proposed that this system (in which a prisoner's progress was measured not so much by length of sentence served as by amount of labour performed, which governed progress through three stages of penal discipline of decreasing severity before release under supervision on a ticket-of-leave) be adapted for use in Victoria. But local circumstances required that variations be made in the implementation, while retaining the central principles — 'individualisation and reclamation of the prisoner' — which were said to be applicable to any country. The colony differed from other countries 'in the varied character of its population, in their social circumstances and industrial pursuits, in its most prevalent crimes, in geographical features and . . . in the facilities for obtaining intoxicating liquors'. It was felt that the colonial context justified rejection of the ticket-of-leave system (the idea of release on licence under supervision) and required much stricter supervision at the pre-release stage since it would be easy for prisoners to escape into 'an inland frontier of very great extent', which did not exist in Ireland.[34]

An important difference between colonial Australian penal systems and those in other places was the virtual absence of private entrepreneurs from the Australian domain. Perhaps this was another area in which the memory of the convict era (when, of course, there had been extensive assignment of labour to private masters) acted as a caution against innovation, but the opposition of business and labour also played their part.[35] New South Wales Comptroller-General Neitenstein noted differences in attitudes towards the role of prison labour during his travels in 1904, leading him to reflect on

33 Victoria, Parliament, *Progress Report of the Royal Commission on Penal and Prison Discipline (Pentridge Penal Establishment)*, VPP, Melbourne, 1870, 2nd session, p. ix.

34 Victoria, Parliament, *Report from the Royal Commission on Penal and Prison Discipline (No. 2) (Penal and Prison Discipline)*, VPP, Melbourne, 1871, p. xvii; the Report included an extended memorandum from Hon. J. D. Wood on the Irish prison system.

35 See, for example, New South Wales Prisons Department, *Annual Report*, Sydney, 1885, p. 2, which reported that parliamentary opposition to establishing a 'local manufacturing trade' in a prison at Mudgee led to its demise. See also New South Wales, *Debates*, 17 November 1914, p. 1176, reporting concern of unions over prison labour; on the 'very common prejudice' regarding prison labour in Western Australia, see Western Australia, Parliament, *Report from the Commission Appointed to Inquire into the Penal System in the Colony*, WAPP, Perth, 1899, p. 2.

the limits placed on 'the field of useful and remunerative occupation' by the protest of 'free against prison labour' in New South Wales.[36] The Australian labour movement as well as centralised government appear to have played a very effective role in limiting the prospects of profitable prison labour on the scale developed, say, in France, where State provision and management of work in prisons was rare as late as the 1890s.[37] Although contracting for the provision of goods to private industry was not unknown in Australia, the rule was generally maintained that prison labour, for a pittance in earnings, should be devoted to the production of goods for use in State institutions. Labour was also thereby almost wholly limited to a punitive (that is, penal) purpose.

What separation and hard labour could not accomplish might be achieved by the severity of discipline. Although, as we will see in Chapter 4, the enthusiasm for corporal punishment was diminishing quickly in the later nineteenth century, the prisons remained one locale in which it might legitimately be used. Three forms of punishment were common: dietary, isolation, and flogging, the last retained as a final resort. Women could not be whipped, and the invention of solitary confinement as a significant punishment was especially targeted at them. Confinement in one's cell, together with dietary punishment — typically a reduction to bread and water for 24 hours or a number of days — was the most common response to offending in the prison. Recorded whippings for prison offences were increasingly rare after the convict period, which perhaps explains the controversy that erupted when they did occur; in New South Wales from the 1870s to the early 1890s there appeared to be a recurrent inclination towards the use of harsh punishments in a regime that imitated the toughness of English imprisonment in the 1870s. The use of the gag as well as solitary confinement and flogging were resorted to by prison administrations as a response to prisoner disturbance and occasional protest — and especially to enhance the deterrent value of punishment. Such practices served as a fitting reminder of the epitaph 'reform through suffering'.[38]

36 See NSW, Parliament, *Report by the Comptroller-General of Prisons on Prisons, Reformatories, and Asylums and other Institutions Recently Visited by Him, in Europe and America*, NSWPP, Sydney, 1904, pp. 3, 5–6; Neitenstein nevertheless observed that some jurisdictions elsewhere (for example, New York) prohibited the competition of prison labour on the open market.

37 O'Brien, *Promise of Punishment*, pp. 152–63.

38 See C. Mead, 'Tough but Fair: Some Practices of Imprisonment in New South Wales 1866–1914', *Journal of the Royal Australian Historical Society*, vol. 77, no. 3, December 1991, pp. 63, 68; Garton 'Bad or Mad?', pp. 94, 97: these practices were raised especially in the course of the Royal Commission into Berrima Gaol in 1879 and again in official correspondence in 1894–5 relating to the use of the 'gag'.

None of this takes account of the *illegal* punishments and abuses that occasionally provoked public inquiry. In South Australia, for example, in 1869, following the death of a prisoner, an inquiry found widespread instances of abuse, including beating of prisoners with musket butts and even the use of bayonets.[39] Physical force of this type was almost certainly sporadic, and the legal disabilities of prisoners[40] left them little recourse other than direct confrontation or attempting to lobby for outside inquiry, as we will consider in Chapter 5.

In an intellectual climate that looked to the experimentations of the United Kingdom and North America as a benchmark against which to measure the performance of colonial institutions, the penal system constructed in the decades of self-government endorsed severity and discipline as the hallmarks of a successful prison. 'Reform through suffering' summed up the era: it captured the aspiration for individual reclamation, but hinted at the more fundamental purpose of punishment in this period (that is, deterrence). Citing the Lord Chief Justice of England, the Victorian Royal Commission in 1871 conceded that the reformation of the prisoner was uncertain, but that 'the impressions produced by suffering, inflicted as the punishment of crime, and the fear of its repetition, are far more likely to be lasting, and much more calculated to counteract the tendency to the renewal of criminal habits'. Suffering had to be certain if moral reformation of criminals was not to undermine the deterrent effects of punishment.[41] Hence, particular attention was paid to developing an architecture of institutions that would secure such contradictory aims.

THE ARCHITECTURE OF PUNISHMENT

The architecture of incarceration in the colonies was not characterised by unity, either in principle or in execution. What historian of prison architecture Robin Evans refers to as a 'fabrication of virtue' was, in the colonies, a many-textured cloth. The symbolism of some prison facades tells one kind

39 South Australia, Parliament, *Report of Stockade Inquiry Board*, South Australian Parliamentary Papers (hereafter SAPP), Adelaide, 1869, no. 55, p. 1.
40 See G. Zdenkowski, 'Judicial Intervention in Prisons', *Monash University Law Review*, vol. 6, 1980, pp. 294–330; and G. Zdenkowski, 'Review of Disciplinary Proceedings in Australian Prisons', *Criminal Law Journal*, vol. 7, 1983, pp. 3–43.
41 *Report from the Royal Commission on Penal and Prison Discipline (No. 2) (Penal and Prison Discipline)*, VPP, Melbourne, 1871, pp. iii–v.

of story, speaking all too obviously of Imperial majesty and the solemnity of custodial justice, exhibited most strikingly in the grand portico that still remains at Bathurst Prison. Visiting this gaol in the 1890s, the Irish MP Michael Davitt thought the entrance extravagant, arousing scepticism about priorities: 'Wherever I see an imposing and ornamental prison exterior I am prepared for some other folly inside in the way of expensive but inefficient treatment of criminals'.[42] On the other hand, the casual architectural style of some prisons in remote Australia suggested other constraints — economic above all. The experience of being removed from the social world into that of custody had, therefore, a variety of meanings and symbols.

The point to make is that there can be no one 'ideal' of the prison because a single model cannot possibly contain the experience of custody in its many and varied forms between the end of the convict period and the 1920s. What we have to note is the very multitude of forms of custody, and of the variety of forms of treatment that were applied to those in custody. Attempts to separate the various classes of persons in custody consistently failed, and the frustrations articulated by prison administrators in numerous late-nineteenth-century inquiries into prisons and punishment reflect this. The evidence suggests that penal policy in Australia throughout this period was capable of recognising differences within prisoner populations, even if resources and policy commitment fell short of separating the different classes of the incarcerated. How many classes there actually were was itself a matter for debate. The Queensland Colonial Architect told an 1868 Select Committee that the colony should provide for at least five different kinds of custodial need:

> (1) Watch-houses on the *separate* system, for all kinds of unconvicted persons; (2) lockups, on the *associated* principle, for offenders convicted of the lightest crimes; (3) houses of correction, on the *associated* principle, for those convicted of more atrocious offences; (4) a penitentiary, on the *solitary, separate* and *associated* principles, for those convicted of the most heinous crimes; and (5) penal depots, on the *associated* principle, for those criminals convicted of heinous crimes and condemned to hard labor on the public works.[43]

The systems of discipline applied in different institutions were far less predictable than this systematic outline recommended, but the range custody types was accurate enough for the colonial period.

42 M. Davitt, *Life and Progress in Australasia*, Methuen, London, 1898, p. 435.
43 Queensland, Parliament, *Report of the Select Committee on Prison Discipline*, QPP, Brisbane, 1868, p. 48.

The prisons of Australia — the ones that housed those committed to terms of imprisonment in the period between about 1850 and 1960 — were largely constructions of the late nineteenth century. There was no shortage of them, especially in New South Wales. 'This colony', noted Michael Davitt dryly,

> is not nearly as criminal as it would make a stranger believe it to be from the number of its prisons. There are no less than twenty-three, not counting police lock-ups . . . This colony has long suffered under a kind of criminal nightmare, and has sought to rid itself of the magnified evil by spreading a crowd of needless gaols over a country one and a half times larger than France.[44]

The design of Australian prisons has been expertly documented by James Kerr,[45] who draws attention to a range of custodial designs, from those of major penitentiaries to individual cells in remote bush locations. We can distinguish three main types of carceral institution according to their functions in relation to custodial stages. The three categories of prisoner included: those convicted of serious crime and sentenced to 'penal servitude', which typically involved some component of 'hard labour'; those convicted of lesser crimes, who were sentenced to shorter periods of up to two or three years, usually without hard labour; and those held in custody pending trial or perhaps incarcerated for short periods for failure to pay a fine. For much of this period, imprisonment for civil debt was also common in some colonies, and such prisoners might be separated from others but within the same institution as ordinary criminal law convictions and remands.[46]

To each of these stages we can match an institutional type. The most imposing institutions — those that were the centrepieces of custodial design and emblems of the complex of punishment — were the penitentiaries, housing some hundreds of long-sentence inmates. More functional were the metropolitan and local prisons, which served the dual purposes of reception and remand, as well as places of custody for short-to-medium-term prisoners. The third type was the police gaol or lock-up, intended to hold no more than about ten inmates in custody pending transfer elsewhere or awaiting local jurisdiction. The

44 Davitt, *Life and Progress*, p. 431.
45 Kerr, *Out of Sight, Out of Mind*.
46 Imprisonment for debt was abolished as early as 1843 in New South Wales — later in other colonies — but remains in place in Western Australia. See Kercher, *An Unruly Child*, p. 115.

kinds of custodial building possible for any of these three types of incarceration, however, were even more diverse. The generic objects of regulation in the *Prisons Regulation Act 1840* (NSW) were 'Gaols Prisons and Houses of Correction'. A 'prison' for the purposes of the Queensland *Prisons Act* of 1890 was '[a]ny gaol, house of correction, penal establishment, penitentiary, police gaol [a lock-up or watchhouse proclaimed as such under the Act], or floating vessel used as a gaol hereinafter called a hulk; including any stockade, airing, or other grounds or buildings occupied, or used for or in connection with any prison, and contiguous thereto'.[47] According to these descriptions, a prison seemed to be defined by a physical structure of some kind, but the very rationale of locations such as that of Rottnest Island Penal Establishment and Reformatory, established for Aboriginal prisoners in Western Australia in 1840, or that of St Helena Penal Establishment in Moreton Bay, was their geographic identity as a prison whose walls were the sea. Such places mimicked the history of New South Wales as an earlier prison without walls, where the tyranny of distance exercised its own discipline.

Even Rottnest and St Helena, however, had their distinctive carceral designs. What is astonishing about nineteenth-century prison architecture is not its predictability but its diversity. Contrary to claims that Bentham's 'circular prison design was adopted as the basis for most prisons in the Western world',[48] the panopticon was evocative as a term and concept, but little used as a design. A simple custodial rationale informed the meaning of prison in many of the locales mentioned in the Table 2.8 — hence, their design emphasised solidity and minimalist functionality.

A large number of custodial structures — police lock-ups or watchhouses — had no more than half a dozen cells or, in some cases, a single cell capable of holding a number of prisoners, often in appalling conditions. The police lock-up cell at Tennant Creek in the Northern Territory, erected in this small town in 1934 and surviving until the 1960s, was 'a small, rectangular, timber framed and corrugated iron structure with a curved roof . . . [with] small barred windows at the

47 section 5.
48 L. Finch, *The Classing Gaze*, Allen & Unwin, Sydney, 1993, p. 7; compare with Evans, *Fabrication of Virtue*, p. 228, which emphasises that the 'inspection principle upon which its design was based' was the key thing.

bottom of each corner and heavy mesh door'.[49] Structures like this, with poor ventilation and confined space, had long been part of the penal landscape in rural Australia. Specific evidence about the conditions of Roebourne Gaol in 1881 came from a government medical officer, who concluded that the cells were the 'cause of the present illness and conducive to the ill-health of any person detained there during the summer months and subjected to the usual prison discipline'. He had taken the temperature in the cells in December, finding the best ventilated one to be 116°F in the day, and possibly 100°F at night, sufficient to 'undermine the health of the most robust'.[50] In spite of the atrocious conditions afforded in such structures, they remained common in remote Australia into the 1990s. The Royal Commission into Aboriginal Deaths in Custody reviewed the conditions in many such cells and lock-ups — at Wujal Wujal, for example, a small Aboriginal community in North Queensland:

> The watchhouse at Wujal Wujal stands in an open unshaded depression about 100 metres from the centre of the community. It is a square concrete building with a galvanised iron roof and metal doors. It comprises two small cells neither of which is fitted with an effective observation window. In each cell there are two small windows: one in the rear wall, the other in the steel door. Each is set so high that none but the tallest inmate could ever glimpse the world outside.
>
> The watchhouse has a concrete floor, no exercise yard, no sanitary provisions other than a bucket, no running water, no internal lighting and no furniture or other fittings. The Coroner who conducted the inquest into the death aptly described the watchhouse as nothing more than a 'primitive dungeon'.[51]

Such conditions were tolerated and continue to be tolerated because of the 'temporary' nature of the detention being served, although in remote areas this might amount to a number of days, or even weeks if somebody

49 D. Carment, *History and the Landscape in Central Australia*, Australian National University and North Australia Research Unit, Canberra, 1991, p. 47. Carment notes that the cell (which remains at the National Trust Museum in Tennant Creek) was only replaced in the early 1960s following 'representations from the normally conservative Country Women's Association about the poor conditions for prisoners'.

50 J. A. O. Meehan to Government Resident, Roebourne, 3 December 1881, Western Australian Archives, Battye Library, Perth, CSO, acc.527, 1881/238/17.

51 Royal Commission into Aboriginal Deaths in Custody, *Report of the Inquiry into the Death of the Young Man who Died at Wujal Wujal on 29 March 1987*, AGPS, Canberra, 1991, sec. 1.8.

Table 2.8 Prisons in Australia, c. 1900

Type of prison	*NSW*	*Victoria*	*Queensland*	*South Australia*	*Western Australia*	*Tasmania*
Penitentiaries and penal establishments involving hard labour sentences	Darlinghurst Goulburn Parramatta Bathurst Berrima Biloela Maitland Trial Bay	Pentridge	St Helena Townsville	Yatala	Rottnest Island	Hobart
Prisons for imprisonment, custody on remand	Albury Armidale Broken Hill Deniliquin Dubbo Forbes Grafton Hay Mudgee Tamworth Wagga Wagga Wilcannia Wollongong Yass Young	Ballarat Beechworth Bendigo Castlemaine Geelong Melbourne Sale Coburg Female	Blackall Brisbane Cairns Cooktown Mackay Normanton Rockhampton Roma Thursday Island Toowoomba	Adelaide Wallaroo Mt Gambier Port Lincoln Port Augusta Gladstone	Fremantle Albany Broome Bunbury Busselton Carnarvon Derby Geraldton Newcastle Roebourne Wyndham York	Launceston
Lockup/Police Gaol	Balranald Bega Bingera Bombala Bourke Braidwood Burrowa Casino	Ararat Hamilton Mansfield Omeo Shepparton Warnambool	Ayr Camooweal Charters Towers Fortitude Valley Herberton Ingham	Fowlers Bay Kingscote Renmark Streaky Bay Tarcoola		

Table 2.8 Prisons in Australia, c. 1900 (*cont.*)

Type of prison	*NSW*	*Victoria*	*Queensland*	*South Australia*	*Western Australia*	*Tasmania*
Lockup/Police Gaol	Cobar					
	Cooma					
	Coonabarabran					
	Coonamble					
	Cootamundra					
	Cowra					
	Glen Innes					
	Grenfell					
	Gundagai					
	Gunnedah					
	Hillston					
	Inverell					
	Kempsey (West)					
	Moree					
	Murrurundi					
	Narrabri					
	Narrandera					
	Newcastle					
	Orange					
	Port Macquarie					
	Singleton					
	Taree					
	Tenterfield					
	Walgett					
	Wellington					
	Wentworth					

Source: Annual Reports of Prisons Departments (1910 for SA; 1905 for Victoria; 1900 for all other states) and Colonial Statistical Registers, 1900

was sentenced to a short term of imprisonment. Remand prisoners might serve longer periods. In Queensland in 1887, a Board of Inquiry reported cases in the western districts of people being in remand for up to three months in such lock-ups.[52]

The distinction between lock-ups and police gaols was, generally, that the former were designed for short-term custody following arrest and on remand and the latter were intended to contain prisoners sentenced to short terms of imprisonment. Distance determined a colony's use of police gaols. As Table 2.8 shows, they were extensively available in New South Wales and, to a lesser extent, Queensland, which both had relatively large rural populations at a considerable distance from Sydney and Brisbane. Their rationale was almost solely economic: the expense and inconvenience of transferring prisoners under police escort was enormous. An additional advantage of retaining prisoners in a local gaol was a reduction in the costs of transporting them back to places of employment or residence after release. Not that this charge on the public purse was always readily admitted; for many years during the nineteenth century, Aboriginal prisoners in Western Australia were incarcerated on Rottnest Island, and the problems of removing them back to their own country were eventually cited as a reason for establishing northern gaols.[53]

Often conditions did not differ much between lock-ups and gaols. After inspecting most of the colony's lock-ups and gaols in 1887, the Queensland Board of Inquiry concluded that 'very few came up to the highest standard of requirement for a tropical and sub-tropical country':

> Perhaps a majority might be regarded as fairly adapted to the purposes for which they were built; in a large minority the provision for the healthy and decent detention of prisoners is utterly inadequate. As a rule the cells are too small . . . In the vast majority of the lockups the ventilation is most imperfect, and the suffering endured by the unfortunate prisoners must be great. . . . we were convinced, after inspection, that confinement for even a limited number of hours in many of the Northern and Western lockups must endanger the lives of prisoners.[54]

52 Queensland, Parliament, *Report from the Board of Inquiry Appointed to Inquire into the General Management of the Gaols, Penal Establishments, and Lockups of the Colony of Queensland*, QPP, Brisbane, 1887, p. xviii.

53 Western Australia, Parliament, *Report of the Royal Commission on the Condition of the Natives*, qu. 1890–4, WAPP, Perth, 1905, p. 14, notes that the Aborigines Department paid at that time to transport the Aborigines back to their country after release. One of the purposes of the Discharged Prisoners and Prison Gate Associations was to assist prisoners in returning to their place of residence or employment.

54 Queensland, Parliament, *Report from the Board of Inquiry Appointed to Inquire into the General Management of the Gaols, Penal Establishments, and Lockups of the Colony of Queensland*, QPP, Brisbane 1887, p. xvii.

Most of those who came into police custody, for whatever cause, spent some time in such watchhouses and small gaols. Fewer, of course, spent long periods in lock-ups, although the Queensland Board reported cases of 'presumably innocent men' spending up to three months in lock-ups on remand, effectively suffering 'imprisonment without trial in badly-constructed cells'.[54] But most of those who were sentenced to terms of imprisonment longer than a week would be transferred to a police gaol or a major prison.

The police gaols were typically more substantial structures located in regional centres, built of stone or brick and designed to maintain secure custody. Many survive today, as museums or having been converted to other functions. In Dubbo the solid urban gaol built between the 1860s and 1887 served as a prison for the mid-west of New South Wales until 1966. It could hold 16–20 prisoners in a sixteen-cell male block, as well as a couple of female cells in a separate building. In spite of its small size, it served the full range of punishment functions: the reconstructed open-air gallows, last used in 1904, shows one end of the spectrum; the library, hospital, and kitchen represent the other.[56] In these institutions the labour was never intense but, rather, closely related to the sustenance of the prison: some tailoring, cooking, cleaning, and general maintenance.[57] The design of these small gaols limited the potential of imprisonment as a means of personal reformation, but this did not prevent an ambitious administrator like Comptroller-General Frederick Neitenstein requiring the introduction of a system of restricted association throughout the smaller, as well as large, institutions from the late 1890s.[58]

As we will see in a later discussion, the nineteenth-century discourse of penology was much preoccupied with the separation of populations within prisons and gaols. The uniform presumption of early Victorian reform was that the separation of prisoners from one another was beneficial. The design of small places of containment nevertheless encouraged frequent breaches of this requirement. While the Dubbo Gaol, for example, preserves evidence of the separation of remand and sentenced prisoners, there was no such separation in Queensland police gaols in the 1880s. In

55 Queensland, Parliament, *Report from the Board of Inquiry Appointed to Inquire into the General Management of the Gaols, Penal Establishments, and Lockups of the Colony of Queensland*, QPP, Brisbane 1887, p. xviii.
56 Information derived from B. Hornadge, *Old Dubbo Gaol*, self-published, Dubbo, NSW [n.d.] and personal inspection, January 1995.
57 See NSW Prisons Department, *Annual Report*, Sydney, 1900, pp. 20–1.
58 NSW Prisons Department, *Annual Report*, Sydney, 1900, p. 5.

South Australia, in spite of regulations requiring classification, a Board of Inquiry into the Stockade (the main penal establishment in the colony) thought that 'it would be attended with some difficulty while there is but one building to confine prisoners, when not at work (except three solitary cells), and whilst there is so little diversity of occupation'.[59]

Nevertheless, by this time there were many examples throughout the colonial penal systems of the separation of populations within prisons, and even of the establishment of separate institutions altogether. This process of distinguishing prisoner populations applied not just to remand and sentenced prisoners: at different stages and in different places from the 1840s to the 1890s, the design and construction of prisons were based on decisions to separate women from men, young from old, and Aboriginal from non-Aboriginal. Such separations prefigured other distinctions that would develop in the early twentieth century, but which were less related to architecture than to the system of discipline and prisoner management.

One example of gaol design being affected by population distinctions was the development of Aboriginal cells and prisons in Western Australia. In the decades following the designation of Rottnest Island as a prison for Aborigines in 1840 colonial administrators debated the desirability of meeting perceived customary needs. Experience with Aboriginal prisoners, especially those removed from their home environs, had early suggested the dangers of such removal to their physical health. The Superintendent of the prison was asked by the Colonial Secretary in 1862 for an opinion on the proposed design for a new prison there, the latter observing that 'confinement in prison has the effect of producing pulmonary affection among the native population'. Hence,

> [i]t has been suggested that a large Circular Stone wall should be built with deep foundations to prevent the natives from burrowing under it, and so high as to preclude their climbing over it. That the native prisoners should be therein confined and allowed to erect their own bush huts. That when an accumulation of dirt occurred, the interior might be set on fire when the natives were out at work, by which the place would be thoroughly cleansed, when fresh huts could be erected.[60]

Superintendent Vincent rejected this innovation, fearing murder in the enclosure as a result of the presence of different tribes, and noting an

59 South Australia, Parliament, *Report of Stockade Inquiry Board*, SAPP, Adelaide, 1869, no. 55, p. 2.

60 R. J. Ferguson, *Rottnest Island: History and Architecture*, University of Western Australia Press, Perth, 1986, pp. 38–9.

absence of suitable materials for the proposed huts and of sufficient firewood to keep the prisoners warm at night. Rottnest instead got an octagonal shaped enclosure, with separate limestone cells. Even so, it is evident that, from the 1880s, there were some adaptations made to accommodate the customs and preference of Aboriginal inmates. The contentious nature of these adaptations was disclosed publicly when a Perth newspaper condemned the allegedly appalling conditions of a sick Aboriginal prisoner on Rottnest. Superintendent Jackson reported to the Colonial Secretary that the facts were more complicated. The prisoner concerned had been placed in a

> [c]ell which is about 10 x 10 with a window 4 x 2 and a large ventilator in the top, the door being left open so that there is plenty of ventilation. The floor is covered on purpose with dry sand and a small fire made in the center of the cell, Native fashion, blankets are given but sick Natives will not use neither [sic] bedding or covering they prefer lying down in the hot sand near the fire and roll in it . . . The tribe friends of the sick are allowed to visit and remain with them, the cell being kept clean and fresh dry sand placed in, the dirty one being removed, this I found is the best for sick natives who will not use any of the comforts given to sick Europeans.[61]

Although there is no evidence of a specific policy to design special Aboriginal or 'native' cells in Western Australian prisons, there is a good deal of evidence of segregation of Aborigines into different cell types in the many prisons established in the north from the 1880s. Official Reports around 1900 distinguished 'native cells' or separate wards for Aboriginal prisoners at Albany, Busselton, and Derby, in addition to the separate Aboriginal prison at Rottnest. Specific features of 'native cells' in some places appear to have been the provision of bars in place of bricks in an attempt to reduce the claustrophobic environment, and the chain bars to which Aboriginal prisoners were attached during their confinement at night, a practice that continued in some places after the Second World War.[62] Despite evidence in some places in Western Australia of prisons being built according to a distinctive design for Aboriginal inmates, it may be that the northern climate and the need to accommodate large numbers of arrested cattle-stealers was more influential than sensitivity to the special needs of a particular

61 Supt Jackson to Colonial Secretary, 5 July 1883, commenting on an article in the *Inquirer and Commercial News*, 27 June 1883, Western Australian Archives, Battye Library, Perth, CSO 1883/1539/90.

62 On the use of the chains at Wyndham Police Gaol in 1929, 1936, and 1947, see Western Australian Archives, Battye Library, Perth, CSO acc. 752, 826/1919; see also Kerr, *Out of Sight, Out of Mind*, pp. 99–100.

population. Racial segregation was nevertheless practised over a long period in the north, where as late as 1946, a 'Native compound' was still in use at Broome.[63] More recently, in the Northern Territory, evidence that racial difference had a positive influence on prison regimes has been argued to have distinguished Aboriginal incarceration in Darwin from the more conventional (and severe) regime in Alice Springs.[64]

Beyond the lock-ups and country gaols, there were the penitentiaries and large urban prisons, which processed thousands of inmates a year. The design of the larger establishments was more purposeful and certainly more expensive. The critical development in the mid-nineteenth century was that of the individual cell, a requirement of the separation of prisoners, of breaking up associations, and of preventing contamination, which became the core principles of Victorian imprisonment. Kerr traces the individual cell's introduction into the colonies to the late convict period, when two Royal Engineers, George Barney and the Governor George Gipps, arrived in New South Wales. They brought with them ideas and prescriptions that had been developed in England through the Society for the Improvement of Prison Discipline.[65] Among those ideas, the dominant one was the principle of subjecting the prisoner to inspection — by warders, by the governor, in the presence or in the imagination of the inmate. It was a principle that Evans suggests was 'the unifying feature of early nineteenth-century prison architecture' and the single aspect of Bentham's Panopticon that survived the collapse of his aspirations.[66]

Far from Bentham's vision of the circular panopticon, in which the interiors of all cells were visible from a central surveillance point (a model pursued in only a small number of institutions elsewhere[67]), the dominant feature of Australia prison design was a corridor of cells, the entrances of which were visible from the end of the corridor.[68] The arrangement of these corridors in prison complexes varied greatly, depending on the decade of construction, the size and topographic location of the prison, and the par-

63 Western Australian Archives, Battye Library, Perth, CSO 278/1946. I have benefited in these comments from the research assistance of Andrew Gill.
64 See B. Tyler, 'Penology on an Australian Frontier', *Journal of Northern Territory History*, vol. 4, 1993, pp. 23–35.
65 Kerr, *Out of Sight, Out of Mind*, p. 37.
66 Evans, *Fabrication of Virtue*, p. 228.
67 See Evans, *Fabrication of Virtue*, pp. 228–35; N. Morris, 'The Contemporary Prison: 1965–Present', in Rothman & Morris, *Oxford History of the Prison*, pp. 227–62, is a study of life in such a prison today: the State Penitentiary, Illinois.
68 In addition to personal observation of some of the surviving prisons, the following owes much to Kerr's account, *Out of Sight, Out of Mind*.

ticular architect involved. In some, such as the original Berrima Gaol in New South Wales (1836–39), the extension to Darlinghurst Gaol in Sydney (1866–72), or the Victorian country prisons of the 1860s (Bendigo, Sandhurst, and so on), the corridors radiated in wings off a central hall. In others, such as the country prisons in New South Wales, the constructions were single storey. In still others — the innovative Female Factory at Parramatta or the Melbourne Gaol, for instance — the corridors became galleries facing onto an open interior in a multi-storied edifice, which in the case of Fremantle Prison (Western Australia), built originally as the Imperial convict depot, amounted to four stories of accommodation.

In the Victorian era much attention was focused on the precise calculation of cell size: what cubic volume of air would be conducive to reformation and preserve health in the conditions of separate treatment, particularly in those penitentiaries in which six–twelve months of a sentence might first be served in almost total isolation? The economics of prison construction almost inevitably meant that cells were smaller than the prescribed models — those spelt out for English prison construction — especially the Pentonville standard of 13 feet x 7 feet. Kerr's comparison of single cell sizes for Australian prison construction shows that the smallest standard cells were those in the Fremantle Convict Depot (1852, 7 feet x 4 feet), while only Bathurst Gaol (c. 1884, 13 feet x 7 feet) reached the Pentonville standard.[69] While the preference was for single occupant cells after the 1840s, multiple occupancy of these single cells was not uncommon — for reasons of classification or overcrowding.

The prison was a community — a closed one — but nevertheless a community that was intended to provide the rudimentary elements of everyday life organised around the requirements of punishing and reforming the convicted criminal. Besides the cell blocks, therefore, most large prisons and even some smaller ones included a range of other buildings: kitchen, dining hall, chapel, hospital or infirmary ward, library, and workshops. Punishment cells were usually incorporated in the cell blocks at the base of the building and, in some cases, without windows or any other source of light, although an early attempt to construct such cells for the purposes of punishment by solitary confinement (by Gipps at the Female Factory in 1838–39) was forbidden by the Imperial authorities as illegal.[70] Beyond the buildings themselves, the prison required outdoor facilities — exercise

69 Kerr, *Out of Sight, Out of Mind*, p. 153.
70 Kerr, *Out of Sight, Out of Mind*, pp. 45–6.

yards at minimum. In some prisons, consistent with the requirements of prohibiting prisoner association, these were major constructions that embodied the inspection principle. The so-called 'panopticons' at Pentridge Prison were circular, roofless buildings divided into radial segments in which prisoners might exercise separately under the observation of warders in a post at the centre of the circle. The most spectacular example of such a structure was built at Parramatta in 1899 and survived to the 1980s, becoming a notorious place of punishment: the 'bull-ring'.[71]

Inner-city prisons like Darlinghurst and Melbourne Gaol scarcely had any room for other facilities, but the original intention of penitentiaries like Pentridge, Long Bay, Yatala, and St Helena was to provide sufficient outdoor space for vegetable gardens that would contribute to the sustenance of the inmates. Hence their substantial grounds, enclosed by high walls, contributed to a sense of domination over the surrounding environment — a relation that deserves attention in its own right.[72] Such dominance was a fitting embodiment of the deterrence principle, but an aggravation to those who later sought a different kind of environment, in which the institution's focus would be rehabilitation of the inmate.

These, then, were simply some of the largest public institutions of the late colonial period — monuments to the importance of punishment in sustaining a social order. The prison-building program of the mid-nineteenth century delivered a fabric that would structure the possibilities of punishment for the following century and more — an architecture that would more often be viewed as an enemy of discipline and rehabilitation rather than as an aid to the original, inspiring principles of modern penitentiary design.

71 Kerr, *Out of Sight, Out of Mind*, p. 119.

72 For an account of the relation between prison and urban setting in Melbourne, see R. Broome, 'The Stigma of Pentridge: The View from Coburg 1850–1987', *Journal of Australian Studies*, no. 22, May 1988, pp. 3–18.

3

THE CRIMINAL

In an international movement of extraordinary reforming energy, beginning in the 1880s, the penal systems of most Western countries began to change. In cultural terms the era was alternately optimistic and pessimistic. Science, social policy, and institutional experience all seemed to show that most wrong-doers' capacity for adjustment and rehabilitation was sufficient to return them to society as equal citizens. Environmentalist theories of human and social development supported the idea that reformers had a positive role to play in attuning the law and social institutions better to the needs of individuals and groups. Against this optimism, the development of an applied science of population characteristics — eugenics — provided a cautionary note on the possibilities of reforming individuals: some individuals were doomed by their heredity to be incapable of partaking in the full range of social endeavour, and would, therefore, need to be segregated. Environmentalism and hereditarianism — these two theories were less opposites than explanations that interacted in different measures to influence the shape of social policy and institutional practice throughout the period from the 1880s to the 1930s.[1]

In the field of punishment, these developments were concentrated in the growth of the science of criminology. The classical theories of punishment that had shaped penality from the later eighteenth century had sought to fit the punishment to the crime as exactly as possible, and no

1 See especially M. J. Wiener, *Reconstructing the Criminal: Culture, Law, and Policy in England, 1830–1914*, Cambridge University Press, Cambridge, 1990; S. Garton, 'Sound Minds and Healthy Bodies: Re-considering Eugenics in Australia, 1914–1940', *Australian Historical Studies*, no. 103, 1994, pp. 163–81; R. A. Nye, *Crime, Madness and Politics in Modern France: The Concept of National Decline*, Princeton University Press, Princeton, NJ, 1984; R. Harris, *Murders and Madness: Medicine, Law and Society in the* Fin de Siecle, Clarendon Press, Oxford, 1989; Radzinowicz & Hood, *The Emergence of Penal Policy*; Garland, *Punishment and Welfare*.

attention was paid, in theory at least, to the character of the offender.[2] The object of the nineteenth-century prison was to preserve the deterrent value of punishment while aiming at the rehabilitation of the prisoner as one who was paying a redemption to society through a lengthy sentence and who had become a productive worker through the routines of gaol life. This abstracts from a more complex reality — evident, for example, in the observations of Sir Alfred Stephen, Chief Justice of New South Wales, who in 1861, after twenty-two years on the bench, emphasised the necessity of judicial discretion in taking account of 'every man's case and character', a view that placed him at odds with his time as far as the administration of prisons went.[3]

In the later nineteenth century, evidence of a decline in serious crime shifted the balance of policy and interest in the functions of punishment and imprisonment. From the 1880s, the science of criminology aspired to determine in what measure the reform of criminals could be achieved by imprisonment and hence adjust institutional training to individual needs. While jurists had shaped the development of classical penality, the late-nineteenth-century development of criminology was influenced by medicine and by the statistical and positivist social science that had been developing since the 1830s. A growing interest in the different characteristics of individuals and of population types was characteristic of these sciences, accelerated by the impact of Darwinism.

A cause of optimism for the late-nineteenth-century reformers who sought to alter the shape and function of penal options was the evidence that this was an age of declining criminality. Prisoner numbers were falling, even before the introduction of legal reforms, which further assisted a decline in incarceration. There were signs of a decline in violence, in the colonies as in other countries. Environmentalists felt that such evidence reflected an improvement in wealth and living standards across the greater part of the population and hence justified further social amelioration. Hereditarians pondered whether the trend resulted from the enforced

2 See Garland, *Punishment and Welfare*, ch. 1.

3 NSW, Parliament, *Report from the Select Committee on the Public Prisons of Sydney and Cumberland*, qu. 4851, NSWPP, Sydney, 1861. Stephen wanted to see some test applied to each prisoner before release, and was thus opposed to the administration of a remission system that had no regard to the prior character of the prisoner. This intuition was consistent with later criminological views, but not linked to a science of the criminal's differences. See, for example, Garland, *Punishment and Welfare*, pp. 82–3.

segregation of offenders in prisons and asylums since the middle of the century, and worried that those who were not caught in the net of social defence that these institutions represented would increase their numbers by reproducing at a faster rate than the respectable classes. Such ideas repeated themselves endlessly over the following decades and shaped the structure of penal institutions accordingly.

In this chapter we look first at the influence of criminology by examining the avenues through which it was transmitted into Australian penal debates and practices. Second, we explore the reform of penal strategies and institutions that were associated with an increasing differentiation of the crime problem and of offending populations. Finally the chapter examines the impact of another science — that of psychology — on debates, policies, and practices of punishment in the first half of this century.

CRIMINOLOGY: FROM CRIME TO CRIMINAL

Penal strategies in the nineteenth century developed as part of an international network, which is an interesting phenomenon in itself. The reform of punishment was a preoccupation of governments, of prison administrators, of scientists and jurists — all of them in constant communication through international travel, conferences, and publishing, as well as through personal communication. In the Australasian context (and, indeed, the British Imperial context), we must add that the international network was one of personnel exchange for positions of employment — the examples of Edmund Du Cane and Alexander Maconochie have been noted earlier. Such facts call into question any approach to colonial history that sees metropolitan influences as flowing down a one-way street. The development of penal strategies was interactive, occurring between jurisdictions; in current management terminology, there was constant benchmarking and consequent change in order to emulate what was seen as best practice. What this meant for prisoners in their cells was another matter.

The structures of this international and intercolonial net of influence and debate are worth detailing. Undoubtedly they intensified in the late nineteenth century, but penology and criminology were the subjects of social science and reform associations in the United Kingdom and North America from the 1850s on. Yet the construction of a new approach, which represented a significant break with mid-Victorian penality, was the achievement of the Italian school of criminology, founded by the former army medical officer Cesare Lombroso. His work was mediated for the English-speaking world especially through the writing of Havelock Ellis. Ellis, who had spent his early adult life working as teacher in rural New South Wales, reworked European criminology in his 1890 epitome, *The Criminal*. In the United Kingdom, influence of a different genealogy was exerted by a doctor, Francis Galton, founder of eugenics, and a mathematician, Karl Pearson, who took statistics beyond description by analysing correlations of population attributes. In addition to their monograph publications, researchers and writers such as these broadcast their message through articles in late-nineteenth-century reviews and, from the early twentieth century, in specialist journals such as the *Eugenics Review*.[4]

International conferences, sometimes associated with trade fairs or conventions, also had their place in ventilating the new criminology. Penology was a subject of international conferences before the birth of criminology. As a discipline, criminology built on earlier gatherings of penal administrators to establish an international debate through conferences devoted to the study of crime and penal methods from the 1860s. Included among colonial prison governors were some assiduous enquirers into contemporary criminology and penology. None of them were major researchers responsible for shaping the field, but through their regular correspondence and travel they helped to shape Australian debates on the punishment of crime and the administration of penal establishments as well as other social institutions. The most notable figure in this regard was the New South Wales Comptroller-General of Prisons (1896–1909), Frederick Neitenstein. His overseas travel and regular correspondence with the new criminologists and penal administrators of his time were discussed in a number of impressive public documents on crime and punishment; after receiving one such report, Michael Davitt later commented that he had 'rarely read a more lucid and enlightened treatise on the whole subject of criminal administration'.[5] Neitenstein's authority in criminological opinion and penal administration was unchallenged

4 A recent publication lists more than 1600 articles on crime, punishment, and policing in nineteenth-century periodicals: E. Palmegiano, *Crime in Victorian Britain: An Annotated Bibliography from Nineteenth-Century British Magazines*, Greenwood Press, London, 1993.

5 Davitt, *Life and Progress*, p. 433; on Neitenstein, see S. Garton, 'Frederick William Neitenstein: Juvenile Reformatory and Prison Reform in NSW 1878–1909', *Journal of the Royal Australian Historical Society*, vol. 75, no. 1, June 1989, pp. 51–64; and M. Sernack, Penal Reform in New South Wales: Frederick William Neitenstein, 1896–1909, PhD thesis, University of Sydney, 1979.

in Australia, with the New South Wales system being regarded by contemporaries 'as the model of Prison management in the Commonwealth' by the end of his term of office and for some time thereafter.[6] Two decades after Neitenstein's retirement, a New South Wales Minister for Justice would still intone that 'probably, in the whole annals of the Public Service of this State there was never an appointment more justified than his', and that his was a name ever to be 'associated with the principle of reform and humanitation [*sic*] of our prisons'.[7]

The influence of international penology and criminology in shaping Australian penology was certainly not initiated by, nor was it limited to, Neitenstein and New South Wales. Earlier colonial interest in the development of new approaches to prisoner-management had been evident in the visit of the New South Wales Sheriff, and later Comptroller-General, Harold Maclean, to England, Ireland, and Scotland in 1869–70. This visit consolidated the mid-Victorian systems of separate treatment, labour discipline, and prisoner classification through progressive stages of control in the New South Wales system. From Ireland, he brought back the idea of a pre-release work prison, based on that operating at Lusk outside Dublin, and developed it into the short-lived Trial Bay Prison.[8] In Victoria, John Dennistoun Wood had been commissioned by the government in 1867 to report on the management of European and North American prisons. His labours informed the work of the Royal Commission on Penal Discipline, especially its 1871 report, to which his detailed observations were appended.[9] Three decades later, the Victorian Inspector-General, J. Evans, reported twice in 1901 on his travels in Europe and North America visiting prisons and reformatories; his second report detailed the somewhat

6 As noted in 'Papers in Connection with Warders' Appeal Provisions', Western Australian Archives, Battye Library, Perth, acc. 968 AN 123/2/1142/1911; *Australian Yearbook*, 1929, p. 472, notes the 'especially prominent' commitment to moral reformation in New South Wales gaols.

7 Hon. J. R. Lee, Modern Methods of Prison Reform, lecture given to Howard Prison Reform League, Sydney, 7 July 1930, copy in National Library of Australia, Canberra. His reputation continues: see D. Grant, *Prisons: The Continuing Crisis in NSW*, Federation Press, Sydney, 1992, pp. 49–51; NSW, Parliament, *Report of the Royal Commission into New South Wales Prisons (Nagle Commission)*, NSWPP, Sydney, 1976–77–78, Appendix, pp. 448–55.

8 Kerr, *Out of Sight, Out of Mind*, pp. 108–9; Mead, 'Tough but Fair', pp. 64–5.

9 Victoria, Parliament, *Report from the Royal Commission on Penal and Prison Discipline (No. 2) (Penal and Prison Discipline)*, VPP, Melbourne, 1871, Appendix (Report of Hon. J. D. Wood on Irish Prison System); I. Petrass, 'Those who Trespass against Us': Women in Victorian Prisons, 1857 to 1873, BA (Hons) history thesis, Monash University, 1989, p. 60.

mixed reputation of the Elmira Reformatory in New York, which had begun in 1876 with much fanfare as an institution that would reform prisoners using methods drawn from the systems of Maconochie and Crofton.[10] In South Australia, the Rev. John Pearce was commissioned by the government to report on prison reform in Great Britain and North America in 1911, reporting back on the reformative, rather than punitive, philosophies that now held sway in other countries. One superintendent had told him, 'I don't want to know the nature of the crime, but the character of the prisoner . . . so that he may receive appropriate treatment'.[11] Around the same time, the Chairman of the recently established Indeterminate Sentences Board of Victoria travelled to the USA, United Kingdom, France, and Belgium to examine the ways in which habitual criminals under indeterminate sentences were managed.[12] While none of these adventurers in the world of penology tackled their task with the same enthusiasm as Neitenstein, their observations helped to transmit innovation and to measure the state of local institutions and practices.

World travel was not the only way of measuring one's progress in penology, nor were prison administrators the only advocates of the new criminology. In the 1890s the new science was honoured in the foundation of Australia's first 'Criminology Society' by Melbourne independent clergyman Dr Charles Strong. In 1902 he spoke of the need for a 'rational and enlightened treatment of prisoners', an issue that was too important to be left just to the technical experts — John Howard and the nineteenth-century Quaker reformer Elizabeth Fry had not been departmental officials. The philosophy of reform in place of punishment found its way into Strong's advocacy of 'enlightened, reformative treatment', and he quoted William Douglas Morrison, an English critic of prisons and former prison chaplain, approvingly: 'the less imprisonment the better'. The Society communicated with — and gained ideas from — like bodies elsewhere. Strong proposed, for instance, that a committee on the treatment of the criminal be set up in Melbourne, similar to the committee that had recently reported to the New York State Conference of Charities

10 See Victoria, Parliament, *Report of the Inspector-General on Prison Systems of Europe and America* and *Report of the Inspector-General on the New York State Reformatory at Elmira*, both in VPP, Melbourne, 1901, vol. 2.

11 South Australia, Parliament, *Report of Rev. John Pearce on Prison Reform, Great Britain and America*, SAPP, Adelaide, 1912, no. 62, p. 3.

12 Victoria, Parliament, *Report of the Chairman, Indeterminate Sentences Board, on Reformatory Prisons and Institutions in Europe and America*, VPP, Melbourne, 1910, vol. 3.

and Correction, the proceedings of which the Melbourne Society had received.[13] The feminist and social reformer Vida Goldstein was one of many active in the cause, being asked to report back on the United States penal system while she was in USA for the International Women Suffrage Conference in 1902.[14]

Lay, rather than technical, readings of criminology also found their advocates in the Western Australian Commission into the Penal System of 1899, which drew conventionally — but with more application than demonstrated by any other contemporary colonial observers except Neitenstein — on advanced thinking about the international state of reform in prisons and punishment. Perhaps the Commission was prompted by stirrings from social reformers such as the radical Thomas Walker, formerly a New South Wales MP, who told a Perth lecture audience at this time that prisons generally manufactured more criminals than they cured, and that there was a new science to guide response to crime — 'criminology and penology'. A few years later, Walker had become Attorney-General and was an influential advocate of 'penological reform in Western Australia'.[15] The third and final report of the Commission was a pastiche of 1890s criminological thinking, which drew 'on the best authorities on criminology, such as Professor Ferri, Lombroso, Du Cane, Tallack, Maudsley, Ellis, Mayhew, and others'. The list suggests eclecticism rather than deep analysis, and the influence of the new thinking on the Commissioners was uneven. Where opportune, they were just as inclined to quote the early nineteenth-century English law reformer Samuel Romilly on the necessity of certainty in punishment (a reminder to us of the durability of classical penality) as they were prone to cite more modern arguments for indeterminate sentences. On the other hand, the report spoke in modern terms of the 'biological factor' in crime, the influence of which meant that certain individuals were disposed by their degeneracy to be more susceptible to the 'stress of circumstances', including poverty. This

13 C. Strong, paper read at general meeting of the Criminology Society of Victoria, 9 May 1902; C. Strong, *Prison Reform* (pamphlet), n.d. (reprinted from *Review of Reviews*) (both in the possession of the Mitchell Library, Sydney).

14 J. M. Bomford, *That Dangerous and Persuasive Woman: Vida Goldstein*, Melbourne University Press, Melbourne, 1993, p. 33.

15 For a report on Walker's lecture, 'The Prison Cure for Crime', given at the Bohemia Hall in Perth, see the *Sunday Times* (Perth), 4 December 1898. For an account of Walker's involvement in prison reform after 1911, see [J. M. Drew], *Penological Reform in Western Australia* (pamphlet), Perth, 1916; and ch. 5 below. See also J. E. Thomas & A. Stewart, *Imprisonment in Western Australia: Evolution, Theory and Practice*, University of Western Australia Press, Perth, 1978.

acknowledgment of dual influences in the production of crime sat comfortably with the generally radical disposition of the Commission, which believed, among other things, that attempts to escape were a sign of positive energy in the inmate, which should not be punished harshly by flogging. The growing enthusiasm of some colonies for indeterminate sentencing was not viewed favourably by the Commission, which was sceptical about the authority of the Superintendent in the Elmira system (again, a criticism that reflected the radical liberal, even libertarian, flavour of some of this Western Australian inquiry's thinking). It recommended sentencing of serious offenders by a 'Board of Medical Jurists', while citing the harmful effects of imprisonment and hence favouring short, sharp, and severe sentences for minor offences.[16]

In this respect the Western Australian Commission illustrates a principle of refraction in the beaming of criminological light into colonial penal systems. Its progressivism with respect to the rights of prisoners, the recommended closure of Rottnest, and its opposition to arbitrary punishment and pointless labour sat side by side with more conventional punitive ideas, including a preference for retaining capital punishment and the retention of flogging for some offences, especially when committed by juvenile offenders. Ferri, Ellis, Du Cane, Morrison, and others were cited repeatedly in footnotes to support aspects of a reform package that was a *bricolage* of progressive and more antiquated ideas.

Such lack of system was not a charge to be directed against the leading Australian administrator of his generation, Frederick Neitenstein, however. Davitt's high opinion has already been quoted — an opinion based on Davitt's reading of a report (virtually a manifesto) on crime and its prevention that Neitenstein appended to his first annual report as Comptroller-General. This was a document that showed how late-nineteenth-century thinking, in its attention to a variety of penal strategies, differed from what had gone before by shifting attention away from the prison to other responses. Especially notable was the strong preventative emphasis in the extended discussion of juvenile crime and 'that form of disorder which we have come to know by the name of "larrikinism"': 'The best way to empty the gaols and to diminish crime is to see that the children grow up trained to religious, moral and industrial habits'.[17] Expressed this way, the prescription was sim-

16 Western Australia, Parliament, *Report from the Commission Appointed to Inquire into the Penal System in the Colony*, WAPP, Perth, 1899, pp. 3 (escapes), 12–13 (Elmira), 18–19 (sentencing by Board), 3–4 (short sentences).

17 NSW, Parliament, *Annual Report on Prisons*, NSWPP, Sydney, 1896, Appendix, p. 62.

ilar to the objectives of the institutions of juvenile reform — the reformatories and industrial schools — since the 1850s. But the variety of remedies went beyond the scope of criminal-justice institutions:

> In the suppression of larrikinism, too much has been left to police and to the prisons; but other measures should be taken before the disease is allowed to attain full development. It is just precisely one of those things where prevention is better than cure . . . the only alternative to the prison which has yet been suggested is the lash.

Instead of such penal methods, which were only last resorts for a 'small residuum' of irreclaimable youth, Neitenstein stressed the potential of preventive action: curfews on the gathering of youths after nightfall; the spread of rational recreation, such as the encouragement of illuminated public parks, which could be frequented at night as he had observed in European cities; the introduction of volunteer military corps; and even, perhaps, universal military service (Neitenstein had been famous for his insistence on drill in managing the juveniles on the '*Sobraon*' reformatory ship in Sydney Harbour).[18] The transitional nature of his reform program is evident in his continued promotion of military training and rational recreation, experiments of the Victorian era. But the careful (if intuitive) analysis of the formation of 'pushes' and of the larrikin disposition — together with the search for non-carceral remedies, which looked towards a more reintegrative response to offending — made this a recognisably modern discussion of social and institutional reform.

In 1904 Neitenstein had the opportunity to build on years of correspondence with prison administrators and 'various leading penologists in Europe and America' by touring prisons and other institutions in England, Scotland, Ireland, France, Belgium, Switzerland, the USA, and Canada, visiting at least forty-one prisons as well as courts and other institutions associated with the criminal-justice system. His 100-page report — illustrated with photographs and prison plans, and accompanied by a number of reports and commentaries, especially on juvenile justice issues — gives a remarkably detailed account of turn-of-the-century penal practice in a large number of countries at this time. Neitenstein did not believe that contemporary penal practice elsewhere justified a 'revolution in our present gaol system' in Australia, but he brought home with him ideas about changes in management that he hoped to see implemented in the new state

18 See Garton, 'Frederick William Neitenstein'; and J. Ramsland, *Children of the Backlanes*, NSW University Press, Sydney, 1986.

penal complex at Little Bay in Sydney. Strategically, he also took with him, and sought endorsement of, ideas about classification and treatment that he wished to introduce. We will return to these proposals later in this chapter.

Did the science of criminology make a difference to penal practice? There are reasons for doubting its impact on everyday life within institutions, however much the occasional innovative administrator such as Neitenstein may have sought to promote it. Neitenstein's expectation was that those employed in penal institutions would be abreast of the latest thinking in penology and criminology, but it took most of the succeeding century to develop in Australia a professional environment in 'corrections', as it became known, founded on tertiary-level education and training.[19] For most of this century, the educational expectations of the prison warders were limited to on-the-job training, with some stimulus to self-education provided through the system of promotion between grades by examination. The Prison Regulations in New South Wales in 1915 reflected Neitenstein's abiding legacy in the requirement that, to be promoted to senior warder, candidates had to undergo an examination in the following subjects: 'Criminology — Du Cane's Punishment and prevention of crime; appendices to reports on New South Wales Prisons, commencing 1896; the Howard Association's Penological Principles; report on prisons, &c. visited by Comptroller-General, 1903'.[20]

The impact of criminology at the macro-level was likely to be more profound: in the disposition of offenders between various, more specialised institutions (including juvenile reformatories and inebriate asylums), in the elaboration of new sentencing possibilities, in the multiplication

19 See Western Australia, Parliament, *Report from the Commission Appointed to Inquire into the Penal System in the Colony*, WAPP, Perth, 1899, p. 22, which cites Neitenstein on the necessity of literate and criminologically aware warders. Visiting Cork Prison in Ireland in 1904, Neitenstein noted that the live-in warders had a library available to them, but that it did not contain 'any penological or criminological works, and there is no warder's examination in those subjects'; in England he saw two prisons with schools for the training of warders, but he did not consider the curriculum 'so extensive as that in operation for training warders in this State, and the theoretical side of the prison officers' profession is not so much dealt upon': NSW, Parliament, *Report by the Comptroller-General of Prisons on Prisons, Reformatories, and Asylums . . .*, NSWPP, Sydney, 1904, pp. 62, 52. On the lack of training for juvenile reformatory workers in NSW in the interwar period, see J. Ramsland & G. A. Cartan, 'The Gosford Farm Home for Boys, Mt Penang, 1912–1940', *Journal of the Royal Australian Historical Society*, vol. 75, no. 1, June 1989, p. 76.

20 NSW, Parliament, Regulations under *Prisons Act, 1899*, to take effect from 1 December 1915, cl. 9, NSWPP, Sydney, 1915–16.

of 'utopias' in which the feeble-minded would be separated out from the healthy citizenry, and in the occasional scientific excursions into the penitentiary to test new, and sometimes old, theories about the making of criminals. The erratic course of some of these developments can be charted in the following pages.

THE INDIVIDUALISATION OF PUNISHMENT?

It has been argued that a key feature of prison and penal reform at the end of the nineteenth century was the 'individualisation' of punishment. The term was used by Raymond Saleilles at the turn of the century in an influential text, which sought to describe the emergence of a new criminology — one that would replace the 'value rationality of traditional penal morality with a new purposive-rationality, which would adopt whatever technical methods were best suited for the control of crime'.[21] To express it less abstractly, the sentencing and punishment of offenders would be guided by their individual circumstances, and their management in or outside institutions would be governed by a science of the criminal. As Saleilles pointed out, 'individualisation' was not in itself new, if this meant the exercise of judicial discretion in discriminating between offenders. We have already noted, for instance, that the New South Wales Chief Justice in 1861 held such a view of sentencing and of the calculation of sanctions: 'that each man's character, and habits, and hopefulness, or the like, will be found to differ from those of others, and that as far as possible there should be an individualization of cases'.[22]

It was this movement toward individualisation that Neitenstein most obviously represented and influenced in Australia. Under the sway of the new criminology, those convicted would no longer be classified according to the nineteenth-century rationale of 'separation' (of individual prisoners from each other, and from any contaminating influences). Rather, each inmate would be classified according to individual needs and capacities,

21 Garland, *Punishment and Modern Society*, p. 185; R. Saleilles, *The Individualisation of Punishment*, Heinemann, London, 1911; in the introduction to the English edition, Roscoe Pound compared Saleilles's project to the operation of equity, a 'system of judicial individualisation' that was distinguished by its getting beyond the application of hard-and-fast rules (p. xvii).

22 NSW, Parliament, *Report of the Select Committee on the Public Prisons in Sydney and Cumberland*, NSWPP, Sydney, qu. 4851. Compare with Saleilles, *Individualization of Punishment*, pp. 46–7.

which would be judged in terms of potential for release back into the community as a useful citizen. While mid-Victorian penality had placed all its faith in hard labour as an instrument of reform, the punishment paradigms of the early twentieth century were more diverse. Labour would be useful for some, education for others, psychiatric treatment for those thought to be subject to mental illness or deficiency. And reformers were eager to assist a trend that, having already gained momentum, was drastically reducing the numbers incarcerated at all, as we have seen.

As is always the case with such reform programs, the resources available to 'individualise' punishment fell far short of those necessary. If the nineteenth-century promise of reform through bricks and mortar fell to pieces in unfinished colonial prisons, the twentieth-century programs of 'treatment' were remarkably long on rhetoric but short on trained personnel and suitable facilities. Up until the 1970s, the autobiographies of prisoners in the system suggest that, in places such as Sydney's major reception facility, Long Bay, the experience of prisoners differed little from that of the inmates of Darlinghurst and Berrima 100 years earlier.[23] Professional enthusiasts from outside the punishment sector occasionally made forays into the prisons or the courts, seeking to test, and occasionally to educate or treat, the criminal subject. But practice within the criminal-justice system in most of the Australian states was long unprofessionalised, with few professionals to work beside the poorly educated warders and their superiors, who were sometimes only slightly better educated. Psychiatrists, psychologists, probation officers, and other professionals, whose role was presaged in the more visionary outlines of a modern penal system after the 1880s, were only occasionally seen in the Australian criminal-justice system before the 1950s.

While this was the overall picture, there were nevertheless exceptions, and we can see the possibilities and limits of change if we examine these

23 See, for example, Anon., *Four Years Experience in Darlinghurst Gaol, by an Ex-Prisoner*, self-published pamphlet, Sydney, n.d. [1868–72]; R. Ross, *Gaol Life: Prison Administration in NSW — The 'Humane' System Criticized*, self-published pamphlet, Sydney, 1908 (on women's imprisonment during Neitenstein's era); V. Marshall, *The World of the Living Dead and Jail from Within*, Wentworth Press, Sydney, 1969 (1919) (for reflections of a 'political prisoner'); J. Garvey, *The Indelible Stamp*, self-published pamphlet, Sydney, n.d. [1936]; L. Newcombe, *Inside Out*, Angus & Robertson, Sydney, 1979 (on Long Bay in the 1950s and Grafton in the 1960s). However, Sernack, Penal Reform in NSW, p. 246, notes that at least one prisoner — Les Nicholas, in *Writings of a Prisoner* [1915–16] — depicted conditions more favourably. For an insider's view on more recent conditions in Long Bay and other prisons, see T. Anderson, *Inside Outlaws: A Prison Diary*, Redfern Legal Centre Publishers, Sydney, 1989.

exceptions in penal practice while appreciating continuities with older regimes. Notably, by the early twentieth century, different groups of prisoners were separated more purposefully, theoretically enabling authorities to pay greater attention to the specific forms of treatment that individual prisoners would undergo. In this history, the development of the indeterminate sentence was the archetypal penalty of individualisation, representing the greatest break from classical penology, with its fixed and known penalties. The premise of the indeterminate sentence was access to a more differentiated prison regime — one that classified prisoners as much as possible according to the number of previous commitments, age, gender (and sexual orientation in some places), and mental state. The larger the jurisdiction, the greater was the potential for elaborate classification: small numbers limited the possibilities, although declining populations in all jurisdictions also freed space for more differentiation. Some classifications had longer histories. The establishment of women's prisons is one instance, and the development of juvenile institutions another; both had their roots firmly embedded in the nineteenth century. Faith in the virtues of rural labour, combined with what were seen to be the ill effects of close incarceration in urban prisons, contributed to the development of prison farms in some states. Beyond the walls of the prison, penal reform also laid the foundations for non-carceral solutions and prescriptions, which helped further diminish the numbers in prison over the first half of the twentieth century.[24]

The indeterminate sentence was introduced in Australia during the first decade of the twentieth century, but in different forms in the various states. It was a controversial measure, and much debated in international criminological circles. After many years of resistance, the International Prison Congress, meeting in Washington in 1910, approved 'the scientific principle of the indeterminate sentence'. It should be applied to 'mental and moral defectives', to juveniles, and to others 'whose offences are chiefly due to circumstances of an individual character'. Cautious about potential abuse of indeterminate sentencing, the Congress recommended that the system's introduction should be conditional on the continuity of 'prevailing conceptions of guilt and punishment', on the assurance of 'an individualised treatment of the offender', and on the supervision of released persons by a board excluding 'all outside influences', but including a prisons administrator, a magistrate, and a doctor.[25]

24 See Garton, 'Bad or Mad?'.

25 Victoria, Parliament, *Report on Penal Establishments and Gaols, 1910*, VPP, Melbourne, 1911, 1st session, vol. 2, pp. 5–9.

By this stage Australian jurisdictions were already enthusiastically embracing the principle of indeterminate sentences, at least for habitual criminals. Although in the United Kingdom the principle of supervising released 'habitual criminals' had been implemented from 1869, such an innovation had not been accepted in Australia, perhaps in part because the system of supervised release on licence imitated too closely the convict era experiments. The trend of declining prison admissions in the last two decades of the nineteenth century accentuated the visibility of repeat offenders, about whom there was much debate. Neitenstein repeated the words of many earlier observers when he attacked the uselessness of short sentences for repeat offenders in his 1896 report on crime and its treatment.[26]

The new criminology sought to address such problems by focusing on the different categories of prisoner. The term 'habitual criminal' did not denote a single type but was a descriptor for a number of characters. The overwhelming number of those arrested by police were men and women arrested on drunkenness, vagrancy, and offensive-behaviour charges. Their processing through the police courts, into gaol on short-term sentences, and out the other door was a distraction and an irritant to the main business of criminal-justice. In attempting to solve 'the habituals problem', the first differentiation was the targeting of drunkenness. This was done through the creation of separate institutions, the inebriate asylums, to which repeat offenders would be committed. Almost universally, these asylums failed, but their establishment as separate institutions was a mark of the times. Medical conceptions were replacing moral ones, although the extent to which medical treatment replaced the penal and moral treatment of the drunkard was limited. In South Australia, for example, the *Convicted Inebriates Act 1913* was applied with considerable vigour in its early years, with significant numbers of inmates being placed in indefinite detention. But the systems at Adelaide and Gladstone gaols were evidently more regimes of penal labour than of medical rehabilitation.[27]

A more sustained attack on serious repeat offending was developed in the early Edwardian years. Habitual criminals legislation was passed in most Australian jurisdictions and in New Zealand between 1905 and 1909, in a movement that John Pratt has linked to the history of the

26 NSW, Parliament, *Annual Report on Prisons, 1896*, NSWPP, Sydney, 1896, Appendix, p. 4.

27 S. Garton, '"Once a Drunkard, Always a Drunkard": Social Reform and the Problem of "Habitual Drunkenness in Australia", 1880–1914', *Labour History*, no. 53, 1987, pp. 38–53; South Australia, Parliament, *Report on Gaols and Prisons for the Year 1915*, SAPP, Adelaide, 1915, vol. 3, pp. 4–8.

concept of dangerousness.[28] The target of this legislation was typically people who had been convicted at least three times of an indictable offence and were considered by the court to be capable of benefiting from reformatory detention. The detention was indefinite, and release was subject to Executive or judicial discretion, with supervision or reporting requirements following release. The Acts varied in their severity in terms of the process of deeming an offender to be a habitual criminal. The New Zealand legislation, for instance, encompassed summary, as well as indictable, offenders. But in Victoria the principle of the indeterminate sentence was embraced most warmly: the 1907 *Indeterminate Sentences Act* empowered judges to declare any person over the age of seventeen years, convicted of a third indictable offence, to be a habitual criminal. In contrast to other jurisdictions, the Act could be (and was) applied to first offenders (specifically to those on multiple charges, bringing public criticism from the prisons department in 1910.[29] The Chairman of the Victorian Indeterminate Sentences Board concluded, after his international travels in 1910, that the Victorian legislation was the most extensive of its type anywhere in Australia, Europe, or North America (though the comparison did not take account of New Zealand, where the ambit of the legislation appeared to be the same).[30] The deeming power of the judge was not the only feature of the Victorian statute: the creation of an Indeterminate Sentences Board — which would oversee the management of those placed in reformatory detention and the proclamation of 'reformatories' for this purpose — was also noteworthy in the Australian context.

The Victorian experiment was, in fact, the beginning of a system of parole, which in later decades was to become characteristic of the management of prisons and of released prisoners in most other jurisdictions. In 1918, similar legislation in Western Australia copied the Victorian experiment, and went even further by empowering prisons administrations to subject ordinary prisoners to reformatory treatment.[31] Yet in the translation of this experiment across the continent, something appears to have changed: by the late 1920s, habitual criminals in Western Australia were

28 J. Pratt, 'Dangerousness, Risk and Technologies of Power', *Australia and New Zealand Journal of Criminology*, vol. 28, no. 1, 1995, pp. 3–31.

29 Victoria, Parliament, *Report on Penal Establishments and Gaols, 1910*, VPP, Melbourne, 1911, 1st session, vol. 2, p. 8.

30 Victoria, Parliament, *Report of the Chairman, Indeterminate Sentences Board, on Reformatory Prisons and Institutions in Europe and America*, VPP, Melbourne, 1910, vol. 3, pp. 4–5.

31 *Prisons Act Amendment Act, 1918*, (WA) s. 64e established the Indeterminate Sentences Board.

more likely to be characterised as beyond reformation. Two types of prisoner were said to be dealt with by the Indeterminate Sentences Board in that state: (a) those sentenced by the Court and (b) those selected by the Board from among all sentenced prisoners:

> While those under (a) are, in most cases, habitual and hardened criminals of a bad type, of whom the reform, if not an entirely hopeless prospect, is a matter of great difficulty and long treatment, those under (b) are specially selected from among all the ordinary prisoners as being of a better disposition and more amenable to reform than the average prisoner.[32]

This local variation on the uses of reformatory treatment reflects the confusion that characterised the whole indeterminate sentencing movement early this century. Many observers — judges, penal administrators, politicians — were simply looking for a means of restraining 'habituals', of limiting the possibility of their continual offending. Other, more optimistic, observers saw indeterminate sentences as having the potential to reform youthful offenders. In Australia, the development of the Victorian program of indeterminate sentencing confused the two objectives; and in Western Australia it seems that the administration sought to make the best of a hopeless situation, selecting the best prospects from the prisons to compensate itself for the hopeless habituals sent by the courts. Indeed, the history of indeterminate sentencing in Western Australia highlights the different perspectives of various state agents on the uses of such legislation. For police, the attraction of habitual criminals legislation was that it kept the criminals off the streets, and preferably out of the state — according to Inspector (and later Commissioner) Connell in 1909, the eastern states' habituals were being driven to the west to avoid legislation that made them liable 'to confinement for an indefinite period, or in criminal parlance to the "Kathleen Mavourneen" sentence (It may be for years or it may be for ever)'. For penal administrators, the legislation's essence was the reconceptualisation of the offender as someone whose future could be moulded by reformatory treatment and subsequent supervision. Hence, Comptroller-General Pennefather framed his advocacy of the indeterminate sentence in terms of changing the offender's character to the point where release was justified.[33]

32 Drew, *Penological Reform in Western Australia*, p. 13.

33 Papers relating to habitual criminals and indeterminate sentence legislation (Connell to Commissioner of Police, 24 August 1909; Pennefather, 29 April 1911), Western Australian Archives, Perth, Battye Library, Acc. 968, AN 123/2/5187/11. Connell's reference to the 'Kathleen Mavourneen' is an early occurrence of the term applied to indefinite prison sentences (also known as 'a Kath'), as noted in other sources from 1914 on; see G. Wilkes, *A Dictionary of Australian Colloquialisms*, Sydney University Press, Sydney, 1978, p. 194.

Apart from indeterminate sentencing, the twentieth century saw various jurisdictions adopt other innovations in the management of prisoners. The Victorian era was characterised by faith in the virtues of prison labour as punishment and vehicle of reform, but typically this labour was carried out in workshops, in cells, or in the prison yards and environs. In the Edwardian period, this practice was transformed, at least for some prisoners. In this age of the Scout — of physical exercise and open air — it was not surprising to see a discourse of reform emerge that emphasised the merits of healthful environments, in which the walls of the prison were less evident and the opportunities for productive agricultural work were abundant. The creation of prison farms revived early nineteenth-century enthusiasms, and their use in prisons administration closely replicated the kind of penal regime developed by Crofton in Ireland, where the prison farm at Lusk had represented the pre-release stage of his system of punishment.[34] The development of the prison farm in twentieth-century Australia was closely linked to the thinking associated with indefinite sentencing. The prison farm was to be a reformatory for prisoners thought to be capable of benefiting from such treatment, or a half-way house prior to release. Its purpose was articulated in recommendations by Tasmania's Chief Justice in 1943: 'The purpose of the prison camp is to translate the prisoner to comparative freedom, and therefore, to comparative fitness for return to society and so overcome the inevitable deteriorating effect of over-regimentation in a prison'.[35] At Pardelup in Western Australia the government established a prison farm in the late 1920s as part of a program of ongoing reform aimed at developing reformatory methods. It was for men 'who exhibit a desire to reform', a place 'where, by their own industry and good conduct, in wholesome and healthful surroundings, they will have the opportunity to redeem the past'.[36] However, the numbers deemed to be suitable for such environments were usually small — only nineteen prisoners at Pardelup in 1928, of whom thirteen were 'reformatory' prisoners on indefinite sentence.[37]

In large systems such as that in Victoria, institutions such as the McLeod 'settlement', established on French Island in the 1920s, represented a more

34 R. Hinde, 'Sir Walter Crofton and the Reform of the Irish Convict System 1854–61', *Irish Jurist*, vol. 12, 1977, pp. 115–47, 295–338.
35 Tasmania, Parliament, *Report of the Royal Commission into Hobart Gaol*, Tasmanian Parliamentary Papers (hereafter TPP), Hobart, 1943, p. 37.
36 J. M. Drew (Chief Secretary), Prison Reform: The Pardelup Farm, 1928, in possession of the Battye Library, Perth, p. 1.
37 Drew, Prison Reform, p. 5.

substantial element of the penal system. McLeod was one of the five reformatories established to house the various categories of indeterminately sentenced prisoners during these decades. In the 1930s Victoria added the Cooriemungle Prison Farm to its stock of prisons. Similar farms were established in other jurisdictions, including New South Wales (where three afforestation camps were established, as well as Emu Plains, where dormitories were replaced by individual huts for each prisoner[38]) and Queensland (Palen Creek and Numinbah). Yet the flush of enthusiasm for open-air reform never came to dominate any penal system, and it is notable that even Neitenstein, who was very favourably impressed in 1904 by the open-air environment at Sherborn Women's Reformatory near Boston, did not proceed to establish a similar institution for women in Sydney, the Long Bay Female Penitentiary falling well short of a Sherborn.[39]

The new science of criminology had seemed to promise a means of carefully estimating individual prisoners' characters and potential, but in the end, male prisons failed to fully deliver on this promise. Outside the establishment of the prison farms, there were few other new establishments — a significant, if undistinguished, exception being the State Reformatory at Long Bay in Sydney, whose opening in 1914 saw the final closure of Darlinghurst as the city's main prison.

Rather, the decline in numbers (and, consequently, greater scope for reorganising those left) combined with new classification systems to develop more refined groupings of prisoners. Neitenstein aspired to a system in which the many establishments in his charge would each hold a different class of prisoner. Within each gaol there would be further classifications according to age, conduct, and disposition. The gaols themselves would be graded 'for hopeful cases and first offenders; for previously convicted, but hopeful cases; for habituals; for feeble minded, including sexual perverts, not actual lunatics or imbeciles; for the incorrigibles as regards behaviour'. The system was organised along these lines for at least the next half-century, until the explosion of prisoner numbers in New South Wales in the 1950s played havoc with such a system.

In 1945 the Premier was advised that the classification of prisoners was effected by 'the use of particular gaols for the detention of general types and the separation within each prison of the different classes'. The general principles of classification at this time were said to be:

38 Tasmania, Parliament, *Report of the Royal Commission into Hobart Gaol*, p. 37, TPP, Hobart, 1943, p. 37.

39 For a very critical account of Neitenstein's reforms from an inmate's perspective, see Ross, *Gaol Life*.

1 The separation of convicted from unconvicted prisoners
2 the separation of those under 25 years of age from those over that age
3 the separation of those who have not been previously imprisoned from those who have
4 the separation of known homosexual perverts from all other prisoners
5 the separation of incorrigible intractable prisoners from all other prisoners
6 the separation of the most trustworthy convicted prisoners from all others
7 the separation of those committed as inebriates, as maintenance confinees, or as debtors from all other prisoners than those of their own class.[40]

Like Neitenstein's classification, this list suggests a system in which a number of rationales were at work, some of them closely related to the development of a more individuated science of the criminal (the 'homosexual pervert'), and others having a more pragmatic rationale (the 'incorrigible intractable'). The real limits of individuation were always disclosed in the makeshift accommodations that sought to fit number of prisoners to available institutions. These limits were occasionally admitted by governments, as in a frank comment made by the Victorian Chief Secretary in 1931 that 'the prisons of Victoria were merely places where offenders were locked up', being out-of-date and 'unfit for modern penal methods'.[41]

Similarly, in Queensland in the 1920s, the 'principal classification [was] according to number of convictions with or without hard labour', but the Comptroller-General thought it would be better 'if the nature of the crime was taken into consideration'. This was a backward-looking comment; future classification criteria were more likely to take some account of psychological disposition and character. The 1959 Queensland Prison Regulations show that some change had taken place since the 1920s: every prisoner as far as practicable was to be separated into a particular class, of which there were eleven:

1 unconvicted and special class (including those with an indefinite sentence and those under the age of seventeen)
2 appellants
3 maintenance confinees and debtors
4 youthful prisoners

40 'Provision of Increased Accommodation at the State Penitentiary and Reformatory, Long Bay', NSW State Archives, Sydney, 7/7133.2.

41 *Argus*, 13 August 1931, p. 6.

5 short-sentenced prisoners
6 remediable prisoners
7 recidivist prisoners
8 intractable prisoners
9 homosexual prisoners (including those deemed so in the opinion of the Comptroller-General, as well as those sentenced for 'any act of homosexuality')
10 psychopaths (deemed so by the medical officer)
11 unclassified prisoners (that is, pending classification into one of the above).[42]

Such categories, however, were largely determined by management criteria rather than the psychological disposition of the offender. No gender distinction was usually made in these systems of classification, but the small numbers of women prisoners in most places prevented any serious classification at all. The individualisation of punishment, however, had a particular meaning when it came to women as a category and to young people, and the early twentieth century saw important developments for each group.

Women in prison

Segregation of women from men had long been an elementary feature of prisons policy. But the separation was fragile, and although some wanted priority to be given to the establishment of completely separate institutions and regimes for women, this objective was especially vulnerable to being pushed aside by the other needs of the moment. A story from Sydney's Long Bay Penitentiary in the 1950s, half a century after the establishment of a dedicated women's prison in New South Wales, demonstrates just how unresolved, at a practical level, the separation of women and men was:

> Inside the church we began sweeping and mopping the floor. It is a two-storey building. At that time the women's prison was a part of the men's, separated by a wall that ran along the far side of the church. They used to attend the same once-a-week movie session but were placed in the sealed-off upstairs section of the church. Often during a Saturday afternoon we would be bombarded by notes fluttering down which were grabbed eagerly by the men. Read in the privacy of the cell, they contained messages of frustration and descriptive passages of how they would react if we could get together for a short time.[43]

42 *Queensland Government Gazette*, 14 March 1959, p. 1631.
43 Newcombe, *Inside Out*, pp. 69–70.

Such a story is reminiscent of the convict ships in evoking a desire to transgress a policy of segregation — a policy that was frequently subverted. The possibility of transgression resulted from the shortcomings of prison architecture and resources, which were in turn the product of economic circumstance and government priorities.

Separation of women was already well established in the convict period: the Female Factories in Sydney and Hobart reflected a more general presumption among early nineteenth-century social reformers that women should be separated from men in penal institutions. In France this presumption was matched by practice, especially from the 1820s, but women and men were separated only sporadically in the United Kingdom, and in the USA the first women's prison was not established until 1835 (remaining the only one in that country until the 1870s).[44] The regime for convicted women that was advocated by the Quaker reformer Elizabeth Fry in the 1820s (and recommended by her to the British government for use in the convict institutions in New South Wales and Tasmania[45]) was a model of separate treatment, but one that was only slowly taken up in Great Britain and Ireland. In all jurisdictions, the much greater numbers of male prisoners seemed to collude with governmental parsimony to delay institutional reform for women prisoners.

The point is illustrated by the long gestation of a separate women's prison in Melbourne.[46] As early as 1855, work had begun on a separate institution under Inspector-General John Price, but it was abandoned for economic reasons. The decision to build a central penitentiary for the colony at Pentridge in 1857 was made with the expectation that both men and women convicts would be incarcerated there. However, a revision of estimates excised the women's institution from this project, and thereafter, women were accommodated under makeshift arrangements for nearly forty years until the completion of a female penitentiary at Pentridge in 1894. Their accommodation in these years included eleven years on the hulks, which had been deemed too unhealthy for the men, a couple of years at Pentridge in the late 1860s, and from December 1870, the overcrowded Melbourne Gaol in the city. Their transfer to Melbourne provoked an immediate crisis of accommodation, as well as disciplinary problems. The

44 O'Brien, *Promise of Punishment*, pp. 61–2; L. Zedner, 'Wayward Sisters', in Morris & Rothman, *Oxford History of the Prison*, pp. 333–8.

45 K. Daniels & M. Murnane (eds), *Uphill All the Way*, University of Queensland Press, St Lucia, 1980, pp. 9–10.

46 See Petrass, '"Those who Trespass against Us"', ch. 5.

diary of the prison governor in the months after their transfer from Pentridge details the constant disciplinary charges that were made against the women prisoners in an effort to prevent their association with the men:

> In the afternoon the Visiting Justice paid a visit & tried some women for various offences. Two charges I brought against women for endeavouring to communicate with the male prisoners were very leniently treated, one woman who pleaded guilty being simply cautioned & the case against the other being dismissed as Mr Sturt considered the evidence insufficient. Of course I do not carp at the Magistrate's decisions though I certainly thought the Case was a good one. It is hard to get even visiting Justices to understand Gaol offences, the charges brought against prisoners frequently appear trumpery, as no doubt they would be out of doors, though they are grave infractions of discipline in Gaol & if allowed would soon put an end to the good government of the prison.[47]

After some months, Governor Castieau ordered louvres to cover the windows through which he had discovered the women were communicating with outsiders.[48] The violence and verbal abuse of one of the women prisoners caused him to long for 'the power to send a couple of strong women into her cell to give her a round smacking'.[49] The short-term sentences of most women prisoners (discussed in chapter 2), the lower value of their prison labour (as well as the limited opportunities for work), and the difficulty of maintaining discipline in a gaol with inadequate facilities all rendered women's incarceration difficult in terms of policy and management. Added to this was the problem of the women prisoners' children. Their plight was a subject of comment in public inquiries — and justification for a special establishment. But none of these arguments held sway against the constant calls for economic constraint until the late 1880s.[50]

Only in New South Wales and Victoria were the numbers of female prisoners ever large enough to put significant pressure on the authorities to establish a major separate establishment. As noted earlier (see Table 2.7, p. 41), the decline in the number of prisoners by the end of the century would seem to have lessened the need for building further establishments of any kind. Yet by 1900 the value of classifying prisoners on ever more refined

47 J. B. Castieau, Diary, in the possession of the National Library of Australia, Mss. 2218, 21 August 1871.
48 Castieau, Diary, 4 Jan 1872.
49 Castieau, Diary, 8 Mar 1872. For similar expressions of frustration in English women's prisons, this time by the female warders themselves, see Zedner, *Women, Crime and Custody*, p. 169.
50 Petrass, '"Those who Trespass against Us"', ch. 5.

criteria had been affirmed, which in fact accentuated the need for separate institutions, although other motives were sometimes involved. In fact, in the twenty years from 1888 to 1908, each of the eastern colonies obtained a newly built women's prison, typically a new division at an existing prison location. In the case of Queensland, the motivation appeared to be as much a desire to remove the Fortitude Valley Gaol (where the Brisbane female prisoners were housed), located as it was beside a school, as any other factor.[51] The result was the construction of Brisbane Gaol's female division, a building that by the interwar period was sometimes empty of prisoners and that rarely housed more than a dozen inmates.[52] Like Queensland, South Australia had few long-term female prisoners, limiting the case for a separate prison for women. When the issue attracted some controversy in 1945, after a young prisoner gave birth unexpectedly in a dark isolation cell, the Premier drew Parliament's attention to the very small numbers of women at the Adelaide Gaol, pointing out that the daily average had been less than ten for eight of the previous ten years.[53] More substantial numbers were housed at the female penitentiaries at Coburg (Pentridge), opened in 1894, and Long Bay, opened in 1908.

In spite of the lack of innovation in its design (the 198-cell block epitomised the late Victorian preoccupation with 'regulation and uniformity' according to Kerr[54]), the advantages of the new Female Prison at Coburg were said to be its healthier situation and its capacity for separation of prisoners, impossible at Melbourne Gaol. But the Inspector-General in Victoria believed that sentencing practices stood in the way of the facility being used effectively. Short sentences for women convicted of minor offences (drunkenness, obscene language, and so on) meant that many of the women processed through the criminal-justice system never arrived at the Female Prison.[55] The tendency towards repeat offending among women prisoners was equally a problem; Neitenstein considered it to be one of the major issues of the day, arising, as he commented in 1904, as much in Canada, the USA, and the United Kingdom as in Sydney, 'where

51 Queensland, Parliament, *Debates*, 24 September 1897, p. 972–4.

52 Queensland Prisons Department, *Annual Reports*, Brisbane, 1926, 1931.

53 South Australia, Parliament, *Debates*, 2 October 1945, p. 362; the record of the debate shows that a range of issues to do with treatment of *women* at Adelaide Gaol were canvassed, including a report by the Chairman of the Central Board of Health on the matter, recommending consideration of a new gaol when circumstances allowed.

54 Kerr, *Out of Sight, Out of Mind*, p. 117.

55 Victoria, Parliament, *Report of the Inspector-General on Penal Establishments and Gaols*, VPP, Melbourne, 1905, p. 1.

habitual drunkards and petty misdemeanants are constantly passing from the street to the prisons and back again under a system as incomprehensible as it is useless'.[56]

The State Female Penitentiary in Sydney was a more considered product of the reform momentum of the late nineteenth century, assisted, on the one hand, by the prison administrator Neitenstein and, on the other, by the activities of a feminist lobby group under the leadership of Rose Scott. The interest of the feminists was in specialising the treatment of women prisoners to a degree that had not been attempted in Australia. A central objective of this campaign was the attendance of women custodians at all stages of the processing of any woman prisoner into custody. Scott was appalled, on her visits to Darlinghurst Gaol in the late 1890s, by the spectacle of women prisoners being subject to the jeers of male prisoners, and by the frequency with which male warders had sole custody of the women. In Victoria, at about the same time, the National Council of Women conducted a lengthy inquiry into the conditions of women in police lock-ups. They conducted interviews and inspected the parade of women regularly brought into Russell Street and other police stations by male police officers, who were responsible for managing those who attempted suicide, were hopelessly drunk, or were so violent that they were 'dragged out and put under the tap' in the yard of the station. The unified call of the reformers was summarised in the Victorian Committee's report: 'the lowest human being calling herself woman has the right to the services of her own sex'.[57]

This view was also shared by Scott, but the conditions facing women in prison, in her opinion, went well beyond the issue of the custodian's sex. Indeed, in visiting the women's quarters at Biloela (the old Cockatoo Island Reformatory, which had also become a temporary women's prison), Scott was specifically critical of the character and behaviour of the women warders, who appeared to be 'of a very inferior type to the men warders . . . in one case the face and manner of the woman warder made us suppose that she had once been a hardened criminal herself, and might be that worst of all tyrants, a one time slave now in authority'.

56 NSW, Parliament, *Report by the Comptroller-General of Prisons on Prisons, Reformatories, and Asylums . . .*, NSWPP, Sydney, 1904, p. 43 (commenting on Ontario Reformatory for Women, Toronto) and pp. 26, 53 (Sherborn Reformatory, Massachusetts, and Holloway in England).

57 National Council of Women, Report of the Sub-Committee of the National Council of Women of Victoria, Regarding Appointment of Police Matrons in City and Suburban Lock-Ups, 1902, in the possession of the Mitchell Library, Sydney.

Commenting on the limited array of occupations, she noted a 'feeling that appears to prevail over the minds of all gaol officials — that women criminals are a hopeless set'. Indeed, '[w]ork in the women's quarters appeared to consist solely of scrubbing, cleaning, washing; and needle work of the most hideous and dreary description . . . could any better preparation be found than this, for scenes of terrible re-action, and outbreaks?' According to Scott's observations, the conditions of women's imprisonment at this time conspired towards further degradation of the woman: 'she is inspired with hopelessness, a misery and depression which calls for drink to dull, or the outlet of some physical energy to relieve the mood; hence outbreaks [of] violence and wild fury'. The solution was 'a better environment as to warders, dress and occupation, an education drawing out the latent powers' of the female prisoner.

Scott was at one with Neitenstein's disposition — and with that of other reformers who saw the revolving door of the short-term prison as the source of many problems — and hence supported a reform program that included the introduction of indeterminate sentences and the use of a 'credit marks' system to stimulate progress through the grades of prison towards successful release back into the community.[58] With such support, Neitenstein found that the conditions were right to build a special institution. When it opened in 1909, one of the first directions of the Comptroller General was to allow the Ladies Committee, Prisoners Aid Association, automatic admission into the gaol at any time.[59]

On his travels to the USA in 1904, Neitenstein took the opportunity to spend time at the Sherborn Reformatory for Women in Massachusetts, with whose superintendents he had consulted regarding plans to distribute women prisoners between Bathurst, Darlinghurst, and Biloela. However, by this time, the government was committed to the construction of a new prison at Little Bay (the first stage of what was to become the Long Bay complex). On his travels, Neitenstein took with him a proposal for the 'treatment and classification' of women prisoners at the new institution: 'they very strongly endorsed my view as to the reformative effect of gardening and other outdoor work for female prisoners'. At Little Bay the Comptroller-General proposed to concentrate all the women prisoners of

58 R. Scott, manuscript notes of recommendations on prison reform, forwarded to a number of politicians following visits to Biloela and Darlinghurst, Rose Scott Papers, Mitchell Library, Sydney, Mss. 38/56, item 2/1–15, n.d. On Scott's work in prison reform, see J. Allen, *Rose Scott: Vision and Revision in Feminism*, Oxford University Press, Melbourne, 1994, pp. 153–9.

59 K. Daniels et al. (eds), *Women in Australia*, vol. 2, AGPS, Canberra, 1977, p. 159.

New South Wales, except those on short sentence in country districts. The specificity of women's offending, as well as the smaller numbers involved, affected Neitenstein's proposed classification. The women were to be divided into four groups, each to be kept apart (as provided in the gaol design): long sentenced; petty larcenists; prostitutes; and special. Neitenstein wanted the 'Routine in the Special division to be on the lines of the Sherborn system', which worked with a three-graded progression of inmates through a series of stages governed by conduct marks, which were accumulated in industrious work, self-education, and recreation. In addition, there was to be a further level of classification within each division, according to age, previous convictions, and conduct.[60]

Neitenstein's system of four divisions was designed for a larger number of prisoners than, in fact, ended up at Long Bay in the following decades. As in the rest of Australia, the female, as well as the male, prison population declined rapidly in the first half of the century. By 1932 the population of the Long Bay Female Penitentiary, built to accommodate 320 women, had declined to an average of 50, at which time the government announced that the women would be moved elsewhere.[61] The falling numbers (see Table 3.1) fostered complacency and indifference to prison programs, sparking criticism in the early 1930s that the women prisoners were subjected to 'drab and uninteresting sewing' while men had a greater range of opportunities, including the prison farms and afforestation stations.[62]

Table 3.1 Daily averages of women in Australian prisons, 1891–1981

	NSW	*Victoria*	*Queensland*	*SA*	*WA*	*Tasmania*
1891	291	350	80	34	13	23
1901	202	200	54	–	–	13
1911	135	100	36	33	–	–
1921	111	54	15	17	14	–
1931	98	50	15	7	–	–
1941	76	50	7	4	–	2
1951	na	52	11	7	12	5
1961	97	30	25	17	36	4
1971	87	41	26	42	73	5
1981	118	54	42	26	63	5

Source: Mukherjee et al., *Source Book*; annual reports of Prison Departments.

60 NSW, Parliament, *Report by the Comptroller-General of Prisons on Prisons, Reformatories, and Asylums . . .*, NSWPP, Sydney, 1904, pp. 24–5, 107.
61 *Sydney Morning Herald*, 8 September 1932, p. 8.
62 *Sydney Morning Herald*, 29 July 1931 (criticism by Feminist Club) and 16 November 1932 (Howard League).

By the 1940s, the purpose-built women's prison at Long Bay was significantly under-utilised, and a familiar pattern reasserted itself: the principle of separation was compromised in order to solve a crisis in accommodation for the greater numbers of males. Officials warned that 'whilst men and women are confined in the one institution, supervision does not prevent clandestine correspondence and the possibility of serious incidents cannot be ignored. It is necessary that the female section should be completely isolated from the male prison'. In considering accommodation needs, departmental officers favoured retaining the Women's Reformatory in the metropolitan area, 'having regard to the whole history of the woman population in gaols, which shows that it is a comparatively small problem'. All the same, support came from the Minister for the building of a 'new reformatory for women', an aspiration that took another twenty years to realise.[63] When it was finally opened in 1969, the 'Training and Detention Centre' at Silverwater began an undistinguished life as a women's prison that was to re-create most of the problems identified in Rose Scott's time and before: infantilism, lack of proper classification, and a stereotyping of inmates for particular life roles. It was also to become the subject of a highly critical assessment in the 1985 Report on Women in Prison.[64]

Did women's prisons make a difference to the treatment of women in prisons? A detailed account of conditions within particular prisons is necessary to answer such a question. The range of offences for which women were convicted and incarcerated was narrower than for men, and continued to be so even when rates of women's imprisonment increased later in this century.[65] The sentences served were shorter, and hence the turnover (but also recidivism rates) was high. This in itself was used to justify indifference on the part of the prison system, since the accepted wisdom — epitomised in the repeated observations of Neitenstein's 1904 Report — was that little, if anything, could be done for short-sentenced prisoners. It was argued that character and moral training were more relevant to offending than social circumstance, and so the penal system's best hope was in trying to

63 Corrective training and educational programs for prisoners, 1927–47, 46/16845 and attachments, in NSW State Archives, Sydney, 7/7133.2.

64 New South Wales Task Force on Women in Prison, *Report*, NSW Government Printer, Sydney, 1985; NSW, Parliament, *Report of the New South Wales Department of Corrective Services, 1970*, NSWPP, Sydney, 1969–70, p. 20.

65 See D. Brown, H. Kramer, & M. Quinn, 'Women in Prison: Task Force Reform', in M. Findlay & R. Hogg (eds), *Understanding Crime and Criminal Justice*, Law Book Co, Sydney, 1988.

retain inmates for as long as possible.[66] By the brevity of their stay, women offended against this cardinal principle of a reformed penal system.

It appears that, as treatment programs were developed in twentieth-century prisons, these programs were more likely to be introduced in longer-stay men's prisons. Victoria provides an example. In 1959, by which time a new and separate women's prison at Fairlea had been opened (with a capacity of 100 places but a daily average of only 37 inmates), a detailed account of training and education programs in Victoria's prisons suggested that women were bypassed in such programs: the chief training officer for the Department of Penal Services reported a range of opportunities at Bendigo, Langi Kal Kal, Beechworth, Pentridge, and the McLeod Training Farm, but none at Fairlea. Instead, in the Department's annual report, the Governor of Fairlea simply noted the 'very wide range of problems' in the prison, and increased output in the workroom and laundry.[67]

The individualisation of punishment appeared to have a limited impact on women's imprisonment. Rather, segregating women had the effect of constituting them as a single problem — just one of a range of classifications. Rarely were the conditions of women prisoners considered in public inquiries: — a paragraph or two in such reports was typical. Sometimes, though, these few paragraphs could be illuminating, as in the report of the 1943 Royal Commission on Hobart Gaol. This recommended that a more diverse array of work and training opportunities be offered to women inmates (as opposed to just 'domestic service') in order to foster their artistic and other talents.[68] Such a situation was, in part, the result of relatively low populations of women inmates. But at a time when male prisoners were increasingly classified into a large number of categories, with corresponding institutional provision, women's prisons were more like the single-purpose institutions of the nineteenth century, a perverse historical outcome of a movement to distinguish women's different needs.[69]

66 Compare with Queensland, Parliament, *Annual Report of the Comptroller-General of Prisons*, QPP, Brisbane, 1960: 'the purpose of social education and trade training of prisoners is to ensure that every prisoner, if possible, leaves prison better equipped to face life than when he entered prison. Little can be done for short-term prisoners', pp. 1–2; Victoria, Parliament, *Report on Penal Establishments, Gaols and Reformatory Prisons*, VPP, Melbourne, 1935, p. 9: 'One cannot emphasize too strongly that it is the moral training of the individual which is the most potent factor in his future life as a citizen, and not the mere bricks and mortar amidst which he lives . . . Criminal acts are very largely a matter of habit due to wrong training in youth'.

67 Victoria, Parliament, *Report of the Director of Penal Services*, 1959–60, VPP, Melbourne, 1960–61, vol. 2, p. 733.

68 Tasmania, Parliament, *Report of the Royal Commission into Hobart Gaol*, TPP, Hobart, 1943, p. 42.

THE JUVENILE AND THE REFORMATORY

Reform of juvenile criminal-justice institutions is another example of the impact of turn-of-the-century changes in criminology and penology. Like women's custody, juvenile institutions already had a long nineteenth-century history, which was closely tied to the activities of social reformers in education and charity work. The same strategies that had stimulated separation of women from men were deployed in the segregation of young offenders and older criminals. One of the earliest such separations occurred when a juvenile convict establishment was opened at Point Puer in 1834 as one element of the Tasmanian convict complex. This opening coincided with the foundation, in France, of the Mettray Agricultural Colony, an institution for juvenile delinquents that was to play an important role as a model for later institutions, and that was commonly taken as a reference point for juvenile custodial treatment.[70]

Recent research has challenged the theory that juvenile delinquency was 'invented' by mid-nineteenth-century British reformers, but the indisputable contribution of British social-reform debates at this time was to create a solution to the problem: the industrial and reformatory schools. Founded on the assumption that separation of juveniles from adult prisoners was necessary to prevent the former's contamination by the latter, these institutions aimed to provide a moral and educational environment that would remedy the deficiencies of the juvenile criminal's background. The translation of metropolitan ideas into a colonial setting was again speedy. In the 1860s most colonies established systems of industrial and reformatory schools — the former to operate as an institution for the education of poor and homeless children, and the latter to function as the juvenile custodial institution.[71]

69 On the necessity of acknowledging the different statuses of women prisoners, see A. Howe, *Punish and Critique: Towards a Feminist Analysis of Penality*, Routledge, London, 1994.

70 J. Ramsland, 'The Agricultural Colony at Mettray: A 19th Century Approach to the Institutionalisation of Delinquent Boys', *Melbourne Studies in Education*, vol. 29, 1987–88.

71 Juvenile justice, welfare policy, and institutions have been studied more intensively than other areas in the historiography of prison and custody in post-convict Australia. Their operation and social context have been the subject of study in a number of states. See, for example, M. Barbalet, *Far from a Low Gutter Girl*, Oxford University Press, Melbourne, 1983; Ramsland, *Children of the Backlanes*; R. van Krieken, *Children and the State: Social Control and the Formation of Australian Child Welfare*, Allen & Unwin, Sydney, 1992; P. Hetherington, 'Australian Colonial Law and the Construction of Childhood', in D. Kirkby (ed.), *Sex, Power and Justice: Historical Perspectives on Law in Australia*, Oxford University Press, Melbourne, 1995.

Education and training for moral character and citizenship were intended to be the core functions of these institutions, but their performance was variable. Under a conscientious and determined superintendent like Neitenstein, the New South Wales boys industrial school, the hulk *Vernon*, seemed to thrive on military discipline, while conditions in the corresponding girls' institution were more brutal.[72]

In Melbourne, the boys' reformatory, Jika, located within the walls of Pentridge, contravened the best principles of juvenile treatment in its dangerous association of the boys with older prisoners. When a brief outbreak of protest at Jika provoked public scrutiny in 1878, investigations revealed a Dickensian institution, with excessive corporal punishment and arbitrary discipline, which included depriving the entire establishment of food. The Board of Inquiry recommended that it be broken up, and the Board's secretary, Marcus Clarke, submitted a detailed report on the 'Family System' that was in practice in the USA, 'the principle of which consists of dividing the children to be reformed into small families, and so dealing with them individually'. Clarke discounted the models of 'such well-known Catholic institutions as Mettray and Albertville' since Victoria was not a Catholic country, but added (at odds with his own modernist agnosticism, which inclined to the triumph of science over the delusion of religion) that religious discipline should be an essential part of reforming and educating 'unformed minds'.[73]

The reformatory and industrial schools were a significant component of the penal system's response to juvenile offending in the latter part of the century. They housed those convicted of criminal offences, or those judged to be neglected, potentially criminal, and in need of care and education. The 177 boys who occupied the Jika reformatory in 1877 were aged from nine to sixteen years, nearly all of them incarcerated for petty thieving. The contrast between the 'criminal' careers of the boys and those of the girls housed in these institutions has been a common theme in the history of reformatories, persisting to the present day. Boys ended up in reformato-

72 Krieken, *Children and the State*, pp. 68–72.

73 Victoria, Parliament, *Report of the Board Appointed to Enquire into the Outbreak of the Inmates . . . at Jika, on the 13th of March 1878*, VPP, Melbourne, 1878, Appendix G; compare with M. Clarke, 'Civilization without Delusion' (originally in *Victorian Review*, 1879), in M. Wilding (ed.) *Marcus Clarke*, University of Queensland Press, St Lucia, 1976. A clue to this contradiction is evident in Clarke's supplementary comment (in the Report on Jika) on religious discipline: 'That discipline is, I think, best which appeals to imagination rather than intellect, and to sympathy rather than fear'. On Clarke and religion, see C. M. H. Clark, *A History of Australia*, vol. 4, Melbourne University Press, 1978, pp. 315–6.

ries after a sequence of usually minor offences, but serious enough to attract the constant attention of police. Girls were more likely to be there for offences associated with sexual misconduct or abuse against them, the reformatory being an institution that would both train them for useful service in adulthood and reduce the risk of their entry into prostitution.

The separation of children and young people from adult offenders was therefore already a well-established feature of penal systems by the early twentieth century. From this point, however, attention increasingly focused on a broader range of strategies. Penal options were just one of many different responses to the phenomenon of juvenile offending. Social strategies included targeting the families of troublesome youngsters through the activities of child welfare departments, which had the power to remove neglected children and foster them elsewhere. Criminal-justice reforms before the First World War completed the separation of children from adults in the processing of offenders, with the creation of children's courts, to which other professionals might be attached. These professionals would advise the court on the best mode of managing the child brought before it. Through the progressive refinement of public education, educational strategies sought to prevent, as best as possible, the factors that lead children to offend.

What role were penal institutions to play in this array of responses? Some outside the justice system (notably the child-welfare doyen in New South Wales Dr Charles Mackellar[74]) sought to separate juveniles altogether from the penal and justice systems, opposing institutionalisation except in the worst cases. Nevertheless, there was a good deal of interest in Australia in one English institutional innovation. The Borstal was an extension of the child reformatory idea to apply to young adults, aged from sixteen to twenty-one. It originated in the considerations of the Gladstone Committee on Prisons in 1894, which among other things, had sought to develop a means of addressing the high rates of offending among late adolescent males, seeking instead to improve their prospects of becoming good citizens. Continuing the principle of separating classes of offenders to limit their contamination by others, the Borstal added to this the requirement of supervision on release. In some respects, therefore, the Borstal was simply a refinement of nineteenth-century ideas: the reformatory had been tried (indeed the new system took some inspiration from the Elmira Reformatory in New York) and so had supervision (of habitual criminals released on licence in England after 1869). But in

74 S. Garton, 'Sir Charles Mackellar: Psychiatry, Eugenics and Child Welfare in New South Wales, 1900–1914', *Australian Historical Studies*, no. 86, 1986, pp. 21–34.

extending the principle of reformatory treatment towards adulthood, the adoption of the Borstal system broke with juridical and penal thinking about an adult's personal responsibility. Once mature, adults had previously been considered fully responsible for their actions and not susceptible to reformatory treatment. Once a break had been achieved in this mode of thinking, it was clear that the specificity of the program — its focus on the education and training of young adult male offenders — made it more in tune with the age of increasing individualisation.[75]

In Australia, as a potential mode of dealing with crime and delinquency, the Borstal became the subject of common debate and observation. As late as 1945 the New South Wales Premier, W. J. McKell, was prompted to report on the workings of the system, which he had investigated during a visit to Great Britain that year: 'The purpose of a Borstal Institution' he reported, citing the prison commissioners, 'is to teach wayward lads to be self-contained men, to train them to be fit for freedom. It is impossible to train men for freedom in a condition of captivity'. In place of the older systems where the lads had been treated either as 'a lump of hard material, yielding only to the hammer', or as a 'lump of putty' to be reduced to a uniform shape, the modern way was 'to regard him as a living organism . . . a lad of many mixtures, with a life and character of his own'. Sentenced to a 'modified indeterminate sentence', the Borstal boy or girl (there was one institution for the latter by this time) served a period of rigorous physical training combined with work, before release on licence to the care of the Borstal Association.[76] The system commended itself to McKell, who had already appointed a committee to report on the treatment of young offenders aged from sixteen to twenty-three years. His committee, reporting late in 1945, supported the principle of a system of 'establishments intermediate between prisons and child welfare institutions', while suggesting that it was neither 'necessary nor desirable to introduce either the terminology of the Borstal system, or to adopt the principles of that system without modification'. Their recommendation instead was the establishment of a 'Young Persons' Rehabili-

75 See R. Hood, *Borstal Reassessed*, Heinemann, London, 1965, ch. 1, for the origins of the system in England and its departure from conventional assumptions about criminal responsibility.

76 NSW, Parliament, *Report by W. J. McKell on the Borstal System (Great Britain) for the Rehabilitation of Young Offenders*, NSWPP, Sydney, 1945; see also Tasmania, Parliament, *Report of the Parliamentary Standing Committee on Public Works (Tasmania): New Gaol Proposal*, TPP, Hobart, 1935, pp. 2–3, recommending trial of the Borstal system.

tation Board', which would supervise the treatment of persons between the ages of sixteen and twenty-three committed by the Courts for such treatment. The Board would oversee a period of brief institutional detention before offenders were released on 'parole' under supervision.[77] In Tasmania the Chief Justice, Sir John Morris, had already recommended the separation of young offenders (between the ages of seventeen and twenty-five) by placing them in a new institution run on Borstal lines, though the small numbers could not justify a complete Borstal system, as in England. Such an institution was to be run on principles that would build personal responsibility and self-control, in an environment of trust.[78]

As we have seen, the Victorian Indeterminate Sentences Act had, from 1907, already fostered such programs of reformatory treatment and supervised release, though not only for young offenders. A condition of effective treatment in reformatories was seen to be the separation of young from old:

> The organisation and management of a reformatory in which are confined men of very various ages will present considerable difficulties, especially if the whole number in the institution is not large; gymnastic exercises, drill parades, sloyd [*sic*] work, recitations, debates, for instance, which are beneficial and interesting to lads and young men, are less necessary and may prove irksome to older men.

British and North American institutions were seen in 1910 as superior, not only in achieving such separation but also in their more developed system of supervising inmates after release: in Victoria they simply reported to police stations every three months; in England the Borstal Association had supervision and control, and similar arrangements were adopted in New York.[79]

Over time, however, the Victorian system became large enough in numbers to allow classification. By the interwar years, the Castlemaine Prison had a separate 'Reformatory' for young people sentenced to indeterminate sentences, while a number of 'reformatories' were established

77 Inter-Departmental Committee, Report (A. W. Hicks, Chairman), 16 September 1945, NSW State Archives, Sydney, AGJ, 7/7133.2.

78 Tasmania, Parliament, *Report of the Royal Commission on Hobart Gaol*, TPP, 1943, p. 33; the recommendation was not taken up, and Kilderry Farm, the proposed institution, continued to be a general purpose gaol farm housing a range of offenders.

79 Victoria, Parliament, *Report of the Chairman, Indeterminate Sentences Board, on Reformatory Prisons and Institutions in Europe and America*, VPP, 1910, vol. 3, p. 405. See also the critical assessment of Victorian indeterminate sentencing in Victoria, Parliament, *Report on Penal Establishments and Gaols, 1910*, VPP, 1911, 1st session, vol. 2, pp. 5–9.

in other prisons, including Pentridge. The success of indeterminate sentencing and growing institutional differentiation in bringing about true individualisation of punishment may be doubted when one examines the routines and control strategies used in some of these institutions: the continuing emphasis on military-style discipline and hard labour, even in welfare custodial institutions like Mt Penang in New South Wales, reflects the limits of individualisation.[80] But individualisation always operated more at the level of discourse and professional practice than in terms of an ideal tailoring of punishment to individual circumstances. In this respect, a critical development of the early twentieth century was the growing role of psychology in explaining crime and guiding the treatment of the criminal.

THE PSYCHOLOGY OF THE CRIMINAL

The growth of psychology from the late nineteenth century was significant for the organisation of punishment, both within prisons and without. Psychology promised to make sense of behaviour and, in some cases, offer remedies, futile though these turned out to be in so many cases.[81] In organisational terms, its impact was most noticeable in the classification of prisoners, though the aspirations of psychologists in this respect were constantly frustrated by the ebb and flow of prisoner populations. But criminal-law reform also bore the footprint of psychology, as did public discourses about criminality, its causes, and its remedies. We examine some of these themes below, in looking at classification of the criminal, at the phenomena of the 'mental defective' and the 'sexual pervert', and at popular opinion about crime and the criminal.

Psychology was only one of the sciences — the 'human sciences' — that focused on the prison and the criminal from the late nineteenth century. Eugenics — a science of populations and their reproduction — flourished from the 1880s to the 1930s, after which its association with Nazi extermination policies discredited it. Its themes of racial degeneration and

80 See Ramsland & Cartan, 'The Gosford Farm Home for Boys'.

81 For an account of the impact of psychology and psychiatry in Australia, see S. Garton, *Medicine and Madness*, University of NSW Press, Sydney, 1988, especially ch. 4; S. Garton, 'The Rise of the Therapeutic State: Psychiatry and the System of Criminal Jurisdiction in New South Wales, 1890–1940', *Australian Journal of Politics and History*, vol. 32, no. 3, 1986, pp. 378–88; M. Lewis, *Managing Madness*, AGPS, Canberra, 1988, pp. 109–11; J. J. Matthews, *Good and Mad Women*, Allen & Unwin, Sydney, 1984.

of the decline of the superior classes infected many debates about punishment in this period, in ways that confuse the distinctions between it and other sciences, including psychology and statistics. Initially, the development of eugenics was closely linked to the refinement of population statistics, another long-standing influence on criminal-justice debates. There was also an overlap between eugenics and anatomy, at least in its anthropometric phase. In Australia the University of Melbourne's Professor of Anatomy, R. J. Berry, busily measured the skull sizes of Pentridge inmates before the First World War.[82]

The most significant impact of eugenics was the role it played in refining segregation as a penal option with significant social functions. At a time of declining prison populations, eugenics helped sustain a rationale for institutionalising those considered most unfit to partake in civic life and, especially, to reproduce another generation — their role in inhibiting the reproduction of criminals was seen as an important rationale for the survival of carceral institutions.[83] Psychology, however, was more responsible for examining what would, or could, be done with prison inmates, as well as making suggestions about managing those at risk of criminality — the juvenile especially — outside institutions.

An example of psychology's influence was evident in the country's smallest jurisdiction, Tasmania. There the powerful influence of an extraordinary intellectual and social reformer, Edmund Morris Miller, helped to shape a distinctive emphasis on penal administration from the 1920s. Miller was one of those 'progressives' whose impact on Australian intellectual, cultural, and administrative life has been traced by Michael Roe.[84] Trained in philosophy, and lecturing in economics at the University of Tasmania, Miller became interested in the uses of psychological testing. He brought to the project a reforming zeal that was not exhausted by his success in pressing the adoption of the *Mental Deficiency Act* in 1920, a piece of legislation that created a means of certifying 'defectives' through the administration of the Mental Deficiency Board, over which he presided

82 M. Cawte, 'Craniotomy and Eugenics in Australia: R. J. A. Berry and the Quest for Social Efficiency', *Australian Historical Studies*, no. 86, 1986, pp. 35–53; for the Pentridge study, see R. J. A. Berry & L. Buchner, 'The Correlation of Size of Head and Intelligence, as Estimated from the Cubic Capacity of Brain of 355 Melbourne Criminals', *Proceedings of the Royal Society of Victoria*, vol. 25, (n.s.), pt 2, 1913, pp. 229–53.

83 For a recent assessment of the impact of eugenics, see Garton, 'Sound Minds and Healthy Bodies'.

84 M. Roe, *Nine Australian Progressives*, University of Queensland Press, St Lucia, 1984, pp. 280–314; and Garton, 'Sound Minds and Healthy Bodies'.

for many years. At Miller's prompting, a survey of the male prisoners in Hobart Gaol was commenced in 1924. Over the following year, Miller and the Gaol Medical Officer assessed the IQ levels of 119 prisoners. The results — which suggested that over half of the prisoners were below normal levels of intelligence — were compared with similar surveys conducted in the USA, as well as at Pentridge by Berry.[85]

Scrutiny of the psychological attributes and capacities of the prisoners at Hobart had an immediate practical effect in the adoption of a new classification system. The previous system, following classical penal theory, was one in which prisoners were assessed solely in terms of their record of offending. Now the prisoners were to be classified (and, ideally, accommodated separately) according to their IQ status, although some residual categories were maintained, including the category of those deemed to be habitual criminals. What material difference such reclassification made requires further inquiry. The answer, probably, is that it did not make much difference at all; inquiries in 1935 and 1943 would both comment on the lack of classification in Hobart Gaol.[86] More significant than its practical effect was the symbolic importance of this measure in reflecting an aspiration to punish according to a calculation of the prisoner's individual attributes — behavioural, psychological, and biological.

While Miller's influence on penal policy and practice had waned by the 1940s, the influence of psychological perspectives remained evident in Tasmania. In 1943 a Royal Commission of Inquiry led by the state's Chief Justice, Sir John Morris, strongly advocated the use of expert classification in prison administration, with a view to individualising the management of prisoners in order to enable their rehabilitation:

> Because the doubtfulness of the deterrent effect of punishment makes the only reasonable purpose of the prison the returning to society of men who will no longer be its enemies, the administration of the prison [should] be regarded as a problem of education in the sense of that term, which includes the development of the individual in such a way as will supply character defects, give him self-respect and enable him to find a place in the community.[87]

85 Tasmania, Parliament, *Report on Criminality and Levels of Intelligence: Being Report of a Mental Survey of the Hobart Gaol*, TPP, Hobart, 1925–26. On testing at Castlemaine Reformatory, see also Victoria, Parliament, *Report and Statistical Tables on Penal Establishments, Gaols and Reformatory Prisons, 1925*, VPP, 1926, Appendix, p. 7; on testing in Parramatta Prison at this time, see Garton, *Medicine and Madness*, p. 85.

86 Royal Commission on Escapes from Hobart Gaol, Report, typescript in Tasmanian State Library, Hobart, 1935; Tasmania, Parliament, *Report of the Royal Commission on the Hobart Gaol*, TPP, Hobart, 1943.

87 Tasmania, Parliament, *Report of the Royal Commission on the Hobart Gaol*, TPP, Hobart, 1943, p. 7.

To this end, the organisation of a prison would include the tailoring of prison life, including work, to the educative and training needs of the individual prisoner — needs assessed in part by psychological assessment. Morris recommended the abolition of the post of Controller of Prisons and the appointment of a Director of Correction to be in charge of all institutions holding 'delinquents'. (This seemed like a far-sighted recommendation, but three decades later the state was still enacting legislation to establish the office of Controller of Prisons.[88])

Morris outlined the role of the Director of Correction as follows:

> It should be the duty of the Director of Correction, immediately upon the conviction of any offender . . . to procure a full case history of the offender from birth. He should arrange for the immediate examination of the offender by a psychologist, psychiatrist, medical officer, and a dentist, and should supply a report to be placed before a sentencing court which the court may make use of as it thinks proper. After sentence the Director should plan a programme of rehabilitation for the offender based upon his estimate of the individual offender's needs.[89]

Coming from the state's Chief Justice, this recommendation suggests just how far medical and psychological postulates about individual behaviour had penetrated official thinking, especially outside penal institutions. For the influence of psychology was very much a movement that grew outside the prisons, seeking to change their direction through legislation, administrative reform, and custodial practice. The permanent appointment of psychologists to prisons services did not come until the 1950s in New South Wales and Victoria, and later in other states. Nevertheless, an organisational influence was notable in New South Wales with a Psychological Clinic being established at Long Bay in 1929, and in 1950, with greater consequence, a Classification Committee was introduced, offering the services of 'an educationist, a psychologist and a trades supervisor'.[90] When prisons did not have their own experts in these areas, it became common for the department to second or contract services as needed. Hence the health and education departments in a number of states became directly involved in the delivery of these services in their respective areas.

The impact of psychology was nevertheless registered in other respects. It was especially evident in the development of policies to identify and manage 'defectives' in prisons, as well as in sentencing reforms during and

88 See *Prison Act 1977* (Tas.), s. 6(1).
89 Tasmania, Parliament, *Report of the Royal Commission on the Hobart Gaol*, TPP, Hobart, 1943, p. 32.
90 NSW, Parliament, *Report of the Royal Commission into New South Wales Prisons (Nagle Commission)*, NSWPP, Sydney, 1976–77–78, Appendix, pp. 459, 461.

after the interwar period that targeted the sexual offender. We have already seen that the rise of the indeterminate sentence had its roots in the recommendations of the new criminology. Psychology, however, was more involved in the construction and identification of the defective and the pervert — the means by which the new criminology could individualise and differentiate the prisoner. These were no mere academic inventions — classifications that never materialised in the social practices of punishment; rather, they became a notable feature of the prison from the 1920s onwards.

The significance of the impact varied between jurisdictions. Tasmania again played an idiosyncratic role, positioning itself at one end of the spectrum when it came to managing the type known as defectives.[91] Under Miller's Mental Deficiency Act, the Mental Deficiency Board was empowered to transfer mental defectives between institutions that were nominated to accommodate them. In the 1920s and 1930s, the Board proceeded to 'make use of this power to transfer defectives to the Hobart Gaol from other institutions as punishment for unruliness or other conduct there. The treatment of such persons at the Hobart Gaol is identical in every respect with the treatment of an ordinary prisoner'.[92] As Morris noted in his inquiry in 1943, the power was a 'serious menace to liberty' and had proved so in practice. He illustrated his point with a case in which a man had been committed by the Board to the gaol as a mental defective and had since been recommitted for a further three years, without ever having been tried or convicted. This apparent return to the promiscuous mingling of populations offended two centuries of disaggregation, and Morris recommended that Hobart Gaol cease operating as an institution for mental defectives immediately.

Not all 'mental defectives' were criminals, and one aim of penologists was to prevent defectives from becoming offenders. In the area of sexual offences, the notion of the defective was used in the interwar years to explain what appeared to be an increase in attacks on women and children. From this concern arose the use of the indeterminate sentence, targeted especially at offenders classified as sexual perverts. The turn-of-the-century debates on habitual offenders had focused on the phenomena of repeat offending; except for the minor offence of drunkenness, they did not focus

91 For the history of legislation and policy regarding 'mental defectives', especially with respect to its eugenic features, see Lewis, *Managing Madness*, pp. 147–9; Garton, *Medicine and Madness*, pp. 60–1, 78–81; Garton, 'Sound Minds and Healthy Bodies'.

92 Tasmania, Parliament, *Report of the Royal Commission on the Hobart Gaol*, TPP, Hobart, 1943, p. 41.

on specific crimes. In the interwar years, there was a heightened awareness of sexual offences, inspired in part by professional developments in the classification of behaviour, but also evident in public concern about attacks reported in the media. One response was to call for the greater use of corporal punishments (to be examined in the next chapter). Alternatively, medical and psychology professionals recommended that sex offenders undergo treatment.

In New South Wales, the *Mental Defectives (Convicted Persons) Act* of 1939 imitated the Tasmanian (1920) and earlier English legislation (1913) in its concern with the mentally deficient, but it limited the State's attention in this respect to those who had already been convicted. The spirit of the legislation was to target sexual offenders, although only the minor offence of obscene exposure was specified, others liable being any person convicted of an offence punishable by death or by prison for not less than two years. Following identification by a judge or prison governor, such offenders could eventually be declared prisoners to be detained 'during the Governor's pleasure'.

The legislation, however, was little used, and in 1946 a number of departmental reports examined the reasons. Their conclusions summarised the expanding definition of the defective type, while the Act focused on the 'mental' defective only:

> Today, criteria of intelligence alone may be looked to to classify a person as a mental defective, and so bring him within the statutory provisions, but it is felt that this affords an incomplete coverage since other classes, victims of emotional and temperamental instability and aberration of the sexual impulse, are equally in need of care, in their own interests, and in the public interest.

These types were the 'social defectives', and there was said to be no treatment available to them in the state's prisons. Such persons, when released from prison, were a potential danger to the community, especially 'in the case of sexual psychopaths'. An interdepartmental committee inquiring into the effectiveness of the legislation concluded that the Act should be extended to include 'social defectives' and that qualified psychiatrists replace general medical practitioners in the process of certification. Such certified persons would be subject to indefinite detention until certified fit for release.[93]

93 Minute regarding Report of Inter-Departmental Committee on Mental Deficiency, 13 August 1946, 46/9008, 7/7133.2, NSW State Archives, Sydney.

The sexual psychopath was precisely the target of Queensland legislation enacted in 1945, under which sexual offenders could be sentenced to detention at His Majesty's pleasure. The incidence of sexual offending had received particular attention in this state during the war. A committee of inquiry into sexual offences had been the forum for generating a proposal for indefinite detention and appropriate treatment of these offenders, though it was sceptical about the success of psychological treatment for most sex offenders and did not consider that they should be detained in separate prison accommodation.[94] Subsequent amendment of the Criminal Code provided for indefinite detention, and for the regular medical and psychiatric assessment of such persons. In 1949, it was being said that Queensland led the nation in successfully responding to sex crimes, which had reportedly increased in all other states. The New South Wales Attorney-General promised that legislation was being prepared.[95]

In the first half of the twentieth century, the most optimistic claims about the future of penality were informed by promises to transform prisons from detention centres to places of treatment leading to successful release. The discourse of treatment reflected the persuasiveness of medical and psychological explanations. But beyond influencing legislation, such as that dealing with sex offences, the practical impact was less striking. The methodologies of research (at first focused on intelligence testing, then on a more clinical evaluation rooted in psychoanalysis) were, in any case, less attuned to successful treatment than to classification and diagnosis.[96] And the resources committed to medical and psychological treatment in prisons would never be adequate to the task.

Nevertheless, since the end of the First World War, the hegemony of psychological ideas in penal reform has been illustrated at many levels of the public culture of punishment. Media reports and debate leave us the most visible evidence of this, but so too do archival traces of the debates and resolutions of political parties, the activities of numerous reform groups, and correspondence to government regarding crime, criminals, and how to prevent the former and deal with the latter.

To take the first of these levels — political parties — it was common in the resolutions of parties on both sides of the political fence to give voice

94 Queensland, Parliament, *Report of Committee of Inquiry Regarding Sex Offences*, QPP, Brisbane, 1944, p. 13 .

95 NSW, *Debates*, 30 Mar 1949, pp. 1725–6.

96 See, for example, the *Argus*, 17 December 1924, p. 9 on the use of intelligence tests in classifying prisoners at Castlemaine Reformatory.

to progressive recommendations articulating modern ideas about the treatment of prisoners. In the late 1930s the United Australia Party in New South Wales — a party in government at the time — regularly considered prison reform at its annual conventions. Party members considered modern innovations, including psychiatric clinics for the classification of prisoners, which helped to separate the 'mentally subnormal' from the 'normal criminal'. A 'Scientific Reformatory Plan for the treatment of all prisoners based upon their mental capacity' would bring the state to the front line of progress in penality.[97] Science and psychology were the touchstones of a modern system of punishment, irrespective, it seemed, of political leaning. Hence cross-party support was evident in debates on measures such as the *New South Wales Prisons Act* of 1952, in which members from the three major parties (Labor in government, and Liberal and Country parties in opposition) competed with each other to affirm their support for modern modes of treatment. These forms of treatment were encapsulated in measures taken by the government in 1950 to establish the Classification Committee (one of the members was a psychiatrist, and the department's psychologist was secretary), a committee that scrutinised the prisoner's background and the results of psychological tests to guide the prisoner's disposal in one of the penal institutions.[98] The only regret expressed was that scientific treatment did not go far enough, and one member elaborated at length on the need for a Department of Criminology at the University of Sydney to stimulate research on the matter of penal reform.[99]

While there was often strong support among politicians for progressive penal reform, the media could be sceptical. Governments were sensitive about making too great a leap forward in adopting the treatment mode of punishment in place of old-fashioned deterrence through severity and certainty of discipline in a conventional prison. In Melbourne the conservative *Argus* opposed leniency in the sentencing of juveniles and the extension of psychiatric treatment to prisoners in general, which it saw as a symptom of a misguided 'wave of pseudo-humanitarianism'.[100] And the message from the psychologists was not always consistent in any case. The

97 Suggested Legislative Amendments proposed by the Annual Conference of the United Australia Party, 1935–39, NSW State Archives, Sydney, 5/7790.3.
98 See debate on the 1952 Prisons Bill, in NSW, *Debates*, 18 March 1952, pp. 5372–94.
99 Mr Hughes, (Armidale), in NSW, *Debates*, 18 March 1952, p. 5387.
100 *Argus*, 22 September 1937, p. 22; 13 December 1937, p. 12 (attacking a proposal by Mr Oldham, MLA, for a select committee to investigate reform in relation to mental hygiene and the penal system).

Argus quoted the Auckland Prison Chaplain on a visit to Melbourne after a year abroad studying prison reform: 'In the prevention of crime we are not paying enough attention to the psychological point of view'.[101] But on other occasions it could also cite Professor F. C. Bartlett, an experimental psychologist in Cambridge who had told the Chief Constables Association meeting that 'if a man deserves a whipping, he should get one straight away'.[102] Bartlett was one of the experts cited by the Queensland Sex Offences Committee of Inquiry in 1944 as authority for the limited results that might be expected from psychological treatment of prisoners.[103]

In an arena in which there were high expectations of psychology, Bartlett's scepticism was unusual. Reform enthusiasts were much inclined to accept that psychology was the way of the future. Hence the Howard Prison Reform League proposed to the New South Wales government in the late 1920s that the office of comptroller-general be replaced by 'a governing board of trained psychologists'.[104] Within penal administration itself, there was little doubting that psychology was the best guide to future management, as the report of a departmental committee on prison reform in New South Wales made clear at this time.[105] Such a presumption — that psychology provides the best guide to the job of managing prisons — was beginning to influence appointment decisions. In Melbourne in 1923 the advertisement for the position of inspector-general of penal establishments looked for a person with a university degree, 'to ensure that a man of suitable personality, and likely to be able to classify prisoners, should be obtained. The degree which would be most useful to applicants was one which had necessitated the study of psychology'.[106] For decades there had been agreement on the relevance of psychology to penology, and against this background, it is no surprise that psychological clinics, classification teams, and consultant psychiatrists had become standard features of the prisons system in all jurisdictions by the 1950s.

101 *Argus*, 6 March 1937, p. 21.

102 *Argus*, 24 June 1939, p. 9. Corporal punishment of adult male offenders was, however, more likely to be rejected by most of those who invoked psychology as a guide to penal reform, as we will see in the next chapter.

103 Queensland, Parliament, *Report of Committee of Inquiry Regarding Sex Offences*, QPP, Brisbane, 1944, p. 13.

104 *Sydney Morning Herald*, 4 October 1928, p. 6.

105 Prison Reform 1925–44: Draft Report of a Committee on Prison Reform, 1928, NSW State Archives, Sydney, 7/7150; see *Sydney Morning Herald*, 31 May 1928, for a report of the Minister announcing the appointment of an expert committee on prison reform.

106 *Argus*, 1 November 1923, p. 5.

In these ways, the organisation of imprisonment was affected by the new sciences of criminology and psychology, though it is unlikely that the majority of inmates' actual experience of incarceration changed much at all. The tedium of prison life, the periodic stories of prison brutality, the frequency of escape attempts, disturbances, and not infrequent riots in the interwar period all constituted a more familiar underlay to the seeming professionalisation of punishment. A familiar dialectic of reform and institutional lethargy seemed to be repeated in every generation, but the broader field of penality was undoubtedly changing, in ways that merit attention in the following chapters.

4

Punishing the Body

The modern era's preoccupation with the redemption or taming of the criminal mind, body, and soul through the instrument of the prison was not exclusive of other approaches to punishment. Over a long period of time, the legitimacy of corporal punishment and execution was challenged in Australia, as elsewhere, yet the practice continued past the mid-twentieth century. A fundamental cultural ambivalence towards punishments of the body is still evident, especially in recurrent calls for the application of both the death penalty and corporal punishment in response to horrific crimes or outbreaks of violence. Hence, the presumption that the decline in punishing the body reflects an irreversible growth in the civilising impulse requires historical examination. Through an understanding of this protracted history, we can also appreciate the influence of some fundamental emotions — emotions to which punishment appeals and that it aspires to satisfy.

Corporal punishment and changing sensibilities

Well before the end of capital punishment in Australia, flogging went out of fashion. By 1967, when Ronald Ryan was hanged in Australia's last execution, corporal punishment was effectively finished as a penalty in criminal-justice sentencing. Like the death penalty, however, flogging remains a significant element of the collective psyche, constantly hovering on the verge of recovery. Calls for its reintroduction show the limits of what is possible in penal reform. Because corporal punishment has passed, we cannot assume that it will not be reintroduced. Moreover, in an age of cultural relativism and of post-Mabo reassessment, the decline of flogging within Australia's European penal system deserves more reflective treatment than we might otherwise expect. The debates in Australia on the legitimacy of corporal punishment in indigenous cultures are current enough to suggest that the basis of non-indigenous attitudes towards the use of such punishment also requires historical analysis.

In the nineteenth century, Australian punishment changed in ways that were also evident in other settler and European societies. But local cultures have their own decisive mechanisms of change. In the case of colonial Australia, the novelist Marcus Clarke was one of the most influential shapers of opinion on the country's immediate past. For Clarke, the use of the lash was an emblem of the brutality and brutalising effects of the convict system. His most famous novel, *For the Term of his Natural Life*, was first serialised in the Melbourne-based *Australian Journal* between 1870 and 1872. To Michael Davitt, visiting Australia in 1895, two decades after Clarke's novel was published, the work was 'immortal' and linked explicitly to the 'reaction in the public mind out there against the horrible outrages which irresponsible prison power committed in the "old days"'.[1] One of the chapters, entitled 'One hundred lashes', depicted the awful spectacle of corporal punishment in a degraded and inhuman institution. Here Clarke used flogging as a device for demonstrating Rufus Dawes's courage and virtue, and then his degradation, all in the same episode. Having been ordered to flog a young fellow-convict, Kirkald, who collapses from the effects, Dawes refuses to flog any further. Then he is flogged himself, though his previous beatings have toughened his back, which enables him to withstand the pain. Eventually, having endured one hundred and twenty lashes in silence, he breaks down, not crying out but swearing oaths and blasphemies against his tormentors: 'he seemed to have abandoned his humanity'.[2] Indeed, a common Victorian objection to flogging was that it debased the humanity, of both the flogged and the flogger.

We will return later to the ambiguities of the community's response to flogging, and to questions of humanity and of manliness. There is no doubting, however, the persuasive power of such depictions of flogging. If the novel is not merely a reflection of opinion but an agent of political and cultural formation in this period, then Clarke's account of the convict

1 Davitt, *Life and Progress*, pp. 414, 418–19.
2 Clarke, *For the Term of his Natural Life*, p. 285.

system helped to create the view that flogging and other such abuses of power, which he saw as inherent in the convict system, were unacceptable.[3]

Yet we know also that Clarke was no distant observer of a long-past practice. His association with the Governor of the Melbourne Gaol, J. B. Castieau — an active one during the years in which *His Natural Life* was written — was recorded in the latter's diaries and suggests the possibility that Clarke drew on images of that institution in his own portrait of the punishment system. On one occasion, in February 1871, Castieau recorded that Clarke attended one of the gaol's occasional floggings:

> There was a man flogged this afternoon. The Members of the Press & the usual 'loafers' were present in addition to the officials. The prisoner was an 'old hand' with a face that would bring in a verdict of 'Guilty' from most Juries. He displayed most stolid endurance without the slightest bravado or flashness & took his fifty lashes without a groan & scarcely a movement except a horrible twitching & trembling in the muscles of his arms which he kept strained to the utmost. This was the most severe flogging I have yet seen administered. Marcus Clark [*sic*] 'The Peripatetic Philosopher' met me in the street this morning & came to the Gaol to see the 'Punishment' this afternoon. I was glad to see he did not believe much in its efficacy as a rule though he believed flogging could occasionally be resorted to with advantage.[4]

This is an illuminating comment. At the very time that Clarke was depicting the awfulness of the convict system as a relic of the past, he was able to witness in Melbourne a flogging punishment and convey his own view of its 'efficacy'.[5] His host, Castieau, was sceptical of its utility and, throughout the following decade, expressed privately in his diary the view that flogging was degrading and ghoulish.

We can see this again in 1872 when Judge Redmond Barry handed down a sentence in a bestiality case in Melbourne, as Castieau recorded:

3 Long after his death, this influence was still evident in the frequency with which Clarke was cited in parliamentary debate on issues of punishment. For example, Mr Styants, MLA Kalgoorlie, in a speech on the Punishment of Whipping Abolition Bill, 1952, said, 'I believe whipping is an outmoded system of punishment. We have read books on the early history of Australia, particularly one called "For the term of his natural life", which reeks of floggings from the front page to the back' Western Australia, *Debates*, 13 November 1952, p. 2101. See also the comments of Mr Cook, MLA, Victoria, who in debate on Supply, Penal Establishments, cites Clarke's novel, in particular the case of Kirkland, to condemn the association of prisoners in the same cell (Victoria, *Debates*, 23 January 1900, p. 3190).

4 Castieau, Diary, 13 February 1871.

5 Clarke's predisposition towards flogging was also evident in some of his journalistic comments on convicts; see B. Elliott, *Marcus Clarke*, Clarendon Press, Oxford, 1958, p. 161.

> The Criminal Sittings commenced this morning & I was at the Court by ten o'clock to be in attendance upon the presiding Judge who this time was Mr Justice Barry. There were no cases of importance; one miserable looking deformed blear eyed youth pleaded Guilty to an Unnatural Offence. He was caught in the act with a Goat. Mr Barry seized the opportunity & dealt out an elaborate sentence, Ten Years on the Roads & to be three times whipped by the Common Hangman, 25 lashes on the breech with a cat o nine tails.

Having indicated his distaste for the severity of such a sentence Castieau elaborated on the circumstances of the boy's upbringing, in a passage that suggests a depth of difference between the judge and the prison governor:

> The horrid part of this matter after all is the statement made by the prisoner when arrested which was that he had learnt the crime he had committed from seeing the boys at Sunbury commit themselves in the same way with the Goats that were about the Station. The sentence of Judge Barry's would have been a righteous one if the culprit had been a man but with this idiotic infant I think it lacketh discretion & will cause the judge tribulation.[6]

It was such conflict between officialdom that helped to shape subsequent penal practice, leading to the eventual demise of corporal punishment.

So how did flogging decline? And why did it retain its appeal, or at least elements of legitimacy, even for those who wanted to condemn it as a sign of a barbaric past? The question is, of course, complex, and it reaches out into areas of cultural history that are only tangentially related to the mechanics of punishment. In documenting the decline, there is also an implicit need to identify the place of flogging in earlier penality.

Early modern European punishment included whipping in various guises. Its uses were mixed: the penalty was an instance of Foucault's semio-technique, demonstrating to the public the awful consequences of breaching the law, thus functioning as both a punishment and deterrent. Exercised more often against petty thieves and lower class offenders, it was a punishment that was increasingly supplemented by others. The combination of whipping and banishment was a common sentence in colonial America for itinerant or foreign offenders, while whipping as well as imprisonment was an option in late-eighteenth- and early-nineteenth-century sentencing in England.[7]

The transformation of bodily punishments was linked to more general changes in sentencing. For centuries, whipping or beating was widely

6 Castieau, Diary, 15 August 1872.
7 D. Rothman, 'Perfecting the Prison', in Morris & Rothman, p. 112; Beattie, *Crime and the Courts*, pp. 461–2, 560–2.

used in summary punishment, before it became a major element in punishment for the more serious category of felony. Its increased use in early modern English penality appears to be linked to the search for alternatives to the death penalty and transportation. As the favoured punishment for the less serious charge of petty larceny, Beattie finds that its use increased in the late seventeenth century. During this period, it appears that juries were looking to reduce the risk of passing a capital sentence on a person convicted of grand larceny. After the Transportation Act of 1718, as transportation to the American colonies became increasingly favoured, the use of whipping declined: the severity of transportation was greater than whipping or branding, while stopping short of the death penalty.[8]

Whipping declined in stages as its application was progressively restricted. The informal exclusion of gentlemen from the classes liable to be publicly whipped was a sign of the transformation to come.[9] Hence, early in the nineteenth century, women and girls were removed from the list of those who could be so punished: the power to order a whipping of females, whether in public or private, was abolished in England and Wales in 1820.[10] Measures against cruelty to animals fit into this sequence of gradual restrictions on physical punishments, with the first statutory prohibitions on cruelty dating from the 1820s. Women's exclusion from the list of those who could be corporally punished appears to be incidentally responsible for the development of a particularly resilient form of prison discipline from the early nineteenth century: solitary confinement. This punishment originated in the need to establish a form of discipline that could replace whipping. Thus, Paula Jane Byrne has suggested, women in the convict colonies were also subjected to the rigours of prison discipline earlier than men.[11]

The result of the progressive restrictions was that, by the second half of the nineteenth century, whipping was confined to specific social groups, and to a great extent to specific offences. Those who remained liable to whipping as a punishment were juvenile males and prisoners. Indeed, the

8 Beattie, *Crime and the Courts*, pp. 485–7; Radzinowicz & Hood, *The Emergence of Penal Policy*, pp. 689 ff.

9 Beattie, *Crime and the Courts*, p. 463.

10 Departmental Committee on Corporal Punishment, *Report*, His Majesty's Stationery Office, London, 1938 is indispensable on the legislative history; see also Radzinowicz & Hood, *The Emergence of Penal Policy*, ch. 21 ('The Mentality of the Cat and the Birch').

11 *Holland and Wife v. The Queen*, (1840) 2 Irish Law Reports, p. 335; P. J. Byrne, 'On her Own Hands: Women and Criminal Law in New South Wales, 1810–1830', in Philips & Davies (eds), *A Nation of Rogues*, pp. 34–5; Salt, *These Outcast Women*, ch. 5.

link between corporal punishment and the need to discipline the behaviour of unruly young males still remains one of the strongest themes in debates about appropriate punishment. The degree to which flogging might still be regarded as appropriate for boys, even when its use on adult males is frowned on, is well illustrated by the debates on discipline in English prisons in the 1850s. By this time, flogging in English prisons was rare — so rare that prisons like Reading Gaol, which was recording three floggings a year, were attracting critical notice. Yet the corporal punishment of boys was still approved by those who otherwise criticised it for men. One prison governor thus urged the necessity of separating boys and men in the gaol, not just because of the danger of contamination — the common reason for such a proposal — but because of the need to discipline them differently. To clarify what he meant when he said 'treat them as boys', Captain Williams was asked by a Select Committee member, 'By treating them as boys you mean now and then flogging them?', to which he agreed. Even so, he wanted to use such a punishment carefully, as its effects varied between individuals. Others felt that flogging juveniles merely 'hardened them'.[12]

Such reservations were also admitted by the authors of the most substantial Australian inquiry into penalties and sentencing in the second half of the nineteenth century: the Victorian Royal Commission on Penal and Prison Discipline (1870–72). The commissioners nevertheless laid their qualms aside in order to avoid the greater evil of imprisoning juveniles with adults. When other social preventive measures against juvenile crime failed — such as public education, and the substitution of 'healthful and rational recreation' for immoral and indecent popular amusements — the commissioners acknowledged the difficulty of summarily punishing juveniles by any means other than 'personal chastisement'. Their reluctance to endorse whipping was evident, since there existed, 'and properly, a strong repugnance to the infliction of corporal punishment on youths'. Among other objections was the criticism that whipping destroyed 'self-respect' and permanently degraded 'the moral feelings'. Endorsement of whipping as a punishment was therefore hedged around with a number of qualifications, including the requirements that two justices, including a police magistrate, order it, and that jurisdiction be limited to proclaimed police districts for a certain time only. The whipping was

12 United Kingdom, Parliament, *Report from the Select Committee on Prison Discipline*, BPP, London, 1850, vol. 17, evidence of Capt. W. Williams, pp. 771–3. Even so, whipping of adult male prisoners was intensively used in English prisons and increased under the Du Cane regime of the 1860s and 1870s; see Radzinowicz & Hood, *Emergence of Penal Policy*, pp. 552–6.

to be by birch rather than lash and limited to a maximum of twenty-five strokes. It is evident that the commissioners saw such whipping as a special resort to deal with what they hoped would be a temporary problem.[13]

Prisoners, but only male ones, were a second category of persons who might be whipped, for offences committed within a prison. Again, the history of this formal punishment extends well into the second half of the twentieth century, although Australian prison governors were mostly disinclined to use such disciplinary means. At Brisbane in 1868 a parliamentary select committee recommended the construction of punishment cells to limit the use of the 'lash', but noted at the same time that the instrument had been used only once in the previous fifteen months.[14] Although, in the 1890s, Michael Davitt noted a number of institutions in which prisoners might still be whipped, the incidence of such formal punishment was very low.[15] In 1944, when John Barry surveyed the state prison administrators in Australia on the uses of corporal punishment, he could find only scanty evidence of its use, even though it remained a formal option. The South Australian authorities regarded it as 'a deterrence against assaults on prison officers', as the United Kingdom's Cadogan Committee had also. In Victoria, the Visiting Justice had no power to order corporal punishment, although whipping as a result of a court sentence (whether for a prison offence or otherwise) still occurred. The Victorian Inspector-General emphasised the relative leniency of those floggings that did take place, stressing instead the effect produced by the 'solemnity of the occasion, the ritual accompanying it, the suspense beforehand and between each stroke'. These comments suggest the depth of the transition from the convict period, when the physical intensity of the whipping, the laying on hard of each stroke, had been a matter of calculation. Other states reported the rarity of corporal punishment in prisons, and in New South Wales there had been no whipping since 1905.[16]

13 Victoria, Parliament, *Report from the Royal Commission on Penal and Prison Discipline (No. 2) (Penal and Prison Discipline)*, VPP, Melbourne, 1871, pp. xii–xiii.

14 Queensland, Parliament, *Report of the Select Committee on Prison Discipline*, QPP, Brisbane, 1868, p. 11.

15 Davitt, *Life and Progress*, pp. 413–55.

16 See Sir John Barry Papers, National Library of Australia, ms 2505/ series 41, fol. 74–109 for a report on the survey, which had been undertaken as preparation for a chapter on prisons and punishment in a book on Australian criminal law. He was writing the book (published as *An Introduction to Australian Criminal Law* in 1947) in collaboration with Professor George Paton and Geoffrey Sawer. On flogging in the colonial period, see especially the reports from magistrates in response to an official circular, 29 August 1833, in *Convict Discipline, 1833*, Gryphon Books, Sydney, 1977, pp. 49 ff.

A third group who remained susceptible to whipping was made up of offenders against specific aspects of the criminal law. Here the definition of those who might be whipped appears to have been the product of particular social anxieties. Hence a specific offence warranting whipping in England and Wales between 1862 and 1947 was that of robbery, in its various forms. The garrotting panic of 1862 and other English debates about violence against women and children had revived faith in the benefits of whipping violent offenders, and this faith was echoed in the recommendations of the Victorian Royal Commission on Penal and Prison Discipline.[17] Endorsing a more clearly defined range of penalties for different scales of violence, the commissioners — led by the Chief Justice, William Stawell — recommended that judges' powers to order private whipping in cases involving personal violence and for unnatural offences 'be extended to aggravated cases of offences against women and children, and to crimes perpetrated under circumstances of cruelty or brutality'.[18] In spite of support for preserving corporal punishment as a sentencing option, the rates of use for those adults convicted under such offences varied noticeably across the period. In England and Wales during the Edwardian period, the whipping of adults convicted for robbery with violence was rare, notably so in comparison with the 1890s and the 1920s.[19] In Australia, despite recommendations such as those of the Victorian Royal Commission, sentencing orders that included whipping continued to be infrequent, although there were exceptions.

Thus in Western Australia — which, like other jurisdictions in the 1880s, had been disinclined to use whipping — there was a revival in its use in the 1890s, especially for the punishment of Aboriginal offenders. Although the official statistics do not record the characteristics of the offenders who were subject to these whippings, it is likely that the great bulk of those who were whipped on summary conviction from 1892 were Aboriginal. In that year the government reversed an 1883 decision to abolish whipping as punishment for 'aboriginal natives'. The Attorney-General justified the revival of whipping on explicitly racialist grounds: 'You can only

17 See J. Davis, 'The London Garotting Panic of 1862', in V. A. C. Gatrell et al. (eds), *Crime and the Law: The Social History of Crime in Western Europe since 1500*, Europa, London, 1980; Radzinowicz & Hood, *Emergence of Penal Policy*, pp. 692–4.

18 Victoria, Parliament, *Report from the Royal Commission on Penal and Prison Discipline (No. 2) (Penal and Prison Discipline)*, VPP, Melbourne, 1871.

19 See Departmental Committee on Corporal Punishment, *Report*, His Majesty's Stationery Office, London, 1938, p. 130.

deal with them ['all these coloured races', including 'blackfellows, or Indians, or Chinamen'] like you deal with naughty children — whip them . . . Give them a little stick when they really deserve it, and it does them a power of good'.[20] On numerous occasions in the 1890s the Western Australia legislature discussed the proposal that whipping be used to control the 'natives' (as a deterrent, for example, instead of sending offenders to the Aboriginal prison on Rottnest Island). The infliction of pain to enforce labour at Rottnest was advocated during a parliamentary discussion in 1895: enforcement of hard labour through flogging and chaining to a wheelbarrow, it was said, would reduce the incidence of spearing cattle.[21]

The reversion to whipping in such cases was a late colonial attempt to revive a punishment that was increasingly deplored in other jurisdictions, including Australian ones. Its exceptional nature belatedly caused one Western Australian MLA to attack the 1892 bill as 'an outrage on humanity'.[22] Only a few years before this, the 1887 Queensland Board of Inquiry into Prisons had considered whether corporal punishment might be an alternative punishment for Aboriginal prisoners — especially in view of the Board's critical assessment of the effects of incarceration on them — but recommended against it, since 'no matter how carefully regulations under which the flogging should be given were framed, abuses would be certain to arise, and unnecessary cruelty be practised'.[23]

The example of whipping demonstrates a common feature of the history of punishment: the idiosyncrasy of sanctions in particular jurisdictions. Precisely because its use became so marginal, the occasions on which whipping was invoked as a penalty point to some of the underlying local conflicts that determine policy and practice. For while Western Australia continued to endorse its use in the case of Aboriginal offenders (somewhat eccentrically in the Australian context), policy recommendations were being made in the same colony that deplored its use in other settings. The 1899 Penal Commission reviewed international evidence on the changing use of corporal punishment, even noting that Italy had banned

20 S. Burt, Attorney-General, in Western Australia, *Debates*, 29 January 1892, p. 398. The *Aboriginal Offenders (Amendment) Act 1892* (WA) prescribed the maximum number of strokes (twenty-five for adult males and twelve for juvenile males) to be used in whipping Aborigines tried summarily. In spite of the Attorney-General's comment, the Act applied to Aboriginal offenders only.

21 Western Australia, *Debates*, 22 August 1895, p. 673.

22 Western Australia, *Debates*, 3 February 1892, pp. 427–30.

23 Queensland, Parliament, *Report from the Board of Inquiry Appointed to Inquire into the General Management of the Gaols, Penal Establishments, and Lockups of the Colony of Queensland*, QPP, Brisbane, 1887, p. xxvi.

Table 4.1 Whipping as a sanction, Western Australia, 1887–1900

Year	*Total number of people whipped**	*Total number of people whipped for property offences*
1887	3	2
1888	5	3
1889	13	4
1890	5	0
1891	4	0
1892	115	104
1893	91	63
1894	111	93
1895	62	48
1896	83	59
1897	41	31
1898	13	9
1899	19	13
1900	10	4

Source: WA Statistical Register, 1896, 1900.

its use by parents. Yet, while the Commission wanted whipping to be retained as an option — believing it had a deterrent effect, and that the use of the birch on youthful offenders was especially worth preserving — it drew the line at its use in prison. Influenced particularly by the Visiting Justice to Fremantle Prison, who had described the flogging of prisoners as degrading, the Commission recommended that it be abolished as a disciplinary instrument within prisons.[24]

Such recommendations for the abolition of corporal punishment were by now mostly consistent with sentencing practice. Occasional flurries of use in relation to juvenile crime are evident — as in South Australia in 1900, when twenty-six juveniles are recorded as having been whipped for larceny offences. But a special provision of the New South Wales *Criminal Law Amendment Act* in 1883, which allowed two justices sitting together to order a whipping, had not been used by 1900. Other jurisdictions were equally disinclined by this time to use whipping at all.

In 1937 an international comparison of the use of whipping (or at least one within the bounds of the old Empire) was conducted for a British committee (the Cadogan Committee). By this time punishment by whipping in Australia (and New Zealand) was rarer still, especially in comparison with other similar settler societies, including Canada and

24 Western Australia, Parliament, *Final Report of the Royal Commission on Fremantle Prison*, WAPP, Perth, 1899, p. 14.

Southern Rhodesia.[25] In that year it was reported that the highest rate of use had been in Victoria, where there had been ten cases in the previous five years. In New South Wales there had been none since 1905, although, as we will see shortly, there were a number of whippings ordered but later remitted. The number of offences for which whipping might be ordered in Australian jurisdictions was formally quite broad. But on the evidence of various cases from the 1870s, it appears that, in some jurisdictions, it was used mostly to punish sexual offenders, — especially homosexuals, but also, in some cases, those convicted of indecent assault, incest, and carnal knowledge. This is a notable contrast to English practice, in which the emphasis was on the use of whipping to control robbery — and where attempts to add whipping to the range of punishments for sexual offences were generally unsuccessful in the later nineteenth century.[26] The link between whipping and sexual offences was nevertheless stubbornly revived from time to time in Australia — even as late as the 1960s in Victoria, when a judge called expert evidence in consideration of a possible order for whipping in a case of robbery in company involving personal violence.[27]

It appears, then, that, while the use of flogging in English-speaking countries was in a long decline, there were nevertheless some interesting and provocative differences between jurisdictions. Moreover, these cultural differences may be much more subtle than we might expect. How do we explain the much greater use of whipping in both criminal sentencing and prison discipline in twentieth-century England, as compared with Australia? Some differences (as we have already noted with regard to late-nineteenth-century Western Australia) appear to have been inflected by the use of racial thresholds to define categories of who should be whipped. Hence, in 1938 the Cadogan Committee reported that annu-

25 See Departmental Committee on Corporal Punishment, *Report*, London, His Majesty's Stationery Office, 1938, Appendices; see also p. 144, which indicates that the situation in the USA was generally even more resistant to flogging as a punishment. On the successes of the ante-bellum campaigns against corporal punishment, see M. C. Glenn, *Campaigns against Corporal Punishment*, State University of New York Press, Albany, NY, 1984. On the rarity of whipping in New Zealand (for property offences, although it had also been extended to some sexual offences in 1868), see Pratt, *Punishment in a Perfect Society*, pp. 91, 149, 207.

26 Radzinowicz & Hood, *Emergence of Penal Policy*, pp. 695–6, 702. An exception was the use of whipping as a punishment for offences under the *White Slave Traffic Act, 1912* (UK).

27 'Whipping as a Penal Sanction: Its Consideration in a Recent Case', *Australian and New Zealand Journal of Criminology*, vol. 1, no. 1, March 1968, pp. 10–25.

ally, on average, 436 whippings were ordered against adult males in Southern Rhodesian courts; not one of these had been ordered against a European. There is some evidence that a similar racial distinction was made in Australia at this time: in the Northern Territory in the 1930s, the corporal punishment of Aboriginal offenders was still regarded as an essential instrument of discipline. T. G. H. Strehlow, a patrol officer who was later to become a distinguished anthropologist, advised in 1936 that his possession of summary corporal punishment powers was 'actually an essential requirement for upholding the authority of the patrol officer', enabling him to control the anarchy of the tribes in the centre.[28]

Apart from such exceptions, the evidence is strong that the incidence of whipping declined in Australia as officialdom became increasingly sensitive to its use. While there remained the occasional whipping judge or magistrate, and inevitably the odd politician or journalist to argue in its favour, it grew more difficult to administer a punishment that many people regarded as distasteful. We can see evidence of this difficulty in the debates that arose over the use of corporal punishment in New South Wales earlier this century.

The altered context for whipping was evident in the obstacles placed in the path of those few judges who wished to see it exercised as a deterrent. There were a number of such cases in New South Wales between 1905 and 1940. In each case, like the Melbourne prison governor Castieau some decades before, prison and other criminal-justice officials in New South Wales expressed distaste for corporal punishment. In 1923, the New South Wales Comptroller General of Prisons, on whom fell the burden of administering such punishments, requested advice from the Justice Department regarding a sentence of whipping on a 47-year-old man found guilty of indecently assaulting a boy of eleven years. He noted that the 'last flogging' for the indecent assault of a male had been in 1900, and the last of any kind (of ten lashes) had been for attempted bestiality. In 1919 a seventeen-year-old youth on a charge of bestiality had been sentenced at Bathurst Quarter Sessions to a week's light labour and ten strokes of the lash; the flogging was remitted by the Executive Council. Not disguising his feeling against the punishment, the Acting Under Secretary of Justice noted that '[a]part from the question of whether flogging a man 47 years of age, which prisoner says he is, I need only say at

28 T. Rowse, 'Strehlow's Strap: Functionalism and Historicism in Colonial Ethnography', in B. Attwood & J. Arnold (eds), *Power, Knowledge and Aborigines*, La Trobe University Press, Melbourne, 1992, p. 91.

this stage that there is no official flagellator and some difficulty would probably arise if a warder were asked to flog a prisoner'.[29] Similar reasoning won the day in the other cases of this kind in the 1920s. If an appeal against the sentence failed, the whipping portion of a sentence was always remitted nevertheless. A gap between some judicial opinion and the justice and prisons bureaucracy became evident. Occasionally judges would resort to the sentence — as did Judge Edwards in a 1925 case, again of an indecent assault on a boy: 'Flogging is the only remedy in cases of this kind. There are far too many of them. It is disgraceful'.[30] But again, in the absence of an 'official flogger', as the Under Secretary of Justice put it, there was an immediate administrative problem in carrying out such an order.

In any case, flogging was no longer the 'only remedy'. Responding to a call in 1937 by a branch of the Country Women's Association for flogging to be introduced as a deterrent against sexual attacks, especially on young girls, the general secretary of the Racial Hygiene Association, Mrs L. E. Goodisson, countered that such offenders should be classed among the mentally unfit — psychiatry and segregation colonies were the remedy.[31] These were not always exclusive remedies, however. In Victoria, in 1923, a rash of attacks on women and children inspired a campaign for penal reform to deal with the issue. Both flogging and psychiatric treatment received support in public meetings and deputations on the issue, although there was also some victim-blaming evident in calls for 'high ideals in dress and conduct'.[32] A mixed response was similarly evident two decades later when, in 1946, the Housewives Association of New South Wales urged that the lash was the 'only means of preventing a repetition of the brutality and cruelty being exercised by some lower classes of the community', but a supplementary resolution called for a psychiatrist to be employed and for second offenders to be segregated for life.[33] As we have seen in the previous chapter, the latter course was in fact the one being taken by the criminal law during this period as legislators sought to refine their response to sexual offences.

29 Minute 16 November 1923, Sexual Offenders, 1919–45, Attorney-General Special Bundles, NSW State Archives, Sydney, 12/1351.1.

30 Minute 11 March 1925, Sexual Offenders, 1919–45, Attorney-General Special Bundles, NSW State Archives, Sydney, 12/1351.1.

31 *Sun* (Sydney), 2 September 1937 (in NSW State Archives, Sydney, AG 12/1351.1).

32 *Argus*, 17 May, 4 June, 11 June, 18 June, 1923.

33 Minute 4 July 1946, 'Sexual Offenders, 1919–45', Attorney-General Special Bundles, NSW State Archives, Sydney, 12/1351.1.

Yet alternative remedies, such as psychiatric treatment or reformatories, failed to deliver the emotional satisfaction that corporal punishment might. Even in the course of repudiating a call for the lash, there might emerge the possibilities of teaching offenders a good lesson through informal physical punishment. On the eve of war in 1939, the New South Wales Minister for Justice received a deputation of the Women Justices Association, who wished to discuss the problem of sexual assaults. Rejecting a call from one woman for the use of the lash, the Minister was asked what the government would do 'if women took the law into their own hands and caught one of these men and dealt with him'. The law was that self-defence justified the use of force in stopping an attack, but the Minister also remembered 'a case where a lot of women got hold of a man who offended and gave him a frightful thrashing. We would not bother our heads in a case like that'.[34] Such a concession suggests something about the limitations of the case against corporal punishment, limitations that allowed the survival of corporal punishment in other kinds of social relations and institutions, especially the family, the school, and non-regulated social life. All the same, what we know about the incidence of bodily punishment suggests, in fact, that women have rarely taken the law into their own hands in this way — especially when one considers the persistence of wife-beating and other abuse later to be termed 'domestic violence'.[35]

This example of women demanding more severe sanctions for violent assault suggests that penal and sentencing practice operated in predictable tension with so-called popular opinion. Every well-publicised case of sexual assault or other violent crime brought out a variety of commentators, who made their views known to government: from individual letter writers through to community groups and political parties. An anonymous letter from 'Humanity' in Sydney urged the government to prevent the whipping of a seventeen-year-old boy for bestiality: 'the sooner this kind of thing is put a stop to the better for *Australia*'. Such appeals against the lash typically recalled its use in slavery or the convict period, or deployed

34 Minutes of deputation 23 March 1939, Sexual Offenders, 1919–45, Attorney-General Special Bundles, NSW State Archives, Sydney, 12/1351.1.

35 On the significance of wife-beating as an exception to the antebellum crusade against corporal punishment, see Glenn, *Campaigns against Corporal Punishment*, ch. 4; on Australia, see J. Allen, *Sex and Secrets: Crimes Involving Australian Women since 1880*, Oxford University Press, Melbourne, 1990, pp. 46–52, and K. Saunders, 'The Study of Domestic Violence in Colonial Queensland', *Historical Studies*, no. 82, 1984, pp. 68–85; on Victorian Kent, see C. Conley, *The Unwritten Law*, Oxford University Press, Oxford, 1991, ch. 3.

arguments dating from early nineteenth-century humanitarian reform movements, in which the lash was said to degrade both the flogger and the flogged. In 1933, calls by Police Commissioner Childs for the reintroduction of the lash prompted the *Tamworth Northern Leader* to cite the diminishing use of the lash since the convict days as authority against its revival: 'All the official records of convictism prove conclusively that flogging never reduced crime, but on the contrary effectually prevented the criminal's reformation'.[36] But enlightened rural opinion was countered by other appeals to history. Writing from Fremantle in Western Australia, a correspondent advised the New South Wales Minister for Justice to look to the lash to remedy the evil of overcrowded gaols: 'it stamped out garrotting in London many years ago and one sentence in Liverpool cured ruffianism' — a reference to a well-worn mythology about the effectiveness of whipping.[37]

There were always, of course, those who would rake up anecdotal evidence of the efficacy of corporal punishment. And, as with hanging, there were those who declared they would not shrink from inflicting such punishment. In 1929, following the New South Wales government's introduction of the lash to counter razor gangs and child molesters, John L., married and the father of five children, offered to solve the government's publicly acknowledged problem of having no 'public flagellator': 'my reason for applying for the position is that I am a strict disciplinarian and I believe in the law being carried out especially on this class of criminal'. He had, he said, seen plenty of birching carried out (perhaps in England, where thousands of birchings were still being administered on juveniles every year up until the 1920s) and thoroughly understood how to carry out the punishment.[38] But other people's memories of flogging convinced them that it was a remnant of a past best forgotten: a branch of the Australasian Society of Patriots reminded the government in 1928 that there had been a public appeal for funds to assist the last man flogged in Sydney.[39]

36 *Tamworth Northern Leader*, 27 June 1933, in NSW State Archives, Sydney, 12/1351.1.

37 Letter of H. B. to the Minister for Justice, 28 May 1930, in NSW State Archives, Sydney, 12/1351.1; see also Radzinowicz & Hood, *Emergence of Penal Policy*, pp. 703–5 on the uses of such arguments in Great Britain.

38 Letter of J. L. to the Minister of Justice, 6 March 1929, in NSW State Archives, Sydney, 12/1351.1; on birching in England, Wales, and Scotland, see Departmental Committee on Corporal Punishment, *Report*, London, His Majesty's Stationery Office, 1938, pp. 19–20.

39 Letter from Australasian Society of Patriots to Minister of Justice, 14 March 1928 in NSW State Archives, Sydney, 12/1351.1.

The decline of whipping has not meant the end of calls for its reintroduction. The issue is periodically raised, in the same circumstances in which it has been raised since the middle of the nineteenth century: usually in response to a particularly violent act, somewhat short of murder, or else in the aftermath of an outburst of juvenile misbehaviour. The image of a vigilante mob gathered outside a court should not be the dominant picture of those who call for whipping. Judges, politicians, and journalists have all been among those who have advocated its use in the last twenty years in Australia. In 1973 the Chief Justice of Victoria, Sir Henry Winneke, suggested that the courts might once again have to consider the birch for some assault cases, and opinion polls reported that over 60 per cent of Australians supported 'the whipping of some convicted bashers'.[40] In 1994 the populist Queensland MP Vince Lester was active in putting a call for the reintroduction of flogging onto a National Party conference agenda. This was just eight years after the National Party government in Queensland had, in fact, been responsible for removing whipping from the sentencing options outlined by the state's Criminal Code.[41] The orthodoxy, however, is that, in Western societies, corporal punishment is now frowned upon — hence the difficulty of recognising punishments such as tribal spearing in indigenous law. Therefore, explanations of the lash's decline must consider both the causes of the decline and corporal punishment's persistent popularity in certain quarters.

A proper historical explanation has to surmount two centuries of rationalism in debates about punishment. The influence of such views is evident, for example, in the explanations of corporal punishment's demise advanced by criminologist and Professor of Law Norval Morris in 1966. Responding to a judge's request for advice during sentencing in a Victorian case, Morris strongly opposed the use of whipping, in spite of the gravity of the associated violence in the case. Morris argued that whipping had fallen into disuse for at least four reasons: statistical evidence that it was useless as a deterrent; statistical evidence that its use contributed to greater brutality of those flogged; its antipathy to 'our professed, and to a degree practised, correctional aims', looking back to vengeance rather than forward to prevention; and, finally, its brutalising effects on the community

40 'Birching, Whipping and Public Comment', *Australian and New Zealand Journal of Criminology*, vol. 6, no. 3, 1973, p. 133; McNair Surveys, press release on Australian Public Opinion Poll, poll no. 05/7/73; interestingly, the strongest opinion against flogging was in NSW (43 per cent) and the weakest in Victoria (28 per cent).

41 *Criminal Code Amendment Act, No. 1, 1986* (Qld)

using it, since in such a situation 'we are the floggers'.[42] Such reasons, however — alternately positivist in their appeal to evidence or rhetorical in their reliance on principle — point more to the marshalling of arguments in favour of, or against, whipping than to explanations of the decline itself.

It was not primarily the voice of reason that brought an end to flogging, but the marshalling of emotions. References to statistics are relevant, but prior to the Cadogan Committee — by which time flogging was in major decline — they had not been seriously examined. The significance of emotions in motivating opposition to flogging lies in the success with which they were used in particular campaigns. In Australia, flogging declined without any explicit policy direction: it simply stopped being used. But it did so in the aftermath of an early nineteenth-century campaign against its use. In the 1820s and 1830s, the flogging of soldiers in the British Army was the subject of a specific reform campaign. Significantly, this occurred at a time when the punishment of convicts was also a preoccupation of public life. Although the flogging of soldiers continued under some restrictions until 1881,[43] the campaign effected a significant reduction in the use of this disciplinary technique. Major figures in penal reform, such as Bentham, had been sympathetic to the campaign. But John Dinwiddy, a historian of the campaign, concludes that rational argument was less effective in this context than 'appeals to visceral feeling'. Indeed, the Duke of Wellington had a statistical advantage in proving flogging's effectiveness in maintaining army discipline, but he and other defenders of the 'hard school' were finding it increasingly difficult to counter emotional appeals focused on the brutalising effects of flogging on all concerned in the exercise.[44]

This history of the success of appealing to the emotions is an important lesson in the Australian context. For we must also explain the demise in Australia of whipping in a juridical context — a context in which the punishment had been a realistic and considered sanction for a long time. Morris's arguments of 1966, in fact, reflect more the influence of two British inquiries — the Cadogan Committee and its successor of 1960, the Barry Committee — than recognition that the demise occurred in some common law jurisdictions long before it occurred in the United Kingdom. On this point, we have strong evidence, marshalled by Cadogan, that corporal punishment was used much less in Australia and New Zealand than

42 'Whipping as a Penal Sanction', p. 23.
43 Dinwiddy, 'The Early Nineteenth-Century Campaign against Flogging'.
44 Dinwiddy, 'The Early Nineteenth-Century Campaign against Flogging', p. 325.

it was in the United Kingdom, Canada, or southern Africa, all of them common law jurisdictions. Morris, in fact, drew attention to the possible significance of this difference: 'Australia has a rich heritage of the lash. It will not further our social history to perseverate [*sic*] that chapter of our history. If there is one lesson that we should have learnt from that history it is that of the futility of the lash'.[45]

To what extent was the memory of the convict era a factor in the demise of flogging after the 1850s? To argue that it was a significant factor would be consistent with what we know of the larger history of changes in modern Western penality. In the last resort, those changes have to be explained not in terms of changing economic modes or the preferences of the judiciary, but in terms of an altered cultural connotation attached to punishments of the body. Changing sensibilities are highly selective, suggests David Garland[46] — hence the differing statuses accorded men, women, children, and certain racial groups in judicial sanctions, as well as in private (non-legal, domestic) punishment. But the long-term changes that saw growing restrictions put on public punishments — including both execution and flogging, as well as the stocks and public penal labour — are an index of alterations in social relations and individual sympathies. The relatively early demise of whipping in Australia may demonstrate a particular cultural context's peculiar power to change decisively the possibilities of punishment. *For the Term of his Natural Life* symbolises the rejection of the convict era's putative brutality. Its critique of the abuses of punishment, coming from one who was not himself totally opposed to flogging, advocates the rejection of flogging from a point of view that was more broadly accepted in later colonial society. By 1900 this rejection was so consolidated that New South Wales and Tasmania had all but seen their last whippings, and other states were not far behind them. Yet was it merely an accident that, by the 1950s, Victoria and South Australia, most free from a convict heritage, were still the places where judicial whipping could be considered? Indeed, in the latter state, there were at least eighteen whippings in the decade up to 1964?[47] In corporal, as in capital, punishment, we observe culture's capacity to disturb our expectations of what constitutes progress and enlightenment. Reason has its role to play in debates on such punishment, but the history of the emotions, and

45 'Whipping as Penal Sanction', p. 23.
46 Garland, *Punishment and Modern Society*, p. 243.
47 N. Morris & C. Howard, *Studies in Criminal Law*, Clarendon Press, Oxford, 1964, p. 161.

of their invocation in public debate, probably has more to tell us about why corporal punishment declined as a sentencing option.

EXECUTION

After seventy-three years as a prison, the Darlinghurst Gaol was opened to the public in July 1914 in an early demonstration of the potential of cultural tourism. Enormous crowds visited the gaol: 14 000 people on the opening day, with the admission charges raising a total of £170 for the Prisoners' Aid Society. After the first week, during which the *Sydney Morning Herald* reported that 100 000 visitors had been through the gaol, the government decided to stop the gala. Particularly disturbing was the macabre interest in the gallows site, where souvenir-hunters had torn off bits of the trap-door at the drop. The Attorney-General was 'disagreeably surprised . . . The popularity of the opening evidenced the existence of a morbid sentiment which it is desirable to suppress rather than encourage'.[48]

There have been few legal executions in Australia in the twentieth century, and none at all since 1967. Yet the 'morbid sentiment' discerned in 1914 and the continuing popularity of the death penalty as a penal option both indicate that the abolition of hanging in Australia was primarily a political act, rather than the result of a wholesale cultural conversion. The possibility of reversion to exemplary punishments of the body remains a real one. This is evident in the example of one of the cultures closest to our own, the USA, as well as in more distant cultures, such as Iran.[49] Opinion poll evidence for Australia suggests that, in spite of the *de jure* as well as de facto extinction of capital punishment, the death penalty is still desired by about half of the Australian population, more in some states than others. This desire increased in the 1980s and after, following a fall in popularity during the 1960s and 1970s. A recent analysis of national attitudinal survey data suggests that the amount of time that had passed since abolition significantly influenced attitudes to reviving the death penalty. Nevertheless, strong popular support for the death penalty (less among women than men) suggests again that sanctions and law reform do not, by any means, reflect mass popular opinion.[50] It is difficult to disagree with these

48 Corrective Services, news cuttings, in NSW State Archives, Sydney, 2/2142; *Sydney Morning Herald*, 21 July 1914 and 28 July 1914.

49 See, for example, R. Hood, *The Death Penalty*, Clarendon Press, Oxford, 1989.

50 J. Kelley & J. Braithwaite, 'Public Opinion and the Death Penalty in Australia', *Justice Quarterly*, vol. 7, no. 3, 1990, pp. 529–63.

researchers that what prevents the death penalty's reintroduction in Australia is the likely resistance of political elites — a coalition crossing conventional political boundaries — as well as the possibility of substantial conflict arising from any use of the penalty (as was evident in the controversy surrounding the hanging of Ronald Ryan in Victoria in 1967).

Does the abolition of execution in Australia really share the same historical space as the demise of corporal punishment? The history of punishment is one of overlapping incidents and practices. It is also a history marked by what appear to be contradictions from one perspective, but harmonies seen from another. From a current viewpoint, the demise of whipping and hanging seem part of the same story: a growing sensitivity (and resistance) to the sight of blood and of human (or even animal) physical suffering explains modern Western intolerance of corporal sanctions such as whipping and hanging. In England especially, there is strong evidence that the eighteenth century saw a significant shift in conceptions of the body, and of its place in the language of politics. Historian Randall McGowen has shown how the political metaphor of the body politic — which characterised capital punishment as an excision of a diseased limb — was challenged by a new psychology of the individual. This psychology emphasised the individual's self-interest and capacity for sympathy, diminishing the rationale for collective rituals of punishment.[51] Yet whipping was able to survive this challenge to some extent, since it was intended to reform as well as deter, and it was conceived in eighteenth-century sentencing practice as one of the alternatives to the death sentence.

The interrelationship of Australia's history of transportation with changing attitudes to the death penalty has already been noted. Transportation was an alternative penalty — more lenient and palatable, but still severe enough to act as a deterrent. Indeed, for those condemned to it, the prospect may well have been more terrifying than death. The search for alternatives to hanging, of which transportation was one, similarly brought the use of whipping to prominence, before a sentence of imprisonment in penal servitude hastened the replacement of both. For the best part of two centuries, however, the new and the old stood side by side. The most severe sanction in the English common law, which was death, was supplemented first by transportation, then by 'penal servitude for life'. The

51 R. McGowen, 'The Body and Punishment in Eighteenth-Century England', *Journal of Modern History*, vol. 59, 1987, pp. 651–79; see also G. T. Smith, 'Civilised People Don't Want to See That Kind of Thing: The Decline of Physical Punishment in London, 1760–1840', in Strange (ed.), *Qualities of Mercy*.

range of capital offences contracted, until only murder and treason earned the penalty But, all the same, for over a century, prisons included special cells for the condemned, as well as whipping posts for those so sentenced.

This range of penalties for serious offences was imitated in the colonies. But in a place in which transportation was already a way of life, the use of the death penalty, if anything, increased in use, as the military governors sought to maintain control over a large body of convicts without the control of prison walls. During the convict years, hanging was used as a criminal-law sanction to a degree that exceeded its use in England in relative terms and even approached it in absolute terms. Although the numbers of executions can be difficult to determine with accuracy, the data suggest that, in New South Wales, and especially in Tasmania, hanging was used to excess up until 1850. Maintaining control through the savage use of hanging as a deterrent became a characteristic of Arthur's governorship in Tasmania — a practice that was continued by Sir John Franklin into the 1840s.[52] In England at this time, the death penalty was used in less than 10 per cent of capital convictions, the great majority of death sentences being commuted to life imprisonment. In Van Diemen's Land, the death penalty was used frequently as part of a persistent attempt by Governor Arthur to secure free settlement in the midst of a penal colony (see Table 4.2).[53]

Table 4.2 Capital punishment in New South Wales, Van Diemen's Land, and England and Wales

Years	*Number of people executed*		
	New South Wales	*Van Diemen's Land*	*England and Wales*
1821–25	127	57	364
1826–30	129	163	307
1831–35	159	54	207
1836–40	87	20	51

Sources: Mukherjee et al., *Source Book*, pp. 651–2; Grabosky, *Sydney in Ferment*, p. 65 for 1829 (for New South Wales and Van Diemen's Land); V. A. C. Gatrell, *The Hanging Tree: Execution and the English People, 1770–1868*, Oxford University Press, Oxford, 1994, p. 617 (for England and Wales).

The relatively intense use of the death penalty did not survive beyond mid-century. A number of conditions had altered. One was the demise of convictism as the dominant force of colonial life; no longer were the colonies characterised by a social system in which political authority had to be exercised with the firmness of martial law and in which the capac-

52 For a detailed account of the execution policy and many case histories, see Davis, *Tasmanian Gallows*, chs 2–3.

53 See Davis, *Tasmanian Gallows*; Robson, *A History of Tasmania*, vol. 1, pp. 147–8.

ity for self-government was limited. The second was the construction of the prisons and the establishment of penal servitude as the dominant criminal sanction. Third, reform of the criminal law, which in England had begun to diminish the number of offences carrying the death penalty, became a significant force in the colonies as well.

The subsequent history of Australian capital punishment was one in which hanging (the only form of execution used) attracting enormous political attention and yet was the penalty in only a minuscule proportion of cases. The abolitionist movement was growing in significance and had many friends in Parliament. At the same time, sections of the media, through their role in publicising the crimes and trials of those sentenced to death, inflamed political controversy over the choices facing governments with the power of mercy in their hands. Every death sentence required Cabinet to consider a stark choice between execution and commutation into life imprisonment. From the 1880s onwards, the parliaments and the press constantly debated the continuation of the death penalty.

Before considering the ultimate victor in this parliamentary battle — the abolitionist movement — the specificity of the death penalty bears some comment. For the reality was that, as the number of capital offences contracted (with, broadly speaking, non-violent offences going first, then rape, leaving only murder and treason), so did the kinds of offending in specific cases that would warrant a death sentence. Judges might exercise their own discretion by awarding a sentence of 'death recorded', a judicial stratagem in non-homicidal cases that effectively advised the government to exercise mercy.[54] Then the Executive might agree that the sentence not be carried out, a judgment that sometimes took place in the context of enormous political pressures from both pro- and anti-hanging forces. The result is that the record of punishment displays certain interesting characteristics with regard to offences and offenders, which we will examine.

A thorough study of the exercise of the death penalty in any Australian jurisdiction is still to be undertaken. Data from South Australia and Victoria provide the most complete overviews available from published research. Seventy-six executions took place in South Australia from 1836 to the last hanging in 1964, and a study of the prison records relating to these executions shows that only two of these persons were women. In a pattern that is replicated elsewhere in Australia, Aborigines were overrepresented:

54 Davis, *Tasmanian Gallows*, p. 39; R. Douglas & K. Laster, 'A Matter of Life and Death: The Victorian Executive and the Decision to Execute, 1842–1967', *Australia and New Zealand Journal of Criminology*, vol. 24, no. 2, 1991, p. 145.

twenty of the seventy-six were Aborigines. Aborigines also benefited, however, from the prerogative of mercy, accounting for twenty-eight of the 108 commutations. Women sentenced to death were very likely, as in all jurisdictions, to receive the benefit of mercy: in South Australia, only two women were executed (a White woman in 1873 and, in 1900, an Indian woman, both for murdering their husbands), while at least nine had their death sentences commuted.[55]

These patterns were replicated in the larger population of Victoria, where 606 people were sentenced to death between 1842 and 1967, of whom 185 were executed (see Tables 4.3 and 4.4). Only five women were hanged in Victoria of the 335 charged with capital offences over the period 1842–1967, and the execution of the death penalty was usually a contentious matter in these cases.[56] Although, in terms of the risk of being executed following a capital charge, some proportional differences between the races are apparent, these are not statistically significant. In fact, Roger Douglas and Kathy Laster's more detailed scrutiny suggests that controlling for time of the trial and other variables reveal 'a (barely significant) relationship between being [A]boriginal and being *acquitted*'. They suggest that racial discrimination operated more subtly than might at first be expected. That is, colonial doubt about whether Aborigines could be regarded as fully equal legal subjects may have facilitated the exercise of mercy.[57]

Table 4.3 Executions in Victoria, 1842–1967, by sex

Sex	*No. charged with a capital offence*	*Percentage acquitted*	*Percentage convicted as charged*	*Percentage executed (of those charged)*
Female	335	53.0	13.5	1.5
Male	2256	38.1	24.6	7.9

Source: adapted from Douglas & Laster, 'A Matter of Life and Death', p. 156.

In South Australia and in other jurisdictions during the early colonial period, the hanging of Aborigines was assumed to be an essential weapon

55 A. R. G. Griffiths, 'Capital Punishment in South Australia, 1836–1964', *Australia and New Zealand Journal of Criminology*, vol. 3, no. 4, December 1970, pp. 214–22.

56 See M. Cannon, *The Woman as Murderer*, Today's Australia Publishing Company, Mornington, Vic. 1994; K. Laster, 'Arbitrary Chivalry: Women and Capital Punishment in Victoria, 1842–1967', in D. Philips & S. Davies (eds), *A Nation of Rogues: Crime, Law And Punishment in Colonial Australia*, Melbourne University Press, Melbourne, 1994.

57 R. Douglas & K. Laster, 'A Matter of Life and Death', pp. 152–3.

Table 4.4 Executions in Victoria, 1842–1967, by race

Sex	*No. charged with a capital offence*	*Percentage acquitted*	*Percentage convicted as charged*	*Percentage executed (of those charged)*
Aboriginal	28	39.3	32.2	10.7
Chinese	30	33.3	36.6	16.7
Other	2533	40.6	24.8	7.1

Source: adapted from Douglas & Laster, 'A Matter of Life and Death', p. 156.

in securing the frontiers of settlement.[58] Nevertheless, arguments about mercy were also commonly advanced in some of these cases, especially in relation to the vexed issue of Aborigines' status at law and their knowledge of White man's law. In some cases, this matter was addressed on explicitly racialist grounds, as suggested by Douglas and Laster in their quotation from an 1897 Victorian petition for mercy 'having regard to the well-known intense animal passions of the Aborigines, their degraded ancestry and evil tribal influences; all so widely different from the heredity and circumstances of white men'.[59]

But there were those who advanced a different argument — one that was more sceptical of the 'facts' of colonisation. A cogent plea on behalf of an Aboriginal defendant was advanced in the South Australian Parliament in 1893 by a vocal opponent of abolition, Mr Solomon. In a number of cases involving both Aborigines and Whites, the Governor had extended mercy. By this time, the Governor had to act on the advice of the Executive, the Cabinet of the day. Solomon was particularly disturbed by what he saw as evidence of different standards being applied to a respectable White farmer, who had committed a wilful and premeditated murder by shooting a girl, and an Aboriginal 'half-caste' convicted of the murder of a cattle station overseer. In terms reminiscent of debate in the famous Stuart case over sixty years later, the Aboriginal prisoner's life history was eloquently laid before the House by Solomon, who had been to the Darwin gaol to interview him. Solomon recounted that Flannagan had been born of a Queensland Aboriginal mother and a White father, taken from his tribe when only a few years old by Queensland overlanders ('some of the Queenslanders in the back blocks were about the lowest scum to be found in the whole of Australia' he added) and 'was brought

58 S. Davies, 'Aborigines, Murder and the Criminal Law in Early Port Phillip, 1841–1851', *Historical Studies*, vol. 22, no 88, 1987, pp. 313–35.
59 Douglas & Laster, 'A Matter of Life and Death', p. 153.

over by these cattle men and travelled between Queensland and the Northern Territory, occasionally changing hands from one brutal master to another'. Having read the details of both cases, Solomon thought mercy had been 'strained' in the case of Page, the White farmer, and that it might now be exercised in favour of Flannagan: 'Flannagan was a half-caste blackboy and was now about 20 years of age, but from his childhood he had been merely a chattel, handed over from one person to another, and he had never had any opportunity of knowing right from wrong or of knowing what our English law was'.[60]

As this case suggests, the debate about capital punishment moved uncertainly between the principles of justice in particular cases and the ethics of capital punishment as a penalty generally. Debates on mercy vented the former and became a vehicle through which the social contexts of criminality and the individualisation of the offender were developed as principles determining degree of culpability and mode of punishment. While the courts were normally the location for such considerations, debates on the death penalty, whether as a moral absolute or as an appropriate penalty in particular cases, broadened the forum of debate on punishment.

The hanging of women inflamed considerable controversy, and by the 1890s the issue had become interwoven with strongly held presumptions about the nature of woman and about her responsibilities and burdens. The Governor of New South Wales, Lord Carrington, made no secret of his great distaste for the part he was duty-bound to play in the political debate that raged in 1888–89 over the prospective hanging of convicted husband-poisoner Louisa Collins. Collins was supported by vocal public advocates of mercy, who deputised Carrington. Carrington, however, also received angry letters from supporters of the death penalty, such as the letter advising him that a public meeting against the death penalty had been filled with 'free thinkers' and 'RCs' (Roman Catholics) — an allegation that unwittingly demonstrates the breadth of the anti-hanging coalition. Women supporters of Collins's case (which had been marked by uncertain forensic evidence and had gone to three juries before conviction) did not disguise the basis of their sympathy: from Gulgong, Mrs Rachel Elliott told the Governor that Collins had already endured the pains of hell five times in bringing five children into the world.[61] In reviewing the five cases of women hanged in Victoria, Laster has documented the intersection of

60 South Australia, *Debates*, 13 July 1893, pp. 397–8.
61 Petitions re commutation of death sentence on Louisa Collins (1887–88), in NSW State Archives, Sydney, 4/895.1.

their fates with the prevalent discourses of femininity, but she notes that, in the end, the decision to carry through the execution of the death penalty was determined by a particular constellation of political forces. Such a conclusion is compellingly demonstrated in Carolyn Strange's recent comparative study of the exercise of mercy in the late nineteenth and early twentieth centuries. However, her detailed study of mercy decisions discloses more than just their political contexts. Equally striking is the evidence that a particular cultural history (in the Australian case, convictism as an element of popular political memory) influenced the outcome of many mercy decisions. Quite simply, she shows that mercy was much more frequently exercised in New South Wales than in Ontario.[62]

As well as femininity and Aboriginality, youth was a factor that was likely to inspire appeals for clemency and associated political controversy. The most famous case involving appeals for mercy on the grounds of the offenders' youth was the Mt Rennie rape case in 1886–87, which again involved Carrington. The controversy exposed significant tensions in colonial life: anxieties about larrikinism and the condition of youth in colonial society; women's demands for protection; the anti-feminism of significant sectors of colonial culture, especially centred around *The Bulletin*; the class tensions that found expression in attacks on the judicial system and on the role of Judge Windeyer in the trial and sentencing decision.[63] The youth of offenders had been the focus of an earlier campaign in 1879. At the Mudgee Assizes, a fourteen-year-old Aboriginal youth and his nineteen-year-old associate had been found guilty of rape. A petition of over 6400 signatures — initiated, it appears, by a group of Sydney lawyers, including a future Prime Minister (barrister Edmund Barton) — was also signed by the Anglican Bishop of Sydney. The petition argued that the colonies should not be executing people for an offence that had been removed from the list of capital offences in the United Kingdom, that the youth of the two convicted was a ground for mercy, and that future

62 See Laster, 'Arbitrary Chivalry', pp. 169, 185; C. Strange, 'Discretionary Justice: Political Culture and the Death Penalty in New South Wales and Ontario, 1890–1920, in Strange (ed.), *Qualities of Mercy*.

63 See D. Walker, 'Youth on Trial: The Mt Rennie Case', *Labour History*, no. 50, 1986, pp. 28–42; Allen, *Sex and Secrets*, pp. 54–64; J. Peers, 'The Tribe of Mary Jane Hicks: Imaging Women through the Mount Rennie Case 1886', *Australian Cultural History: Crimes and Trials*, vol. 12, 1993, pp. 127–44; D. Philips, 'Anatomy of a Rape Case 1888: Sex, Race, Violence and the Criminal Law in Victoria', in Philips & Davies (eds), *A Nation of Rogues*, pp. 108–10.

juries would be reluctant to convict on a charge of rape if the likely consequence was the carrying out of the death penalty.[64] There is strong evidence that, in their calculations of guilt, juries were sensitive to a prospective death sentence, especially in the case of a rape charge, which survived as a capital offence in Australian jurisdictions for many decades after its removal in England in 1841.[65]

These were among the more cogent arguments put forward in favour of abolition, an issue that became part of Australian political debate over the next eighty years. The abolitionist case had already been advanced in the late convict era, as part of the movement of 'moral enlightenment' — a movement to which Michael Roe has traced many of the institutional reforms that took place in New South Wales and Tasmania before self-government in the 1850s.[66] Yet abolition was a long time in coming. Why was this so? The durability of hanging as a punishment of last resort is particularly striking in the light of the relatively speedy demise of whipping. True, both punishments were rarely used by the 1920s, and in most jurisdictions neither was formally abolished by this time. But in the debates on punishment, there is a sense that whipping had become almost unthinkable long before the cessation of the death penalty. Indeed, exchanges in the Victorian Legislative Council in 1959 illustrated just that presumption, with the persistent Labor abolitionist J. W. Galbally chiding the Country Party's D. J. Walters — a defender of both capital and corporal punishment — in disbelief: 'do not tell me that you are in favour of whipping now'.[67]

In examining the different rationales underlying each punishment, the reasons for this discrepancy may be plumbed at some depth. Whipping, as we have seen, was increasingly restricted to a number of subject populations: juveniles, male prisoners for prison offences, and (in Australia) sex offenders. In each case, its purpose was manifold: to set an example and to deter, but also to help change the behaviour of the prisoner. In this last respect, its use remained consistent with more general changes in punishment towards reformation of the individual offender. The readiness

64 Petition in Case of an Aboriginal Alexander Metcalf and of Charles E. Wilkinson (1879), NSW State Archives, Sydney, 4/6029.

65 See especially R. Barber, 'Rape as a Capital Offence in Nineteenth Century Queensland', *Australian Journal of Politics and History*, vol. 21, no. 1, 1975, pp. 31–41; Douglas & Laster, 'A Matter of Life and Death', pp. 153–4.

66 M. Roe, *Quest for Authority in Eastern Australia, 1835–1851*, Melbourne University Press, Melbourne, 1965, especially pp. 197–8.

67 Victoria, *Debates*, 21 October 1959, p. 799.

with which latter day advocates of corporal punishment nostalgically recall their own character-forming experiences under the paternalistic hand of a parent, teacher, or policeman is also consistent with this view of whipping as an essentially reformative, even character-forming, punishment.

The application of the death penalty, on the other hand, precludes such a possibility. Its finality indicates other purposes — purposes of ancient lineage, which continue to be evoked in the passionate and angry debates that are occasioned by horrific crimes. To surrender such responses — to abandon the eye for an eye approach — required substantial cultural and personal change. To the audience of a book like this in a country like Australia, abolition is usually such an element of faith that its rationale does not need to be rehearsed. We can gain a greater understanding of capital punishment's long survival, and of why some continue to hanker after it, by examining the rhetoric of those who opposed the frequent legislative attempts to abolish the death penalty in the Australian states.

The eighteenth-century movement against bodily punishment was marked by a changing conception of the body itself, paralleling a challenge to an organic conception of the body politic,[68] although that movement by no means succeeded in wholly transforming the way popular and political discourses conceived of the uses of capital punishment. The overwhelming characteristic of anti-abolitionist opinion, however, was its increasing incoherence, especially when ranged against the often learned arguments of the proponents of abolition. Faith in the stability of the common law and its defence of the community was pitted against the rationalist arguments of abolitionists, who increasingly could marshal evidence of jurisdictions that had ceased executions without aggravating their crime rates. Both sides called on religious traditions — the Mosaic law, and its interpretation as a rationale for retribution, being a common cause of dispute[69] — while more general principles of respect for life and of the justification for killing in canonical, secular, and international law were also debated at length. In Melbourne, up until the 1950s, the *Argus* consistently upheld the retentionist cause, bringing a panoply of opinion in behind it. To the *Argus*, the death penalty was an immutable part of the common law tradition, and evidence of its decline as a penalty was just seen as confirmation of a deteriorating social order:

68 McGowen, 'The Body and Punishment'.

69 See especially South Australia, *Debates*, 12 August 1891, p. 717; on a motion by Mr V. L. Solomon (MHA for the Northern Territory) for the abolition of capital punishment, see South Australia, *Debates*, 4 November 1891, p. 1869.

> A labour party governed only by its own crude impulses and unchecked by the salutary discipline of a Parliamentary second chamber has already abolished the death penalty in Queensland . . . There should be no weakening of moral fibre when capital punishment is considered in the abstract . . . Has society not a right and a duty to protect its members by the most efficacious methods against its enemies? Unquestionably it has.[70]

When the New South Wales government refused to commute the death sentence on a seventeen-year-old in 1936, the *Argus* applauded it for upholding the authority of the law — a law which allowed the exercise of mercy only in the most deserving or doubtful cases. One correspondent supported capital punishment, not as retaliation, but because violent criminals were 'not fit to live in a civilised State', while others appealed to religious authority (although the Bible was quoted on both sides). 'Christian Conscience' cited Genesis 9:6 — 'Whoso sheddeth man's blood by man shall his blood be shed' — and warned that 'Humanitarianism, when it seeks to override God's word, is nothing less than an insult to the Almighty'.[71]

By the 1950s, however, debates centred largely on the deterrent value of capital punishment. The value of the death penalty as retribution or denunciation was not wholly dismissed, especially in judging the types of crime that merited hanging. For instance, Lord Denning's exposition of denunciation as the ultimate justification for punishment, in his evidence to the United Kingdom Royal Commission into Capital Punishment, was picked up by Australian defenders of the death penalty.[72] But few advocates of hanging were prepared to rely on retribution as the core of their case, however much it may survive as a popular justification.[73] Instead, resis-

70 *Argus*, 6 July 1936, p. 8. The Queensland Labor government had abolished the death penalty in 1922, becoming the first state in Australia to do so — see R. N. Barber, 'The Labor Party and the Abolition of Capital Punishment in Queensland 1899–1922', *Queensland Heritage*, November 1968, pp. 3–12.

71 On the case of Edward Hickey, see the *Argus*, 13 May 1936, p. 6; 21 May 1936, p. 10; 23 May 1936, p. 24.

72 See Victoria, *Debates*, 21 October 1959, in which R. J. Hamer, MLA, quotes Denning: 'The ultimate justification of any punishment is not that it is a deterrent, but that it is the emphatic denunciation by the community of a crime; and from this point of view, there are some murders which, in the present state of public opinion, demand the most emphatic denunciation of all, namely the death penalty'. The same passage was cited with approval in the almost contemporaneous debate in the South Australian parliament — see South Australia, *Debates*, 16 September 1959, p. 759 (Mr Jenkins, MHA).

73 This is consistent with other evidence on the context of mid-twentieth-century decision-making in capital cases. According to the reminiscences of Sir Rupert Hamer, the Victorian premier who eventually sponsored the parliamentary bill abolishing the death penalty, during the controversial Tait case in 1962 he 'never heard Bolte or other ministers express any savage determination that Tait should be executed'; see Cannon, *The Woman as Murderer*, p. 228.

tance to abolition in postwar Australia appears to have become centred on a compact between the State and its security arms — the police and prison officers. In this respect, it was noteworthy that the last person to be hanged was convicted of killing a warder during an escape. The decision of the Victorian government to proceed with the hanging of Ronald Ryan was, in fact, the denouement of a script of statist defence that had been written by Australian conservative leaders over the previous decade.

The significance of this accord between conservative government and the police and prison officers may be seen in the responses of two leading politicians to abolitionist arguments in 1959. In that year, well-known Labor abolitionists John Galbally in Victoria and Don Dunstan in South Australia each attempted to enact a bill to further the abolitionist cause. As he did a number of times before and after, Galbally introduced a straightforward 'abolition of capital punishment' bill into the Legislative Council as a private member. In an attempt to achieve the same end, but by different means, Dunstan sought to remove the provisions for the death penalty in relation to particular offences from the state's criminal law acts. Each of the abolitionists referred extensively to international debate on the issue over the previous decade. Influential support for their case was drawn from two inquiries: the United Kingdom Royal Commission on Capital Punishment (1949–53), which had undertaken an extensive international inquiry, and a more recent commission to inquire into the possible restoration of the death penalty in Ceylon, which was chaired by Norval Morris, formerly of the Melbourne University Criminology Department and, in 1959, a Professor of Law at the University of Adelaide. As Dunstan repeatedly pressed, it was not within the scope of the United Kingdom Commission to make a recommendation on the death penalty, although the trend of its Report was against it; the Ceylon Commission, however, recommended strongly against restoration. Much of the debate was spent reviewing the statistical evidence of murder rates before and after abolition in different jurisdictions, including Queensland (abolition in 1922) and New South Wales (no execution since 1939 and statutory abolition in 1955).

The weight of international evidence and the weakness of various pro-hanging arguments was reflected in the response of the Liberal Party's Rupert Hamer, who spoke against abolition but nevertheless conceded most of the ground to Galbally — indeed, one member suggested that Hamer might have been speaking in support of abolition. Hamer was to become Victorian Premier in 1973 and enact abolition, but he was also a minister in the government that decided Ryan should hang, a decision he opposed in Cabinet. In 1959, however, he could not give way completely. On this matter, he felt, citing part of the United Kingdom Commission's Report, a government should not advance too far ahead of public opinion, which in Australia was still clearly in favour of retention. But the conclusive point for Hamer was the possible deterrent value in special cases. He believed particularly that the government should not remove the deterrent of the death penalty, which offered protection 'to police officers and warders in the course of performing their duties'. The future premier wanted Parliament to remember the number of men who had received life imprisonment for murder, 'and for whom there is no other deterrent whatsoever to the committing of murder in, say, an attempt to escape'.[74] By 1966, he had evidently changed his opinion on this fundamental point. According to his later account of the Ryan case, Hamer had argued that a number of more repulsive murders had resulted in commutation, but the Cabinet was persuaded by the Attorney-General that the 'government must be seen to be "protecting the protectors"' — such as the prison warder who was murdered during Ryan's escape from Pentridge. The Premier, Henry Bolte, was also unusually 'outspoken' on this occasion, believing that 'the public's guardians such as police and warders must be safeguarded at all costs'.[75]

Protecting the protectors had also become the final weapon in the armoury of arguments against abolition in South Australia. The Premier, Sir Thomas Playford, insisted on retention as the ultimate deterrent, in spite of the United Kingdom Royal Commission's explicit demonstration of the weakness of this argument, which had been strongly urged by police. Parliament, Playford said, had not only a strong moral obligation to protect innocent people from crimes of violence, 'but also a particular obligation to members of our Police Force, who, because of the very nature of their profession, are most concerned in this matter'. His case was strengthened by reference to the Westminster Parliament's retention in the *Homicide Act 1957* of the death penalty for a restricted number of offences, including murder of a police officer on duty.[76] The retentionist imagination had long postulated the threats to social order that would emerge once the restraint of the noose was removed. Hence, in 1929 the conservative Melbourne *Argus* quoted an English writer on the dangers of abolition: 'so long as the legal punishment for treason and murder is death, the 'Red' agitator will have difficulty in finding tools to carry on

74 Victoria, *Debates*, 21 October 1959, p. 797.
75 Cannon, *The Woman as Murderer*, pp. 228–9.
76 South Australia, *Debates*, 26 August 1959, p. 618.

the 'heavy civil war' hoped for by Moscow; once that punishment is reduced to imprisonment for life, there will be no lack of ruffians willing to shoot policemen and other Government servants in the back'.[77] Perhaps it was precisely this focus on the defence of the State that doomed the retentionist argument — for political decision-makers had gradually surrendered the death penalty for most capital offences, however grave and shocking their violence. Australia was on the eve of major social conflict over the role of the police —conflict that would erupt from the late 1960s on. It says much about the close alliance between government and police in this era that the last political argument in defence of the death penalty centred not on the violence of a criminal act but on the broader threat to the State if its officials were rendered more vulnerable by abolition. With the passing of the old guard of Bolte and Playford, however, and in the face of the lack of real evidence to support the worst fears of police and their political allies, even this argument lost its cogency.[78]

The abolition of the death penalty illustrates, in fact, the power of the political process in determining an outcome that would by no means have flowed from a referendum of popular opinion. It is true that abolition took place in Australia at what appeared to be a particularly low ebb in the popularity of the death penalty. But the demise of the penalty had begun well in advance of popular opinion, if we think of popular opinion as a single voice. Of course, it was not a single voice, and never was, which was one of the reasons that abolition emerged as something more than a utopian wish, in spite of substantial support for hanging. Some writers see the administration of capital punishment as a sentencing option — with its shift from the judicial arena into the political arena for adjudication on the mercy prerogative — as having been one of the penalty's most offensive characteristics.[79] On the other hand, we should not allow such a perspective to obscure the ways in which the death penalty and its politics epitomise what punishment is, what purposes it serves, and what limits must be put on it.

77 *Argus*, 5 January 1929, p. 8, citing W. G. Carleton Hall, writing in the *English Review*.

78 After the decision to proceed with Ryan's execution, Stanley W. Johnston of the University of Melbourne's Criminology Department commented on the lack of evidence on the deterrent value of the death penalty in relation to the killing of police and prison warders — see S. W. Johnston, 'Why Can't We be Reasonable about Hanging?', *Australian*, 17 December 1966, reprinted in B. Jones (ed.), *The Penalty is Death*, Sun Books, Melbourne, 1968.

79 See, for example, Laster, 'Arbitrary Chivalry'; Douglas & Laster, 'A Matter of Life and Death'; Gatrell, *Hanging Tree*.

5

THE POLITICS OF PUNISHMENT

Like policing, punishment is a subject that fascinates the media and politicians as much as it does the general public. It is a topic that touches emotional chords (of sympathy, empathy, fear, loathing, disgust, and anger, in victims and their associates as much as in the opponents and voyeurs of punishment). It also constitutes a significant function of the modern State. As such, punishment has been an important object of political attention. This concluding chapter examines a specific question relating to the politics of punishment through imprisonment: under what influences has imprisonment changed? The macro-historical answer to this question must be traced over centuries; it is the kind of answer that Durkheim, Elias, or Foucault trace in their work. But we can also examine a more local process, in which changes in institutions and practices take place at an observable level — and in which resistance to change and the limits of change become visible. It is this local process that we seek to document here, while acknowledging that, inevitably, the local process is part of the larger transformation that Elias or Foucault might describe.

Since so much of this book has been about the prison, and about the role of penal administrators in managing and occasionally changing the prison, it is appropriate now to ask a question about the role of prisoners themselves. Like so much in the history of Australian punishment, this is uncharted water, but once one looks for it, the evidence is visible enough. Three decades of modern social history have taught us the historical importance of resistance from below, and this theme is certainly no less relevant to the history of the prison.

The second purpose of this chapter is to look at penal reform as a social movement. This is more familiar territory, and some mention has already been made in earlier chapters of the kinds of debates and political pressures that have affected the prison as a mode of punishment. It is time now to estimate the significance of the forces of civic culture in changing punishment, as well as in maintaining it. Inevitably these forces encompass the media — a critical forum for constituting the field of punishment. For how else would the majority of people, at any stage in the last two centuries, have been made aware of the incidence and incidents of offending, and of the penalties applied in response?

Resistance from below

The impact of the reform movement from the end of the nineteenth century can be measured by the change in status accorded to prisoners. Let us be clear that this was not a change for the better in terms of prisoner self-esteem. The language of the reformatory — the presumption that the task of prison was to 're-form' the prisoner into a citizen, or even to create one where there had been none before — implied an infantilisation of the prisoner, compared with the freedoms of a century before. This is not to say that prison conditions were worse than they had been a century before; they probably were not, but that is always a matter for local inquiry. Yet the standing of the prisoner *as* a citizen was, in fact, diminished as soon as a program for making the prisoner *into* a citizen was adopted. The significance of the change was not lost on those who extended the reformatory idea into young, and not-so-young, adulthood — as we have seen earlier in discussion of the Borstal idea. Making prisoners 'irresponsible', and therefore subject to treatment, also diminished the need to listen to them.

Perhaps this is why, during the interwar period — in which the pressure of prison population was diminishing and the variety of institutions increasing (but only for male inmates) — there was nevertheless a continuing incidence of prison riots and disturbances in Australian prisons. It is difficult to say whether such prisoner behaviour actually increased or not: not surprisingly, the annual reports do not record the incidence of riots, although muted comment is made about the most public events, and the official record of prison punishments gives some clues to levels of aggravation in prisons. But the press reports of the time contain regular references to prisoner outbreaks. In New South Wales the ultimate response of authorities was the declaration in 1943 that Grafton Gaol was to be an institution for 'intractables', following yet another outbreak of trouble at Bathurst. Three decades of subsequent abuse of power at Grafton only came to substantial public attention with the Royal Commission into the New South Wales Prison in the late 1970s. This change in the management of punishment had resulted from inmate resistance, but it was not a change to boast about.

The Bathurst riot that provoked the decision to send intractables to Grafton was not the first one at that institution. Indeed, it had been troubled for at least two decades, in ways that had come to public notice. In 1924 a disturbance at the gaol, provoked by the treatment of one of the prisoners, inspired an internal inquiry, which was taking place when another outbreak occurred. A large number of prisoners refused to return to their cells, and warders and police were called in, using bayonets to force them back to their cells, with some prisoners sustaining 'small wounds'. Subsequently 194 prisoners were disciplined.[1] Four years later, another disturbance took place during an inquiry by the Comptroller-General into lack of discipline at the prison. This time the outbreak seemed to confirm the need for departmental action against the prison governor, which had already been under way at the time of the disturbance. The governor was suspended and then transferred to another gaol.[2] Other incidents involving a number of prisoners occurred in January 1932, and again in November 1938 and January 1939. After the incident in November 1938, in which the tailor's shop was wrecked, an official inquiry concluded that the root cause of the riot was a 20 per cent cut in prisoner earnings. The cut had been imposed in 1931, at the height of the Great Depression, following an agreement made at the Premiers' Conference to reduce government outlays; the prisoners' rates had never been restored.[3]

Bathurst was not alone in its troubles: the press reported disturbances at Parramatta in 1926, 1931, 1934, and 1938, and at Goulburn in 1939. Nor was New South Wales the only jurisdiction beset by prisoner protest and attacks on warders of a kind that seemed to indicate organised action. Four times between 1931 and 1935 the Hobart Gaol recorded incidents involving small explosions of gelignite; in 1936 a prisoner on hunger strike over prison conditions was eventually force fed under medical supervision; and in 1939 a 'demonstration' of prisoners was heard from outside

1 For summary of the official report into the 'Gaol Mutiny', see *Argus*, 31 May 1924, p. 31; and for press clippings regarding the incident, see NSW State Archives, Sydney, 7/7151.

2 *Sydney Morning Herald*, 22 May 1928, p. 11.

3 Bathurst and Parramatta Gaols: disturbances 1938–40, 40/3635, in NSW State Archives, Sydney, 7/7160.1; *Sydney Morning Herald*, 15 January 1932.

the gaol.[4] There was trouble at St Helena in Moreton Bay in 1926, Pentridge in 1926, Fremantle in 1930, and Yatala on a series of occasions in 1930 and 1931.[5] None of these protests, demonstrations, and occasional riots was on the scale of the January 1932 mutiny of prisoners at Dartmoor in England, or that at the Kingston Penitentiary in Ontario in October of the same year, both involving hundreds of prisoners and serious injuries on both sides.[6] But the Australian disturbances were almost all incidents in which prisoners had an express grievance: the quality of food, the rates of earnings for their labour, the ill-treatment of one of their number by staff, or going back further, Captain Neitenstein's 'drillology', which one ex-prisoner recalled as the stimulus for a 'Maitland Riot'.[7]

Rarely did these incidents seem to provoke concern over institutional conditions, and there was no public inquiry into prisons in these decades. A political consensus on progressive penal reform largely distracted attention from any potential review of conditions within institutions. Seen against this background, it is understandable that the declaration of Grafton as a separate institution for intractables should have created the conditions for substantial abuse of prisoners in years to come. It followed a serious riot at Bathurst on 30 June 1942, an incident that prompted the government to take note of the recent Royal Commission into the Canadian Penal System, which had recommended the segregation of intractables in one institution. The Minister for Justice decided that Grafton should be kept for the 'incarceration of known troublemakers where they could be held and employed under strict supervision and where any disaffection could not spread to ordinarily well conducted and industrious men'.[8] This was the

4 Re prisoner Jack Anderson, Prisons, Hobart Gaol, Tasmanian State Archives, Hobart, 10/595; *Argus*, 25 September 1939 (Hobart); *Argus*, 3 September 1935 and 14 October 1935 (Hobart); Tasmania, Parliament, *Report of Board of Inquiry on Riot at Hobart Gaol*, TPP, Hobart, 1939.

5 *Argus*, 9 March 1926 (Parramatta), 27 March 1926 (St Helena), 3 May 1926 (Pentridge), 5 April 1930 (Yatala); *Sydney Morning Herald*, 5 March 1931 and 31 January 1934 (Parramatta), 10 April 1931, and 1 May 1931 (Yatala).

6 These 'mutinies' were widely reported in the Australian press. See *Argus*, 26 January 1932; *Sydney Morning Herald*, 19 October, 22 October, and 24 October 1932.

7 J. Garvey, *The Indelible Stamp* (pamphlet), Redfern [1936], in the possession of the Mitchell Library, Sydney.

8 New South Wales Prisons Department, *Annual Report*, Sydney, 1942–43, copy in Barry Papers, National Library of Australia, Canberra, MSS 2505/41/16–26; for details of three separate disturbances, at Parramatta (August 1938 and January 1939) and Bathurst (November 1938), see Bathurst and Parramatta Gaols, 1938–40, NSW State Archives, Sydney, 7/7160.1.

kind of result that protesting prisoners could have done without. In the long run, it purchased discipline at a very high price, as the Nagle Commission into Prisons unveiled in the late 1970s. The subordinate position of prisoners, and this history of resistance and toughening discipline during the interwar years, was nevertheless striking in the age of the 'reformatory'. It is especially noteworthy that, in this era, the prisoner's voice was little noticed and certainly rarely publicised — a contrast with the readiness with which prisoners had access to public inquiry and political forums in the post-convict era.

Convicts in early penal New South Wales had successfully obtained access to the courts. Thereby, they helped to shape colonial politics and the rule of law in what seemed, initially, to be an environment least hospitable to such aspirations.[9] The legal structures of the penitentiary and prison after the convict era envisaged few, if any, legal rights for prisoners, and the severe constraints placed on prisoners in seeking legal redress of their grievances are a notorious phenomenon.[10] The culture of nineteenth-century incarceration nevertheless created other forums for addressing grievances. A number of the most important inquiries in the self-governing colonies up to 1900 paid particular attention to the grievances of prisoners. They included the New South Wales Select Committee on Public Prisons in Sydney and Cumberland of 1861. Chaired by Henry Parkes, this committee pursued its task by personal visits to all the prisons and watchhouses of the region, uncovering conditions that were, and still are, shocking to read. In addition to interviewing most of the senior officers and many warders, the Committee recorded interviews and received statements from 136 prisoners. Their complaints ranged from the illegality of their detention as a result of unjust sentences to abuse within the prisons. A particular grievance was the inequality of treatment entailed by the abolition of remission from 1 June 1858, which effectively created two classes of prisoner. The prisoners of Cockatoo Island were especially articulate in expressing their grievances, electing two of their number to petition the Committee on a wide range of issues, including remissions, alleged illegal treatment and prolonged detention, physical coercion, and a lack of complaints mechanisms. Their petition was specific in its

9 See especially Neal, *Rule of Law*; Kercher, *An Unruly Child*; Byrne, *Criminal Law and Colonial Subject*.

10 See Zdenkowski, 'Judicial Intervention in Prisons'; and G. Zdenkowski & D. Brown, *The Prison Struggle: Changing Australia's Penal System*, Penguin Books, Melbourne, 1982.

detail, but also rhetorical both in its appeal for justice and (referring to the murder of Inspector-General John Price by convicts at Melbourne a few years earlier) in its implicit threat of the consequences of indifference:

> We have become as men having no hope, in fine, we have become desperate. The records which survive of the treatment experienced by the prisoners subjected to the tyranny of those unfeeling monsters at Melbourne are replete with lamentations and it is to be hoped, that when they can be prevented, they will not be allowed to be enacted here, for the threshold of danger being once entered, terror ceases to exercise its grim sway.[11]

Although the Committee regarded these statements 'in some cases with distrust, and in all with a feeling of caution', it published the evidence of the prisoners, calling the House especially to 'notice the revolting character of some of the evidence received; its very enormity is submitted in justification of its publication, as the ends of truth in disclosing the actual state of our prison establishments must suffer by its being suppressed or modified'.[12] The Committee's report summarised a case for reform, which helped to shape the structure of the New South Wales system over the next thirty years.

This was only the first of a number of major colonial inquiries that recognised the legitimacy of prisoner evidence. Some, however, were striking in their disregard for the views of prisoners. The New South Wales Select Committee conducted extensive visits to the prisons and lock-ups around Sydney over a period of eight days, and the Queensland inquiry in 1887 heard evidence from prisoners during its visits to no less than forty-eight separate prisons, gaols, and lock-ups all over Queensland. The major Victorian Royal Commission of 1870–72, however, heard no prisoner evidence, focusing instead on the opinions of senior judges, doctors, and penal administrators. In this respect the Victorian inquiry might be regarded as an exception to the rule that inmates' opinions were a significant source for inquiry into colonial penality. Certainly that was the view of the Fremantle Prison Commission at the end of the century, which, like its New South Wales predecessor of 1861, actively sought and published the summaries of prisoner evidence and statements. If anything, the Fremantle Commission was even more impressed with the value of prisoner evidence as a guide to carceral realities. From the prisoners, the commissioners

11 NSW, Parliament, *Report of the Select Committee on the Public Prisons in Sydney and Cumberland*, NSWPP, Sydney, 1861, p. 246.

12 NSW, Parliament, *Report of the Select Committee on the Public Prisons in Sydney and Cumberland*, NSWPP, Sydney, 1861, p. 6.

reported, they were 'enabled to procure a great deal of valuable evidence, which will serve as the groundwork for their future investigations into the penal system of the colony'.[13] The reach of prisoner grievances extended well beyond the walls of the prison to issues related to their arrest, conviction, and sentence. The individual cases of a number of inmates received attention in a progress report, which resulted in sentence reductions in some cases. The openness of the Commission to prisoner testimony was of the same order as their view that the flogging of prisoners who escaped was an enormity, administered on the very prisoners who might have the best prospects of becoming 'energetic and useful citizens' on release. Although sometimes sceptical of the reliability of the prisoners' evidence, the Commission seemed to rely principally on that evidence in concluding that justice within the gaol was uncertain: 'verbal rules and instructions had been permitted to take the place of definite and fixed rules for the guidance of both officers and prisoners'.[14]

A readiness to acknowledge prisoner testimony was also evident in some prison administrations, such as that of Hobart Gaol, where in the 1890s prisoners were able to cross-examine warders and others who gave evidence at hearings of charges brought against prisoners.[15] But in an external forum, the Fremantle Commission appeared to be the last such official inquiry for many decades to give serious consideration to the prisoner's own experience of the system. It was not until the 1970s, when prisoner frustration resulted in the burning down of Bathurst Prison, that political conditions favoured a new investigation of imprisonment. This investigation was informed as much by the need to take account of standards of fairness and justice within the prison as by the recognition that prison was an element of a penal system with a variety of purposes. The conditions under which the prison system in Australia reached this new stage of public scrutiny, in which the prisoner's experience rather than the abstract functions of punishment became the focus of attention, have been explored elsewhere and do not require elaboration here.[16] But it is

13 West Australia, Parliament, *Report from the Commission Appointed to Inquire into the Penal System in the Colony*, WAPP, Perth, 1899, p. 1.

14 West Australia, Parliament, *Report from the Commission Appointed to Inquire into the Penal System in the Colony*, WAPP, Perth, 1899, p. 23.

15 Minutes of hearings of charges against prisoners, heard by Supt, 1893–98, Prisons, Tasmanian State Archives, Hobart, GD/106/4.

16 See especially Zdenkowski & Brown, *Prison Struggle*; M. Finnane, 'After the Convicts: Towards a History of Imprisonment in Australia', *Australian and New Zealand Journal of Criminology*, vol. 24, no. 2, 1991, pp. 105–18; T. Vinson, *Wilful Obstruction: The Frustration of Prison Reform*, Methuen, Sydney, 1982.

evident that a penal system in which the prisoner is subject to supervision for the purpose of reform is one in which the capacity to be heard is severely diminished. This much, at least, is clear from the history of prisoner resistance and protest after the convict era.

CHANGING THE SYSTEM?

Barring a dramatic event, such as a major riot, in which prisoners bring their case or frustrations to public notice, the persistent story of penal reform is one in which a large number of non-prisoner interest groups have played an instrumental role, alongside the initiatives of innovative prison administrators. Prisoner input into these groups has been part of this history, but not a dominant part by any means. Religion has had a strong influence. The role of Quakers in early nineteenth-century British and North American reform is an outstanding example of a pattern that has persisted. But free thought, radical politics, and oppositional dissent have all played their part as well. We have already briefly explored some of the important streams of reform and change that were associated with new sciences and with governmental administration. In one sense, the history of the prison and of changing penal policies has been almost indistinguishable from the broader history of social reform in all its post-Enlightenment diversity; it has shared an agenda with education, medical reform, and population policy, as well as having more obvious links with policing. It goes without saying that this is a history whose lines do not travel in one direction, especially not in the direction of progress. Conflicts between an individual concept of liberty, due process and the rule of law, and the collectivist rationales of social policy have characterised penal history since the early nineteenth century. Such conflict is embedded in the politics of prison reform. It is reflected in the limited success of progressive strategies for improving prison conditions and of meeting the objectives of penal reform.

Penal reform, as a positive political activity, has been a marker of progressive politics for two centuries. The institution of the prison emerged in response to penal reform and changed as a result of it. While prisoners themselves were included by the critics of prison conditions in the second half of the nineteenth century, the actions of reform groups from the 1890s onwards were focused on struggles within and against the stream of government policy and political power. Typically, penal reform was the business of activist coalitions, drawing members from the fields of party politics, academic research, social reform and philanthropy, and religious leaders. Professionals working in the field — either as practitioners, researchers, or teachers of professionals — increasingly became significant players, but in the early decades there were few who could be described as such. We can see some of these coalitions at work in examples drawn from a number of jurisdictions in the 1890s and after.

In South Australia there were a number of penal reform groups active from the 1890s to the 1950s. Their names indicate the array of possible lineages that influenced penal reform. The Criminological Society of South Australia was active in the late 1890s, evidently drawing its inspiration from the Criminology Society of Melbourne. The Melbourne Society's object was the 'Study and Promotion of the Best Methods for the Prevention and Treatment of Crime', and its president was the leading social reformer and founder of the Australian Church Dr Charles Strong, who addressed the inaugural meeting of the Adelaide group.[17] The name suggests the intellectual authority of the new science of criminology, and the society's activities in 1897 reflected contemporary interests in marginal populations and in the health and development of children. In that year the Society hosted lectures by some of the colony's leading social reformers and professionals. Thomas Rhodes, JP, was President of the State Children's Council — responsible for managing child welfare, including boarding out and institutional care — and lectured on 'Our Juvenile Delinquents'. Catherine Helen Spence, the leading feminist and social reformer, and also a member of the State Children's Council, spoke on 'Heredity and Environment', while Dr J. B. Cleland, the Medical Superintendent of Parkside Lunatic Asylum, drew together the premier preoccupations of turn-of-the-century social reformers in his address on 'The Chronic Insane, the Habitual Offender and the Endemic Unemployed'. Rabbi Boas lectured on 'Capital Punishment from a Jewish Point of View', and Rev. J. Day Thompson spoke on 'The Elmira System of Criminal Reform'. There were no surprises here: the range of topics placed the society firmly at the centre of contemporary debates on punishment, welfare, and penal reform. The various speakers' positive engagement with penal reform was not a passing fad. Catherine Helen Spence, for exam-

17 The Melbourne Criminology Society was active for at least two decades under Strong's leadership. For an account of Strong, as president of the Criminology Society, appealing for the commutation of a death sentence, see *Argus*, 13 April 1918, p. 17; C. Strong, paper read at general meeting of the Criminology Society of Victoria, 9 May 1902, in the possession of the Mitchell Library, Sydney. See also ch. 3 above.

ple, maintained her involvement in this area, publishing, a few years later, a detailed appraisal of Neitenstein's 1904 New South Wales Report, which drew attention particularly to fines and probation as alternatives to imprisonment.[18] To say that this group was influential in the political arena is almost a tautology: the members of the Society were those who shaped the local institutions of the welfare state.[19] A decade later, one member — Frederick Wallis — had become the state's Chief Secretary as part of a Labor government, responsible for the penal and welfare systems. By that time the Society appears to have transformed itself into a 'Penal Reform Association', the members of which were actively lobbying the government on issues such as the probation of offenders, a measure that was eventually introduced in 1913.[20]

John Howard's pre-eminence as the archetypal prison reformer was recognised in the United Kingdom by the establishment of the Howard Association, which was dedicated to penal reform and the improvement of prisons. This was one of the groups to which reform associations such as the South Australian Criminological Society constantly made reference, and with whom they corresponded. In the 1940s, South Australia saw the establishment of its own Howard Society, known later as the Howard League for Penal Reform. Like its 1890s predecessor, it constantly referred to the practice and agendas of other jurisdictions (there were similar societies in Victoria and New South Wales by this time[21]). Unlike the earlier group, its agenda cut more across the grain of contemporary penal practice, and the Society's records suggest that it played an important role in agitating on issues that would become the staple fare of Australian penal and legal reform two and three decades later. In 1952, for example, the Society actively sought to publicise a riot that had taken place at Yatala prison in May and opposed the recommendations of the South Australian Sexual Offences Committee, which had endorsed police opinion on the

18 *Adelaide Register*, 7 March 1905 — significantly this press clipping is included among the papers of New South Wales feminist and, among other things, prison reformer Rose Scott, Mitchell Library, Sydney, Mss. 38/56.

19 Criminological Society of South Australia, *First Report*, [1897], in the possession of the South Australian State Library, Adelaide. On Rhodes and Spence, see B. Dickey, *Rations, Residence, Resources: A History of Social Welfare in South Australia since 1836*, Wakefield Press, Adelaide, 1986, especially ch. 8 on the State Children's Council.

20 Correspondence re. 1910 Penal Reform Association, in John Howard Society of South Australia Records, SRG 138/6, South Australian State Library, Adelaide.

21 See, for example, the *Argus*, 3 August 1928, p. 9 on Victoria; on New South Wales, see footnote 29.

desirability of suppressing homosexuality (an issue that had already provoked spirited debate within the Society). On other issues, the Society advocated a number of progressive reforms that had long been part of the criminal-justice policy agenda: medical and psychological treatment for juvenile delinquents and sex offenders, for example. Like its predecessor in the 1890s, the Society was also a forum in which influential politicians could share and shape their political agendas. Don Dunstan, MLA, was a young member of the Society when he spoke in 1959 on 'Capital Punishment', the abolition of which he had already urged in the Parliament, as noted previously. In 1976, as Premier of South Australia, he would see its abolition enacted. Other members of the Society included professionals and academics who were active in promoting criminal-justice and penal reform in their respective fields. A new member in 1959 was historian Dr Ken Inglis, whose book *The Stuart Case*, published in that year, documented at length, and for the first time, the abuse of Aboriginal people in the criminal-justice system. Another active member of the Society in the early years was Dr Constance Davey, a psychologist with the Department of Education, who was almost certainly influential in the Society's promotion of medical and psychological services in prisons and courts.[22]

Hence, the penal reform movement acted as a means of spreading ideas and practices from one jurisdiction to another, as well as acting as a relatively independent critic of local practice. It is important to stress that such movements were only *relatively* independent: they could also become too close to power to function as effective critics, their energies being sapped by the work of continually exposing abuse, or being evaporated as their reform agendas became the new orthodoxy. Of course, South Australia was not the only place where reform activists were able to translate their critiques into policy. The example of Western Australia in the 1890s has already been discussed. It is worth revisiting, however, for this was an

22 The minutes of the Society, 1946–59, in John Howard Society of South Australia Records, SRG 138/2, South Australian State Library, Adelaide, are an invaluable source; for Dunstan's views on capital punishment, see above, p. 137, and South Australia, *Debates*, 23 May 1956, p. 203; K. Inglis, *The Stuart Case*, Melbourne University Press, Melbourne, 1959; on Constance Davey, see Dickey, *Rations, Residence, Resources*, p. 198, and Davey's history of children and the law in South Australia, *Children and their Law-Makers*, self-published, Adelaide, 1956, especially pp. 34–5, where she discusses the committee (of which she was a member) appointed to inquire into delinquent and other children in the care of the state. This committee recommended the abolition of corporal punishment and major initiatives involving a psychological clinic and other interventions around delinquency.

instance in which reform agendas were nurtured through political conflict — conflict that nevertheless recognised prisoners' personal experiences of the criminal-justice system. Critiques of the Fremantle Prison and penal methods in Western Australia were pronouncedly libertarian in their initial phase and were only slowly transformed to accord with a more 'criminological' position, as criminology's advocates shaped their ideas into an agenda for reform. Support for the Royal Commission was garnered through the criticism of radical journalist-politicians such as Frederick Charles Vosper, who moved in Parliament that the inquiry into Fremantle prison be established. He sought to distance himself from the charge that the movement was overly sympathetic to criminals, for it was the flogging of prisoners within Fremantle and other such abuses that had initially prompted the agitation. Vosper argued the case for 'a reformatory prison . . . on principles of modern penology'. His knowledge of the prison system was not abstract — he had served three months in a Queensland prison after being convicted for inciting a riot during a miners' strike in 1892.[23] Before Vosper, the case for an inquiry had been made by other politicians, such as the lawyer and independent liberal politician Walter James, later Premier of the state, who protested against the flogging of prison escapees in July 1897. Outside Parliament, another young journalist, J. M. Drew, formed his initial impressions of the need for reform when, in 1895, he served a term for contempt of court in the Perth Waterside Lock-up. Over a number of months, Drew published a 'Jail Journal', which was not a solipsistic reflection, like John Mitchel's famous tract of the same name, but a record of conversations with other inmates, perhaps inspiring the Commission's openness to hearing the evidence of prisoners. To these activists and spokesmen for reform were added other journalists, such as E. S. Emmerson of the *Sunday Chronicle* and Thomas Walker, a radical, and free thinker of impeccable credentials. A one-time New South Wales MLA, Walker moved to Western Australia and edited the *Sunday Times* before going on to resume a career in politics.[24] His 1898 lecture 'Prison Cure for Crime' helped to generate the agenda for penal reform adopted by the Commission. The result of this energetic work by 1890s reformers was some years in the making, but finally arrived

23 Entry on F. C. B. Vosper (1869–91), *Australian Dictionary of Biography*, vol. 12, Melbourne University Press, Melbourne, 1990, pp. 334–5.

24 Entry on Thomas Walker (1858–1932), *Australian Dictionary of Biography*, vol. 6, 1976, pp. 342–4. Walker's colourful career as a spiritualist, birth-control campaigner, poet, dramatist, journalist, lecturer, and politician also included an active role in campaigns against hanging.

after 1910: Drew became Colonial Secretary and Walker the Attorney-General in the Scaddan Labor government, during which time and after, Drew pushed forward the reformatory idea as well as other changes, against the wishes of the Comptroller-General.[25]

Being close to power was, and is, a condition of penal reform. Reform of prisons or of the criminal law might be the focus of a life's work, such as that of prison administrators Neitenstein and, before him, Maconochie. Or it might be just one dimension of a broader campaign, the rationale of which may be derived from a more general critique of the uses and abuses of power. Not surprisingly, turn-of-the-century feminists saw criminal-justice reform as one aspect of social change predicated on women's advancement towards social as well as political equality. Catherine Helen Spence in South Australia, Vida Goldstein in Victoria, and Rose Scott in New South Wales were all leading feminists of their generation who took an active interest in prison reform, as well as in the reform of criminal law and procedure as it affected women. Of them all, Scott was pre-eminent in her focus and impact on this aspect of social reform. Working from within the system, as well as from outside it, she developed a formidable reputation and respect, which earned her personal access at any time to police lock-ups in New South Wales.[26] Responding to the reformism of the new Comptroller-General of Prisons, Frederick Neitenstein, Scott involved herself in prison reform from the late 1890s through the Ladies' Committee of the Prisoners' Aid Association. In this role, she visited prisons and communicated to close political associates the difficulties and disadvantages of women in prison. While her critique of women's position was radical, there was little that could be regarded as exceptional in Scott's program of reform: it was thoroughly 'modern' in its attachment to indeterminate sentences and the reformatory ideal, and in its associated rhetoric of reformation (as opposed to punishment), with 'the factors of reform — love for freedom, love of work — all tending towards the development of self-respect and the awakening of a sense of duty to others'.[27] Working through the establishment, and deploying her social elevation and cultural capital to the maximum in the cause of women's advancement, Scott

25 See especially L. J. Stevenson, Fremantle Prison in the 1890s, MA thesis, University of Western Australia, Perth, 1983, pp. 6–9; on Drew's and Walker's reforms, see above, p. 151.

26 See especially Allen, *Rose Scott*, pp. 153–7; For the visiting card approved by Edmund Fosbery, Inspector-General of police, see Rose Scott Papers, Mitchell Library, Sydney, Mss. 38/56, Item 2/197.

27 Rose Scott Papers, Mitchell Library, Sydney, Mss. 38/56, item 2/15.

was an archetypal prison reformer — the kind that had helped to transform punishment and build the prison as a modern institution. But such people could not control the future — a future in which the separate women's reformatory at Long Bay was never to achieve the objectives set out for it, and was to become itself the object of reform campaigns.[28]

The conditions of women's imprisonment would again become a cause for reformers in the 1940s. In the immediate postwar period, New South Wales possessed not one but two prison reform groups, with some overlapping membership. The Howard tradition had its local representative in the Howard Prison Reform League, which had been formed in 1924.[29] Records dating from 1936 note a distinguished list of members: among them were James Dunlop, former managing director of the leading industrial company Edwards Dunlop Pty Ltd; A. B. Piddington, eminent arbitration court judge and leading liberal; maverick Labor parliamentarian Eddie Ward; and conservative politician Sir Benjamin Fuller. The position of secretary was filled for many years by Norman Sachisthal, who had been an officer in the Child Welfare Department, while other members included Pearl Gibbs, a leading Aboriginal activist (described inaccurately in the members' book as Secretary of the 'Citizens Aboriginal Association'[30]), and Ruby Rich of the Racial Hygiene Association. The League's role was more in the tradition of citizen's watchdog (for example, in its consistent opposition to the death penalty and corporal punishment, its openness to prisoners' own statements of their experience, and its criticism of the association of juveniles with adults in prisons). In a deputation to the federal Attorney-General in 1939, the League sought (unsuccessfully) an undertaking that the Commonwealth would abolish capital punishment throughout Australia.

28 On the failure of bricks-and-mortar solutions, from Rose Scott to Mulawa, see the speech of Wendy Bacon, 1983, quoted in Brown, Kramer, & Quinn, 'Women in Prison', p. 287.

29 *Sydney Morning Herald*, 28 February 1924 reports on a newly formed Howard League for Penal Reform, incorporating the Prisons Reform Society — addresses by members included Miss Rivett, MA, Cantab, on 'The Psychological Aspect of our Prisons'; on the League's continuing role in the late 1920s, see Lee, Modern Methods of Prison Reform.

30 This appears to be a conflation of two organisations that Pearl Gibbs was closely involved with: the Aboriginals Progressive Association, of which she was secretary at one time, and the Committee for Aboriginal Citizen Rights, formed from church, women's, and workers' organisations. See H. Goodall, *Invasion to Embassy: Land in Aboriginal Politics in New South Wales, 1770–1972*, Allen & Unwin, Sydney, 1996, pp. 230–3; and K. Gilbert, J. Horner, & H. Goodall, 'Three Tributes to Pearl Gibbs (1901–1983)', *Aboriginal History*, vol. 7, no. 1, 1983, pp. 4–22.

Among the deputation was Gibbs, who was reported as saying that she spoke 'as an Aboriginal woman' against the capital punishment of Aborigines, as 'the tribalised or half tribalised aboriginal did not understand hanging or the white man's law', especially since the missionaries taught another doctrine — the 'forgiveness of sin'.[31] This group, which had among its members a number of people familiar with the world of politics and business, also enjoyed access to power. The respect with which it was treated was reflected in its members being granted access to gaols, among them the state's most severe — Grafton, — in 1948.[32]

Another society, contemporaneous with the Howard League, was the Prison Reform Council of New South Wales, whose campaigns appeared to be particularly targeted at sustaining the Labor government's belated penal reform efforts in the postwar period. Its President was University of Sydney Professor of Philosophy A. K. Stout, a civil libertarian who was also active in campaigns about police behaviour in demonstrations. The Council's overlap with the Howard League was evident in the membership of Norma Parker, who was Secretary in 1947. A pioneer in professional and academic social work, Parker had already been involved, as a member of 'Catholic Action', with the Howard League since 1941.[33] In April 1947 the Council published a comprehensive critique of prisons in the state, under the title *Forgotten Men*, although some of its most stringent criticism was reserved for the conditions of women in prison. Repeating the now well-worn cry that the object of prison should be to 'reform not punish', the pamphlet included testimony from visitors, prisoners, and an ex-warder in developing its cases for reform on a number of fronts. Stout's foreword stated the rationale for reform in a context familiar to all prison reformers:

> The advocate of prison reform has to overcome considerable public apathy and sometimes open hostility. He is accused of being an unrealistic sentimentalist who is misguided enough to be more interested in the criminal than in the protection of the public. The straight answer

31 *Sydney Morning Herald*, 27 February 1939, p. 13.

32 Howard Prison Reform League, Mitchell Library, Mss. 1034. These papers include a membership book, minute book, and other miscellaneous items, covering the period 1936–52.

33 On Norma Parker's career (which concluded with her appointment as first Head of the School of Social Work at University of New South Wales), see R. J. Lawrence (ed. & compiled), *Norma Parker's Record of Service*, self-published, 1969 (Mitchell Library, Sydney). Her long service was memorialised in an ambiguous gesture: the naming of a women's minimum-security prison in New South Wales the 'Norma Parker Centre'.

to this is that our penal system, as it now works, very inadequately protects the public against the criminal.[34]

Some measure of the difference between this group and the Howard League was the reference in its reform agenda to 'modification of the severe conditions in the punishment section at Grafton Gaol'; the Howard League members who visited in 1948 do not appear to have been alert to conditions at Grafton, which remained contentious for another three decades.[35]

As these comments on a range of prison- and penal-reform groups imply, the objectives of reform must always be situated in their conditions of possibility. Not surprisingly, a popular radical position of the post-Vietnam years was abolition of the prison — a seemingly hopeless and utopian idea at a time when incarceration rates were accelerating. If there was a time since the 1780s when prison might have been abolished, it was around the turn of the century or, even better, between the wars. For a complex of reasons, prison populations had dropped to unusually low levels, and as we have seen, the numbers of women prisoners in the smaller Australian jurisdictions made separate accommodation virtually unviable. Reform campaigns at the turn of the century, however, enhanced the development of the prison, making it into an instrument of greater precision, or so it was hoped. The prison as punishment was diversified as reformers, within and without government, sought to develop modes of incarceration that would foster the reform of the prisoner into a sober and useful citizen, someone who, in Rose Scott's words, would possess self-respect arising from a love for freedom and a love of work. Punishment in this frame was 'individualised', but the language of reformers, prior to the emergence of a serious libertarianism in the 1960s, was primarily one that emphasised the collective good over any notion of individual rights. Hence Stout had to resort to a defensive rationale for the work of prison reform: one that was justified by its appeal to the protection of the public.

The role of organised action groups — lobbies of informed citizens of diverse interests and backgrounds, but all focused on the one object — is one part of the history of prison and penal reform. Another force, which we have already noted in passing, must also be included in this survey of influences on punishment: the media. The role of the media has been critical in generating public discourse on crime and penality for two

34 F. Snow (ed.), *Forgotten Men* (pamphlet), Prison Reform Council of New South Wales, Sydney, 1947 (Mitchell Library, Sydney).

35 See Howard League minute book, 1948, Howard Prison Reform League, Mitchell Library, Mss. 1034.

centuries. It has been no less significant in Australia than elsewhere. Journalism, as a profession, was the seedbed of many political careers, in the nineteenth century especially, and our discussion of prison reform in Western Australia in the 1890s has noted some examples. Prisons, no less than policing, have been a staple diet of newspaper readers. Through editorials, through special features, and through the correspondence columns, the press has maintained the visibility of punishment in a way that belies the phrase 'out of sight, out of mind', so commonly applied to carceral institutions, and much more true of asylums, orphanages, and old people's homes than of prisons.

The variety of media engagements with the prison and punishment systems defies simple summary. The significance of its role in the construction of punishment and crime is a staple of contemporary research in criminology and cultural studies, but less research has been pursued in the historical domain, and then it has mostly been in the study of crime.[36] In the domain of prisons and punishment, two kinds of contribution were characteristic of the media role in Australia. The tradition of muckraking journalism — conventionally associated, from the 1890s, with newspapers like *Truth* — was preceded by other attempts to uncover the curious, and perhaps sordid, world of the prison and its inhabitants. The 'Vagabond' in Melbourne, pseudonym of one of this genre's most famous practitioners, pursued his innovative style of investigative journalism in the 1870s through an early form of participant observation. There was a strong element of voyeurism in the practice of the 'slumming journalists', as Marcus Clarke and the Vagabond have been described, but there was also a link to the liberal programs of social reform of institutions, and amelioration of the conditions of poverty and hopelessness in the nineteenth-century city.[37] From time to time the Vagabond's exploits would be repeated, though not always with the same flair. Nevertheless, the watchful journalist or editor was generally quick to pick up allegations of abuse or ill-treatment in prisons — or, on the other hand, evidence of lack of system and of real punishment — and air them in a manner that

36 See, for example, the essays in *Australian Cultural History: Crimes and Trials*, vol. 12, 1993; for a contemporary study, see P. Grabosky & P. Wilson, *Journalism and Justice*, Pluto Press, Sydney, 1989.

37 See, for example, G. Davison & D. Dunstan, '"This Moral Pandemonium": Images of Low Life', in G. Davison, D. Dunstan, & C. McConville (eds), *The Outcasts of Melbourne: Essays in Social History*, Allen & Unwin, Sydney, 1985, p. 41. The Vagabond was John Stanley James; see M. Cannon (ed.), *The Vagabond Papers*, Melbourne University Press, Melbourne, 1969.

typically prompted parliamentary questions and occasionally more significant inquiry, as we have seen earlier.[38]

Alternatively, the media were more purposefully deployed in pursuing a particular program of reform or in addressing problems in the system. The activists whose efforts we have noted in this chapter — both prisoners and those outside the system — typically included people who accommodated themselves easily to the genre of media debate, using the media to communicate their views on the big issues of punishment and on the problems of a system seemingly always in need of reform. Joseph Bragg was such a person. A one-time 'street Arab', he was recommended for permanent imprisonment while still a juvenile. As a prisoner, he became a key figure in prompting the 1878 Berrima Gaol Inquiry into the use of the gag and other punishments. By the mid-1880s he had embarked on a personal campaign for prison reform, which received wide press coverage. His public addresses on his life of crime and punishment were published extensively in both newspaper and pamphlet form, and are an example of a late Victorian discourse on the virtues of moral reformation.[39]

Other campaigns mounted in the media were consciously articulated to progressive reform agendas, and aimed to influence a new minister or government. A campaign by the anonymous 'Reformer' in Sydney's *Sunday Times* in 1923 was based on the conventional study of 'defects in our prison system' and urged that the failure of prisons to 'reform criminals' was a question of 'national importance'. The campaign was a product of its time in favouring the application of psychological medicine in penal practice. 'Reformer' was also concerned to see a more uniform approach to corrections across the Australian states, a start on which would be made through an interstate conference under the direction of a 'mental alienist' (a psychiatrist). Prisons needed 'technically qualified men to deal with

38 See above, pp. 108–26, on corporal punishment, and pp. 116–17 on the Western Australian Commission of 1899.

39 See J. Bragg, *The Confessions of a Thief*, Sydney, 1886 (Mitchell Library, Sydney). The pamphlet summarises Bragg's life and his opinions on imprisonment and criminality, the subject of his public lectures in April 1886, which were also published in the press; see *Town and Country Journal*, 15 May 1886; *Evening News*, 27 April, 4 May 1886. The pamphlet was also the subject of comment by Havelock Ellis in his regular review of 'Criminal Anthropology', *Journal of Mental Science*, vol. 39, 1893, p. 137, after Ellis was sent the pamphlet by George Ardill, Director of the Sydney Rescue Work Society and prominent charity reformer. On Bragg at the Berrima Gaol Inquiry Commission, see NSW, Parliament, *Report of the Berrima Gaol Inquiry Commission*, NSWPP, Sydney, 1878–79, vol. 3, ev. 3055–3371.

the solution of problems which require . . . experts in mental maladies, men who know about moral defects, and how to attempt their cure'.[40]

As a vehicle for reform, the media were always an uncertain ally. The importance of the exposé cannot be underestimated: the tabloid press especially was ever watchful for eye-catching tales of abuse that conjured up their readers' worst fears about the reality of prisons. Long before the advent of press secretaries and ministers' minders, the government had a system for managing the dangers of bad media publicity: the responsible departments rigorously scrutinised the press for stories concerning prisons, preparing responses for the inevitable parliamentary questions that followed, but which rarely went further.[41]

When more serious allegations were aired, the government's capacity to manage the problem was substantial. In 1955 the *Sunday Telegraph*, which was part of the Packer group and a lively interrogator of police and prison practices at the time,[42] ran a story on the Grafton system, detailing evidence of the physical abuse of prisoners — abuse that would take another two decades to be addressed. Subsequently the editor received an anonymous letter alleging that prisoners had been bashed at Long Bay. He passed the letter on to the Comptroller-General, who found enough substance in the allegations to recommend to the Public Service Board that a warder be charged with misconduct for striking a prisoner. The Board's inquiry, however, dismissed the allegations entirely, explaining that the 'only allegations were made by young men with very long criminal records' (records attached showed they all had histories since childhood) and that psychologists and others who knew them reported that they were willing to lie. The Chair of the Public Service Board reported to the Minister that the warder concerned was 'a man with an unblemished record in the Prison Service, with an excellent war record in the last war, not only in the expeditionary forces, but in the permanent forces.'[43] Allegations of abuse could readily find their way into the press, but the path from media attention to satisfactory redress was strewn with numerous hurdles, includ-

40 'Reformer', *Crime and Criminals: Study of Defects in our Prison System*, [1923], a pamphlet derived from a series of articles first published in the *Sunday Times*, (Mitchell Library, Sydney).

41 On NSW, see Corrective Services, press-cuttings, NSW State Archives, Sydney, 2/2124–6.

42 See M. Finnane, *Police and Government: Histories of Policing in Australia*, Oxford University Press, Melbourne, 1994, p. 168.

43 Correspondence re Long Bay, 1953–57, Corrective Services, NSW State Archives, Sydney, 5/3728.2.

ing the ambivalence of the media itself with regard to prisoners and punishment. For every campaign mounted in favour of reform, or drawing attention to abuses in the system, there was another invoking the need for stricter punishment, for making prison a punishment that 'meant something'. The media have been a crucial fabricator of the conditions of punishment, and of their reform, in Australia. But in both respects they were primarily a vehicle through which other forces worked — an imperfect forum of debate, as well as a stage on which both grievances and righteousness could be paraded.

Conclusion: The Possibilities of Change

This book has considered the history of punishment in Australia in just some of its aspects, and mainly those concerned with the history of the prison. My comments on patterns of sentencing, however, and my discussion of corporal and capital punishment, have suggested that other modes of punishment were important in Australian history. In Chapter 5 I have briefly considered the conditions under which some arguments about reform of the prison have climbed onto the political stage, as well as some reasons why they might or might not succeed in producing change. Today's criminologists — unlike those of the 1890s, who were brim full of confidence that they knew what would work — often say that 'nothing works'. This position may be excessively pessimistic, may justify inaction, and certainly implies that perhaps the only thing that is worth doing is trying to ensure that any new changes do not bring more people into the punishment system.

At a certain level, the belief that nothing works is nonsense. Such a judgment is made from inside a field of reference whose boundaries are defined by the objectives of the criminal-justice system. But the importance of the phenomena of punishment goes beyond the particular perspectives of those seeking to find a way of reducing crime or of preventing people from re-entering prison. We do not have to agree with Durkheim that crime plays a normal role in social life, or that there is a single collective conscience, to recognise nevertheless the value of his postulate that 'punishment constitutes essentially a passionate reaction, graduated in intensity, which society exerts through the mediation of an organised body over those of its members who have violated certain rules of conduct'.[1] The modern history of punishment is the study of those

1 As quoted in S. Lukes & A. Scull (eds), *Durkheim and the Law*, Martin Robertson, Oxford, 1983, p. 68.

reactions, of the forces that modulate the intensity of the reactions, and of the changes in the rules of conduct that simultaneously express and construct reactions, either of the popular majority or of particular social groups. In this conclusion it might be beneficial to take stock briefly of some of the changes that have been, and are, taking place in the modes of punishment in twentieth-century Australia. These changes sometimes have longer histories than we suspect, or else they seek to introduce something very new into the culture.

If there is a single word that constitutes a rallying call in current debates in criminal justice, it is 'community'. The concept of 'community' justifies truth in sentencing and increased use of imprisonment; it explains what is wrong with current policing; it points to a new future for the management of offending and for addressing the harm done to victims of crime. A government can come to power compromised by a secret deal done with a police union — a deal that it justifies in the name of protecting the community — and at the same time contemplate returning the power to punish under customary law to indigenous communities.[2] 'Community' lacks a solid reference point, and is thereby capable of justifying both reactionary and progressive justice policies. In criminal justice today, however, this concept is most commonly associated with a movement to develop new alternatives to the prison. Community-justice mechanisms are sought in order to minimise the harm done to offenders exposed to the abuse of power in total institutions and to address more effectively the needs of victims and their associates.[3]

If we want to think historically about the significance of this phenomenon, we can recognise that what defines community is best expressed in criminal-justice policy as the opposite to prison. Prison was an invention that sought to remove offenders from the community, from its observation, and from its participation in their punishment. Community,

2 Queenslanders in 1996 witnessed both these examples: on the planned return of customary law in 'isolated black communities', see the *Australian*, 8 August 1996.

3 I have been aided in these comments on the uses of 'community' in these debates, especially by D. Moore, Emotions and Social Regulation, PhD thesis in preparation, Griffith University, Brisbane. See also the influential work of J. Braithwaite, *Crime, Shame and Reintegration*, Cambridge University Press, Melbourne, 1989. For a positive evaluation of the restorative-justice initiatives, see C. La Prairie, 'Altering Course: New Directions in Criminal Justice — Sentencing Circles and Family Group Conferences', in D. Dixon (ed.), *Crime, Criminology and Public Policy: Special Supplementary Issue, Australia and New Zealand Journal of Criminology*, 1995, pp. 78–99; and for a more cautious assessment, see J. Bargen, 'A Critical View of Conferencing', in the same volume, pp. 100–3.

conceived more narrowly as the social bonds of offenders with their associates and localities, was even the enemy of possible reform. Hence, the prison took offenders out of the various communities, real and more abstract, of which they had been part. In the extreme prison conditions of total isolation and silence, the opposition of prison and community was magnified.

Such an opposition could never be sustained for long in practice. Its limit was the reality that prisoners, at some stage, had to be returned to the community whence they came. The prison as a total institution had hardly been refined in the 1840s when policy measures were being explored by which prisoners might be returned to the community. The innovative ticket-of-leave system in the Australian convict colonies was adapted to become the basis for supervising released prisoners in England and Wales after 1869. Beyond this experiment, however, there was little initiative taken in penal policy between the 1840s and the 1890s. As we have seen in chapters 2 and 3, there were some gestures towards the future in the rhetoric of individual punishment, but little by way of practical effect.

The genesis of current alternatives to imprisonment may be seen as having passed through three stages since the 1890s, each of them overlapping to create a complex justice framework, with the myriad of sentencing options that we have today. Only some of these options are explicitly linked to the concept of community, but all are posited on the failure of imprisonment to secure the reform of the offender and guarantee the safety of the community.

The reforms of the two decades before the First World War secured a reduction in the uses of imprisonment, which complemented a simultaneous decline in the rate of imprisonment. That is, the introduction of part payment of fines, the use of probation for first offenders, and the removal of some previously indictable offences into summary jurisdiction were all consistent with a diversification of responses to offending.

The trends of reform were not all in the direction of 'decarceration' as it was much later to become known. The differentiation of offenders, which was characteristic of the growth of the welfare complex from the later nineteenth century, also involved institutional reform that maintained carceral solutions: the establishment of inebriate asylums, of women's penitentiaries, of juvenile reformatories.[4] Yet seemingly

4 See especially Garton, 'Bad or Mad?' for an outline of the changes in NSW during this period.

even more in contradiction with the justice reforms aimed at keeping people out of prison were those that sought to hold them indefinitely — or at least until they were fit to leave. This was arguably only an apparent contradiction, since the underlying assumptions about the relation of the criminal-justice system to social order acknowledged the interactions between the two. The same logic of the 'social' that justified part payment of fines, or probation for first offenders — the system should not needlessly aggravate a breakdown in offenders' social relations with their dependent families or their capacity to continue useful and self-supporting labour — also justified the introduction of indefinite sentences, and the de facto introduction of parole. These innovations would resolve the problem of habitual offenders serving endless short sentences and then being returned to the community, only to recommit the same offences. Society would both be protected from repeat offences and receive reconstituted citizens back into itself at a future stage.

The notion of conditionally releasing such prisoners was of considerable appeal to early twentieth-century reformers and prison administrators. Parole, in fact, was introduced by degrees, and through policy more than legislation. In New South Wales the release-on-licence system was altered in 1908 so that even prisoners released as a result of remission of sentence were required to be on good behaviour, reporting to police regularly; previously these prisoners had been released unconditionally.[5] In some areas the conditions of release could go well beyond the requirement of good behaviour. Hence, in Tasmania, the administration of ticket of leave, and later of parole, provides evidence of cases in which a residential or behavioural condition was imposed. For example, in 1877 a released prisoner was required to reside 'north of Oatlands'. In 1920 a woman sentenced to six months for 'concealment of birth' was released on condition of 'marrying within one calendar month, the man responsible for her trouble'.[6] It is necessary to recall that the concept of conditional release has, in fact, had considerable longevity in Australian criminal-justice history. In the case of women convicts in Tasmania before 1850, it appears that a

5 Papers re changes in release on licence scheme, Attorney-General and Justice, NSW State Archives, Sydney, 7/5436. The correspondence suggests that police were concerned about this policy change, presumably because of the increased workload.

6 Cases of DA (released on ticket of leave, 1877) and IA (released on parole, 1920), Prisons, Tasmanian State Archives, Hobart, GD/61.

considerable number of releases to freedom were contingent on marriage to an appropriate man.[7]

In this earlier period, the 'public' was being protected by a State that had virtually exclusive control of the administration of sanctions. Even bodies such as the Prisoners Aid Society and the Discharged Prisoners' Society were closely integrated in the administration of imprisonment and the criminal-justice system, as their records and leadership suggest. The second phase of decarceration, involving the development of 'community-based sanctions', dates from the 1950s in Australia and sees the bureaucratisation, on a large scale, of the non-carceral management of offenders. Parole and probation came into their own, with specialised officers managing large case-loads. Later, the introduction of periodic-detention orders and community-service orders suggested some enhancement of the anti-carceral cause. In the case of community-service orders, there is a gestural link established between the 'community' and the 'offender', one in which the 'community' (typically a service organisation or a school) is recompensed for the harm done by the offender, while the latter avoids the harm of imprisonment and is presumed to learn a moral lesson through labour in the service of the community. The 'community', in this sense, is still an abstract concept, a unity over which the State still exercises a guardianship, and a strong control. Although decarceration, as a long-term, objective phenomenon, was an undoubted reality for some decades, the community-orientation of sentencing was scarcely advanced by the extension of so-called community-based sanctions (and the limited penetration of so-named 'community-service orders' suggested as much).[8] State domination of the penal terrain was undisputed.

The third stage in the development of non-carceral modes of penality is very recent. The introduction of community-justice mechanisms — of 'restorative' justice and of family or community conferencing — is said

7 See, for example, the many cases in Tardif, *Notorious Strumpets*. On the history of ticket of leave and its relevance to more recent 'back end' release schemes, see J. Chan, *Doing Less Time: Penal Reform in Crisis*, Institute of Criminology, Sydney, 1992; and J. Chan, 'Decarceration and Imprisonment in New South Wales: A Historical Analysis of Early Release', *University of New South Wales Law Journal*, vol. 13, no. 2, 1991, pp. 393–416.

8 See especially J. Chan & G. Zdenkowski, 'Just Alternatives', parts I & II, *Australian and New Zealand Journal of Criminology*, vol. 19, no. 2, 1986, pp. 67–90, and vol. 19, no. 3, 1986, pp. 131–54; J. Braithwaite, 'The Political Economy of Punishment', in E. Wheelwright & K. Buckley (eds), *The Political Economy of Australian Capitalism*, vol. 3, ANZ Books, Sydney, 1980; S. Garton, 'The State, Labour Markets and Incarceration: A Critique', in M. Findlay & R. Hogg (eds), *Understanding Crime and Criminal Justice*, Law Book Co., Sydney, 1988.

to bring the community back into the system of responding to offending. Is this development distinctive enough to justify separation as a new stage? The notion of diversion from the criminal-justice system is not enough to distinguish recent innovation from earlier periods, since that has been the aim of reform at least since the introduction of first offenders' probation in the 1880s. Neither is the notion of community involvement a sufficient differentiator, since that rhetoric has been associated with sanction innovations since the 1960s.

More significant and innovative is the appearance of a new party in the debate over responding to crime: the victim. The emergence of the victim — as an independent actor for whom the State is no longer presumed to speak conclusively — is possibly the most substantial change to occur in criminal-justice debate and policy since the emergence of the prison as the centrepiece of the State's response to crime. The attempt to involve victims in a process of reconciliation with the offender is equally a signal development in the range of responses to crime and harmful acts. Certainly, before this, in the post-convict period, there have been those who have sought to speak for victims — notably for women in the 1900s and 1930s, as the debates on corporal punishment and sexual offences testify.[9] The solution then, however, was essentially one of a greater punitiveness, of seeking to persuade the State to act more effectively to deter potential offenders. Today's reformers are yet to establish the limits of restorative justice's potential. It is yet to be determined whether — through an alternative mechanism involving both victims and offenders, as well as their close social affiliates — restorative justice can adequately address the needs of victims. The hopes of those who would like to see the State more removed from the process of punishment — or to see punishment replaced by reintegration as a rhetoric and practice in response to offending — are, of course, a long way from being realised. Whether the general emotional interests served by punishment, as well as the State interests committed to punishment, can shift sufficiently to allow more innovative responses to offending remains a moot point. The re-emergence in the last decade of punitive State policies is hardly an auspicious sign.[10]

A different kind of opportunity for the development of community-based punishment is offered in Australia by the historical legacy of settlement and dispossession. Punishment, as we have observed in earlier

9 See above, chs 4 and 5.
10 D. Garland, 'The Limits of the Sovereign State', *British Journal of Criminology*, vol. 36, no. 4, 1996, pp. 445–71.

chapters, was organised with the particular objective of controlling Aboriginal people in ways that would secure settlement. In the wake of the extension of citizenship, and a coincident collapse of economic opportunities in rural and remote Australia, punishment through imprisonment has become an experience shared by Aboriginal people to an extent unknown to the rest of the Australian community. While the imprisonment of many indigenous people is largely the result of offending within their own communities, for many others it has been the result of offending against standards of propriety in non-Aboriginal communities.[11] In both these situations, the potential of a notion of community justice to alter a damaging and often fatal pattern of offending and incarceration is appealing. On the one hand, restoring to self-governing communities the power to administer justice according to locally administered processes and standards has been contemplated as a means of enhancing individual and community well-being. On the other hand, to address intercultural conflict over drinking in public places and other such causes of needless incarceration, even more challenging obstacles must be surmounted in the way of defining what community means in Australia today. Historically, again and again, attempts to alter the culture of response to crime and offending have exposed the limits of 'community'. At its various levels, the Australian State has been the captive of a partial community interest, and reforms that would reduce incarceration and enhance a more complete sense of justice have been jettisoned.[12]

Contemporary commentary on punishment reflects the uncertainty that now characterises State intervention.[13] The failure of penal sanctions to address offending is seen by some to justify the search for alternative responses, through self-regulation in some areas, and through decriminalisation or privatisation of the social arena in others. But remembering

11 Royal Commission into Aboriginal Deaths in Custody, *National Report.*

12 For commentary on the aftermath of the Royal Commission, see C. Cunneen (ed.), *Aboriginal Perspectives on Criminal Justice,* Institute of Criminology, Sydney, 1992; Harding et al., Aboriginal Contact with the Criminal Justice System; Aboriginal and Torres Strait Islander Overview Committee, *First Report,* Department of Families, Youth and Community Care, Brisbane, 1996; Cunneen & McDonald, *Keeping Aboriginal and Torres Strait Islander People out of Custody.*

13 See, for example, Howe, *Punish and Critique,* ch. 6; P. O'Malley, 'Post-Social Criminologies: Some Implications of Current Political Trends for Criminological Theory and Practice', *Current Issues in Criminal Justice,* vol. 8, no. 1, 1996, pp. 26–38; R. Hogg, 'Criminological Failure and Governmental Effect', *Current Issues in Criminal Justice,* vol. 8, no. 1, 1996, pp. 43–59; Garland, 'Limits of the Sovereign State'.

that the Western State, especially in common law countries, originally emerged as a vehicle for enhancing (indeed constructing) rights and as a mechanism for their protection, there are reasons to be cautious about a too-hasty removal of the State's power to punish. Australia, as a settler society whose origins lie in a massive penal experiment — and which at the end of the twentieth century witnesses the ignoble mass incarceration of dispossessed peoples — is particularly obliged to pay attention to such debates and to resolve them in ways that will enhance justice for all its communities.

BIBLIOGRAPHY

Aboriginal and Torres Strait Islander Overview Committee, *First Report*, Department of Families, Youth and Community Care, Brisbane, 1996.

Alford, K., 'Convicts and Immigrant Women Before 1851', in J. Jupp (ed.), *The Australian People: An Encyclopedia of the Nation, its People and their Origins*, Angus & Robertson, Sydney, 1988.

Allen, J., *Rose Scott: Vision and Revision in Feminism,* Oxford University Press, Melbourne, 1994.

Allen, J., *Sex and Secrets: Crime Involving Australian Women since 1880*, Oxford University Press, Melbourne, 1990

Anderson, T., *Inside Outlaws: A Prison Diary*, Redfern Legal Centre Publishing, Sydney, 1989.

Anon., *Four Years Experience in Darlinghurst Gaol, by an Ex-Prisoner*, self-published pamphlet, Sydney, n.d. [1868–72].

Atkinson, A., 'Four Patterns of Convict Protest', *Labour History*, no. 37, November 1979, pp. 28–51.

—— 'The Free-Born Englishman Transported: Convict Rights as a Measure of Eighteenth-Century Empire', *Past & Present,* no. 144, August 1994, pp. 88–115.

Australian Cultural History: Crimes and Trials, vol. 12, 1993.

Australian Dictionary of Biography, Melbourne University Press, Melbourne, 1976–90.

Australian Yearbook (various years)

Aveling, M., 'Bending the Bars: Convict Women and the State', in K. Saunders & R. Evans (eds), *Gender Relations in Australia,* Harcourt Brace Jovanovich, Sydney, 1992.

Barbalet, M., *Far from a Low Gutter Girl*, Oxford University Press, Melbourne, 1983.

Barber, R. N., 'The Labor Party and the Abolition of Capital Punishment in Queensland 1899–1922', *Queensland Heritage*, November 1968, pp. 3–12.

—— 'Rape as a Capital Offence in Nineteenth Century Queensland', *Australian Journal of Politics and History*, vol. 21, no. 1, 1975, pp. 31–41.

Bargen, J., 'A Critical View of Conferencing', in D. Dixon (ed.), *Crime, Criminology and Public Policy: Special Supplementary Issue, Australia and New Zealand Journal of Criminology*, 1995, pp. 100–3.

Barry, J. V. W., *Alexander Maconochie of Norfolk Island*, Oxford University Press, Melbourne, 1958.

—— *The Life and Death of John Price: A Study of the Exercise of Naked Power*, Melbourne University Press, Melbourne, 1964.

Beattie, J., *Crime and the Courts in England 1660–1800,* Clarendon Press, Oxford, 1986.

Berry, R. J. A. & Buchner, L., 'The Correlation of Size of Head and Intelligence, as Estimated from the Cubic Capacity of Brain of 355 Melbourne Criminals', *Proceedings of the Royal Society of Victoria,* vol. 25, 1913, pp. 229–53.

'Birching, Whipping and Public Comment', *Australian and New Zealand Journal of Criminology*, vol. 6, no. 3, 1973.

Biskup, P., *Not Slaves Not Citizens,* University of Queensland Press, St Lucia, 1973.

Bolton, G. C., 'The Fenians Are Coming, The Fenians Are Coming', in *Studies in Western Australian History*, vol. 4, December 1981, pp. 62–7.

Bomford, J. M., *That Dangerous and Persuasive Woman: Vida Goldstein*, Melbourne University Press, Melbourne, 1993.

Bragg, J., *The Confessions of a Thief,* Sydney, 1886 (Mitchell Library, Sydney).

Braithwaite, J., 'The Political Economy of Punishment', in E. Wheelwright & K. Buckley (eds), *The Political Economy of Australian Capitalism*, vol. 3, ANZ Books, Sydney, 1980.

—— *Crime, Shame and Reintegration*, Cambridge University Press, Melbourne, 1989.

Broadhurst, R., 'Imprisonment of the Aborigine in Western Australia, 1957–1985', in K. Hazlehurst (ed.), *Ivory Scales: Black Australians and the Law*, NSW University Press, Kensington, 1987.

Broome, R., 'The Stigma of Pentridge: The View from Coburg 1850–1987', *Journal of Australian Studies,* no. 22, May 1988, pp. 3–18.

Brown, D., Kramer, H., & Quinn, M., 'Women in Prison: Task Force Reform', in M. Findlay & R. Hogg (eds), *Understanding Crime and Criminal Justice*, Law Book Co., Sydney, 1988.

Byrne, P. J., *Criminal Law and Colonial Subject: New South Wales, 1810–1830,* Cambridge University Press, Melbourne, 1993.

—— 'On Her Own Hands: Women and Criminal Law in New South Wales, 1810–1830', in D. Philips & S. Davies (eds), *A Nation of Rogues? Crime, Law and Punishment in Colonial Australia,* Melbourne University Press, Melbourne, 1994.

Cannon, M. (ed.), *The Vagabond Papers*, Melbourne University Press, Melbourne, 1969.

—— *The Woman as Murderer*, Today's Australia Publishing Company, Mornington, Vic. 1994

Carment, D., *History and the Landscape in Central Australia*, Australian National University and Northern Australian Research Unit, 1991.

Castieau, J. B., Diary, in the possession of the National Library of Australia, Ms. 2218.

Cawte, M., 'Craniotomy and Eugenics in Australia: R. J. A. Berry and the Quest for Social Efficiency', *Australian Historical Studies*, no. 86, 1986, pp. 35–53.

Chan, J., 'Decarceration and Imprisonment in New South Wales: A Historical Analysis of Early Release', *University of New South Wales Law Journal*, vol. 13, no. 2, 1991, pp. 393–416.

—— *Doing Less Time: Penal Reform in Crisis*, Institute of Criminology, Sydney, 1992.

Chan, J. & Zdenkowski, G., 'Just Alternatives', parts I & II, *Australian and New Zealand Journal of Criminology*, vol. 19, no. 2, 1986, pp. 67–90, and vol. 19, no. 3, 1986, pp. 131–54.

Clark, C. M. H., 'The Origins of the Convicts Transported to Eastern Australia, 1787–1852', *Historical Studies,* Part 1, vol. 7, no. 26, May 1956, pp. 121–35; Part 2, vol. 7, no. 27, November 1956, pp. 315–27.

—— *A History of Australia*, vol. 4, Melbourne University Press, 1978.

Clarke, M., 'Civilization without Delusion' (originally in *Victorian Review*, 1879), in M. Wilding (ed.) *Marcus Clarke*, University of Queensland Press, St Lucia, 1976.

—— *For the Term of his Natural Life*, University of Queensland Press, St Lucia, 1976 (1874).

Conley, C., *The Unwritten Law*, Oxford University Press, Oxford, 1991.

Convict Discipline, 1833, Gryphon Books, Sydney, 1977.

Criminological Society of South Australia, *First Report*, [1897], in the possession of the South Australian State Library, Adelaide.

Cunneen, C. (ed.), *Aboriginal Perspectives on Criminal Justice*, Institute of Criminology, Sydney, 1992.

Cunneen, C. & McDonald, D., *Keeping Aboriginal and Torres Strait Islander People out of Custody: An Evaluation of the Implementation of the Recommendations of the Royal Commission in Aboriginal Deaths in Custody*, Aboriginal and Torres Strait Islander Commission, Canberra, 1997.

Daniels, K., Murnane, M., & Picot, A. (eds), *Women in Australia*, vol. 2, AGPS, Canberra, 1977.

Daniels, K. & Murnane, M.(eds), *Uphill All the Way*, University of Queensland Press, St Lucia, 1980, pp. 9–10.

Davey, C., *Children and their Law-Makers*, self-published, Adelaide, 1956.

Davies, S., 'Aborigines, Murder and the Criminal Law in Early Port Phillip, 1841–1851', *Australian Historical Studies*, no 88, 1987, pp. 313–35.

—— '"Ragged, Dirty . . . Infamous and Obscene": The "Vagrant" in Late-Nineteenth-Century Melbourne', in D. Philips & S. Davies (eds), *A Nation of Rogues? Crime, Law and Punishment in Colonial Australia,* Melbourne University Press, Melbourne, 1994.

Davis, J., 'The London Garotting Panic of 1862', in V. A. C. Gatrell et al. (eds), *Crime and the Law: The Social History of Crime in Western Europe since 1500*, Europa, London, 1980.

Davis, R. P., *The Tasmanian Gallows: A Study of Capital Punishment,* Cat & Fiddle Press, Hobart, 1974.

—— 'Victims or Initiators? Three Irish Women Convicts of Van Diemen's Land', in B. Reece (ed.), *Irish Convict Lives*, Crossing Press, Sydney, 1994.

Davison, G. & Dunstan, D., '"This Moral Pandemonium": Images of Low Life', in G. Davison, D. Dunstan, & C. McConville (eds), *The Outcasts of Melbourne: Essays in Social History*, Allen & Unwin, Sydney, 1985.

Davitt, M., *Life and Progress in Australasia*, Methuen, London, 1898.

Dening, G., *Mr Bligh's Bad Language,* Cambridge University Press, Cambridge, 1992.

Departmental Committee on Corporal Punishment (Cadogan Committee), *Report*, His Majesty's Stationery Office, London, 1938.

Devereaux, S., 'In Place of Death: Transportation, Penal Practices and the English State, 1770–1830', in C. Strange (ed.), *Qualities of Mercy: Justice, Punishment and Discretion,* UBC Press, Vancouver, 1996.

Dickey, B., *Rations, Residence, Resources: A History of Social Welfare in South Australia since 1836,* Wakefield Press, Adelaide, 1986.

Dinwiddy, J., 'The Early Nineteenth-Century Campaign against Flogging in the Army', *English Historical Review*, vol. 97, 1982, pp. 308–31.

Douglas, R. & Laster, K., 'A Matter of Life and Death: The Victorian Executive and the Decision to Execute, 1842–1967', *Australia and New Zealand Journal of Criminology*, vol. 24, no. 2, 1991.

[Drew. J. M.], *Penological Reform in Western Australia* (pamphlet), Perth, 1916.

—— Prison Reform: The Pardelup Farm, 1928, in possession of the Battye Library, Perth.

B. Dyster, 'Public Employment and Assignment to Private Masters, 1788–1821', in S. Nicholas (ed.), *Convict Workers: Re-interpreting Australia's Past*, Cambridge University Press, Melbourne, 1988, pp. 127–53.

—— 'Convicts', *Labour History*, no. 67, November 1994, pp. 74–83.

Ekirch, A. R., *Bound for America: The Transportation of British Convicts to the Colonies, 1718–1775*, Clarendon Press, Oxford, 1987.

Elliott, B., *Marcus Clarke*, Clarendon Press, Oxford, 1958.

Ellis, H., 'Criminal Anthropology', *Journal of Mental Science*, vol. 39, 1893, pp. 137–40.

Emsley, C., *Crime and Society in England 1750–1900*, 2nd edn, Longman, London, 1996.

Evans, R., *The Fabrication of Virtue: English Prison Architecture, 1750–1840*, Cambridge University Press, Cambridge, 1982.

Evans, R. & Thorpe, W., 'Power, Punishment and Penal Labour: Convict Workers and Moreton Bay', *Australian Historical Studies*, no. 98, 1992, pp. 90–111.

Ferguson, R. J., *Rottnest Island: History and Architecture*, University of Western Australia Press, Perth, 1986.

Finch, L., *The Classing Gaze*, Allen & Unwin, Sydney, 1993.

Finnane, M., 'After the Convicts: Towards a History of Imprisonment in Australia', *Australian and New Zealand Journal of Criminology*, vol. 24, no. 2, 1991, pp. 105–18.

—— *Police and Government: Histories of Policing in Australia*, Oxford University Press, Melbourne, 1994.

Forster, C., *France and Botany Bay*, Melbourne University Press, Melbourne, 1996.

Foucault, M., *Discipline and Punish: The Birth of the Prison*, Pantheon Books, New York, 1977.

Friedman, L. M. *Crime and Punishment in American History*, Basic Books, New York, 1993.

Frost, A., *Botany Bay Mirages*, Melbourne University Press, Melbourne, 1994.

Galbally, A., *Redmond Barry*, Melbourne University Press, Melbourne, 1995.

Garland, D., *Punishment and Modern Society*, Clarendon Press, Oxford, 1990.

—— 'The Criminal and his Science', *The British Journal of Criminology*, vol. 25, no. 2, April 1985, pp. 109–37.

—— *Punishment and Welfare: A History of Penal Strategies*, Gower, Aldershot, UK, 1985.

—— 'The Limits of the Sovereign State', *British Journal of Criminology*, vol. 36, no. 4, 1996, pp. 445–71.

Garton, S., 'Bad or Mad? Developments in Incarceration in NSW, 1880–1920', in Sydney Labour History Group (ed.), *What Rough Beast?*, Allen & Unwin, Sydney, 1982.

—— 'The Rise of the Therapeutic State: Psychiatry and the System of Criminal Jurisdiction in New South Wales, 1890–1940', *Australian Journal of Politics and History*, vol. 32, no. 3, 1986, pp. 378–88.

—— '"Once a Drunkard, Always a Drunkard": Social Reform and the Problem of "Habitual Drunkenness in Australia", 1880–1914', *Labour History*, no. 53, 1987, pp. 38–53.

—— *Medicine and Madness*, University of NSW Press, Sydney, 1988.

—— 'The State, Labour Markets and Incarceration: A Critique', in M. Findlay & R. Hogg (eds), *Understanding Crime and Criminal Justice*, Law Book Co., Sydney, 1988.

—— 'Frederick William Neitenstein : Juvenile Reformatory and Prison Reform in NSW 1878–1909', *Journal of the Royal Australian Historical Society*, vol. 75, no. 1, June 1989, pp. 51–64.

—— 'The Convict Origins Debate: Historians and the Problem of the "Criminal Class"', *ANZ Journal of Criminology*, vol. 24, no. 2, 1991, pp. 66–82.

—— 'Sir Charles Mackellar: Psychiatry, Eugenics and Child Welfare in New South Wales, 1900–1914', *Australian Historical Studies*, no. 86, 1986, pp. 21–34.

—— 'Sound Minds and Healthy Bodies: Re-considering Eugenics in Australia, 1914–1940', *Australian Historical Studies*, no. 103, 1994, pp. 163–81.

Garvey, J., *The Indelible Stamp*, self-published pamphlet, Sydney, n.d. [1936].

Gatrell, V. A. C., *The Hanging Tree: Execution and the English People, 1770–1868*, Oxford University Press, Oxford, 1994.

Gilbert, K., Horner, J., & Goodall, H., 'Three Tributes to Pearl Gibbs (1901–1983)', *Aboriginal History*, vol. 7, no. 1, 1983, pp. 4–22.

Glenn, M. C., 'The Naval Reform Campaign against Flogging: A Case Study in Changing Attitudes toward Corporal Punishment, 1830–1850', *American Quarterly*, vol. 35, Fall 1983, pp. 408–15.

—— *Campaigns against Corporal Punishment*, State University of New York Press, Albany, NY, 1984.

Goodall, H., *Invasion to Embassy: Land in Aboriginal Politics in New South Wales, 1770–1972*, Allen & Unwin, Sydney, 1996.

Grabosky, P., *Sydney in Ferment*, ANU Press, Canberra, 1977.

Grabosky, P. & Wilson, P., *Journalism and Justice*, Pluto Press, Sydney, 1989.

Grant, D., *Prisons: The Continuing Crisis in NSW*, Federation Press, Sydney, 1992.

Green, N., *The Forrest River Massacres*, Fremantle Arts Centre Press, Fremantle, 1995.

Griffiths, A. R. G., 'Capital Punishment in South Australia, 1836–1964', *Australia and New Zealand Journal of Criminology*, vol. 3, no. 4, December 1970, pp. 214–22.

Grimshaw, P., Lake, M., McGrath, A., & Quartly, M., *Creating a Nation: 1788–1990*, McPhee Gribble, Melbourne, 1994.

Harding, R., Broadhurst, R, Ferrante, A., & Loh, N., *Aboriginal Contact with the Criminal Justice System and the Impact of the Royal Commission into Aboriginal Deaths in Custody*, The Hawkins Press, Sydney, 1995.

Harris, R., *Murders and Madness: Medicine, Law and Society in the* Fin de Siecle, Clarendon Press, Oxford, 1989.

Hasluck, A., *Royal Engineer: A Life of Sir Edmund Du Cane*, Angus & Robertson, Sydney, 1973.

—— *Unwilling Emigrants*, Fremantle Arts Centre Press, Fremantle, 1991 (1959).

Hergenhan, L., *Unnatural Lives*, University of Queensland Press, St Lucia, 1993.

Hetherington, P., 'Australian Colonial Law and the Construction of Childhood', in D. Kirkby (ed.), *Sex, Power and Justice: Historical Perspectives on Law in Australia*, Oxford University Press, Melbourne, 1995.

Hinde, R., 'Sir Walter Crofton and the Reform of the Irish Convict System 1854–61', *Irish Jurist,* vol. 12, 1977.

Hirst, J. B., *Convict Society and its Enemies: A History of Early New South Wales,* Allen & Unwin, Sydney, 1983.

—— 'Or None of the Above: A Reply', *Historical Studies*, no. 89, October 1987, pp. 519–24.

Hobsbawm, E. J. & Rudé, G., *Captain Swing,* Lawrence & Wishart, London, 1969.

Hodge, B. & Mishra, V., *Dark Side of the Dream*, Allen & Unwin, Sydney, 1990.

Hogg, R., 'Criminological Failure and Governmental Effect', *Current Issues in Criminal Justice*, vol. 8, no. 1, 1996, pp. 43–59.

Holtzendorff, F. von, *Die Deportation als Strafmitteln in alter und Neuer Zeit und die Verbrecher colonien der Engländer und Franzosen*, Verlag von Johann Ambrosius Barth, Leipzig, 1859.

Hood, R., *Borstal Reassessed*, Heinemann, London, 1965.

—— *The Death Penalty*, Clarendon Press, Oxford, 1989.

Hornadge, B., *Old Dubbo Gaol*, Dubbo, NSW [n.d.].

Howe, A., *Punish and Critique: Towards a Feminist Analysis of Penality*, Routledge, London, 1994.

Hughes, R., *The Fatal Shore: A History of Transportation of Convicts to Australia 1787–1868*, Collins Harvill, London, 1987.

Ignatieff, M., *A Just Measure of Pain: The Penitentiary in the Industrial Revolution*, Penguin, London, 1989 (1978).

Inglis, K., *The Stuart Case*, Melbourne University Press, Melbourne, 1959.

Johnston, S. W., 'Why Can't We be Reasonable about Hanging?', *Australian*, 17 December 1966, reprinted in B. Jones (ed.), *The Penalty is Death*, Sun Books, Melbourne, 1968.

Kelley, J. & Braithwaite, J., 'Public Opinion and the Death Penalty in Australia', *Justice Quarterly*, vol. 7, no. 3, 1990, pp. 529–63.

Kercher, B., *An Unruly Child: A History of Law in Australia*, Allen & Unwin, Sydney, 1995.

Kerr, J. S., *Design for Convicts,* Library for Australian History, Sydney, 1984.

—— *Out of Sight, Out of Mind (Australia's Places of Confinement, 1788–1988)*, S. H. Ervin Gallery, National Trust of Australia (NSW), Sydney, 1988.

Krieken, R. van, *Children and the State: Social Control and the Formation of Australian Child Welfare*, Allen & Unwin, Sydney, 1992.

La Prairie, C., 'Altering Course: New Directions in Criminal Justice — Sentencing Circles and Family Group Conferences', in D. Dixon (ed.), *Crime, Criminology and Public Policy: Special Supplementary Issue, Australia and New Zealand Journal of Criminology*, 1995, pp. 78–99.

Laster, K., 'Arbitrary Chivalry: Women and Capital Punishment in Victoria, 1842–1967', in D. Philips & S. Davies (eds), *A Nation of Rogues: Crime, Law And Punishment in Colonial Australia*, Melbourne University Press, Melbourne, 1994.

Lawrence, R. J. (ed. & compiled), *Norma Parker's Record of Service*, self-published, 1969 (Mitchell Library, Sydney).

Lee, Hon. J. R., Modern Methods of Prison Reform, lecture given to Howard Prison Reform League, Sydney, 7 July 1930, copy in National Library of Australia, Canberra.

Lewis, M., *Managing Madness*, AGPS, Canberra, 1988.

Luddy, M., *Women and Philanthropy in Nineteenth-Century Ireland*, Cambridge University Press, Cambridge, 1995.

Lukes, S. & Scull, A. (eds), *Durkheim and the Law*, Martin Robertson, Oxford, 1983.

McGowen, R., 'The Body and Punishment in Eighteenth-Century England', *Journal of Modern History*, vol. 59, 1987, pp. 651–79.

McGuire, J., Race and Capital Punishment in Australia, paper presented to the Law and History Conference, Brisbane, July 1996.

Marshall, V., *The World of the Living Dead and Jail from Within*, Wentworth Press, Sydney, 1969 (1919).

Martin, A. W., *Henry Parkes*, Melbourne University Press, Melbourne, 1980.

Martin, G. (ed.), *The Botany Bay Debate*, University of Queensland Press, St Lucia, 1974.

Matthews, J. J., *Good and Mad Women*, Allen & Unwin, Sydney, 1984.

Mead, C., 'Tough but Fair: Some Practices of Imprisonment in New South Wales 1866–1914', *Journal of the Royal Australian Historical Society*, vol. 77, no. 3, December 1991, pp. 57–79.

Meredith, D., 'Full circle? Contemporary Views on Transportation', in S. Nicholas (ed.), *Convict Workers: Re-interpreting Australia's Past*, Cambridge University Press, Melbourne, 1988, pp. 14–24.

Morris, N., *The Habitual Criminal*, Longmans Green & Co., London, 1951.

—— 'The Contemporary Prison: 1965–Present', in N. Morris & D. J. Rothman (eds), *The Oxford History of the Prison: The Practice of Punishment in Western Society*, Oxford University Press, Oxford, 1995.

Morris, N. & Howard, C., *Studies in Criminal Law*, Clarendon Press, Oxford, 1964.

Morris, N. & Rothman, D. J. (eds), *The Oxford History of the Prison: The Practice of Punishment in Western Society*, Oxford University Press, Oxford, 1995.

Mukherjee, S., Scandia, A., Dagger, D., & Matthews, W., *Source Book of Australian Criminal and Social Statistics 1804–1988*, Australian Institute of Criminology, Canberra, 1988.

National Council of Women, Report of the Sub-Committee of the National Council of Women of Victoria, Regarding Appointment of Police Matrons in City and Suburban Lock-Ups, 1902, in the possession of the Mitchell Library, Sydney.

Neal, D. J., 'Free Society, Penal Colony, Slave Society, Prison?' *Historical Studies*, no. 89, October 1987, pp. 497–518.

—— *The Rule of Law in a Penal Colony: Law and Power in Early New South Wales*, Cambridge University Press, Melbourne, 1991.

New South Wales, Parliament, *Report of the Select Committee on Secondary Punishment*, NSW Parliamentary Papers, Sydney 1857.

—— *Report of the Select Committee on the Public Prisons in Sydney and Cumberland*, NSW Parliamentary Papers, Sydney, 1861.

—— *Report of the Berrima Gaol Inquiry Commission*, NSW Parliamentary Papers, Sydney, 1878–79.

—— *Report by the Comptroller-General of Prisons on Prisons, Reformatories, and Asylums and other Institutions Recently Visited by Him, in Europe and America*, NSW Parliamentary Papers, Sydney, 1904.

—— *Report by W. J. McKell on the Borstal System (Great Britain) for the Rehabilitation of Young Offenders*, NSW Parliamentary Papers, Sydney, 1945.

—— *Report of the Royal Commission into New South Wales Prisons (Nagle Commission)*, NSW Parliamentary Papers, Sydney, 1976–77–78.

New South Wales Task Force on Women in Prison, *Report*, NSW Government Printer, Sydney, 1985.

Newcombe, L., *Inside Out*, Angus & Robertson, Sydney, 1979.

Nicholas, S. (ed.), *Convict Workers: Re-interpreting Australia's Past*, Cambridge University Press, Melbourne, 1988.

Nicholas, S. & Shergold, P. R., 'The Convict Period', in J. Jupp (ed.), *The Australian People: An Encyclopedia of the Nation, its People and their Origins*, Angus & Robertson, Sydney, 1988.

Nye, R. A., *Crime, Madness and Politics in Modern France: The Concept of National Decline*, Princeton University Press, Princeton, NJ, 1984.

O'Brien, P., *The Promise of Punishment*, Princeton University Press, Princeton, NJ, 1982.

O'Malley, P., 'Post-Social Criminologies: Some Implications of Current Political Trends for Criminological Theory and Practice', *Current Issues in Criminal Justice*, vol. 8, no. 1, 1996, pp. 26–38.

Oxley, D., 'Gendered Images and Realities', *Australian and New Zealand Journal of Criminology*, vol. 24, no. 2, July 1991, pp. 83–98.

—— *Convict Maids: The Forced Migration of Women to Australia*, Cambridge University Press, Melbourne, 1996.

Palmegiano, E., *Crime in Victorian Britain: An Annotated Bibliography from Nineteenth-Century British Magazines*, Greenwood Press, London, 1993.

Peers, J., 'The Tribe of Mary Jane Hicks: Imaging Women through the Mount Rennie Case 1886', *Australian Cultural History: Crimes and Trials*, vol. 12, 1993, pp. 127–44.

Petrass, I., 'Those who Trespass against Us': Women in Victorian Prisons, 1857 to 1873, BA (Hons) history thesis, Monash University, 1989.

Philips, D., 'Anatomy of a Rape Case 1888: Sex, Race, Violence and the Criminal Law in Victoria', in D. Philips & S. Davies (eds), *A Nation of Rogues? Crime, Law and Punishment in Colonial Australia*, Melbourne University Press, Melbourne, 1994.

Philips, D. & Davies, S. (eds), *A Nation of Rogues? Crime, Law and Punishment in Colonial Australia*, Melbourne University Press, Melbourne, 1994.

Pratt, J., *Punishment in a Perfect Society: The New Zealand Penal System, 1840–1939*, Victoria University Press, Wellington, 1992.

—— '"This is Not a Prison": Foucault, the Panopticon and Pentonville', *Social and Legal Studies*, vol. 2, 1993, pp. 373–95.

—— 'Dangerousness, Risk and Technologies of Power', *Australia and New Zealand Journal of Criminology*, vol. 28, no. 1, 1995, pp. 3–31.

Purdy, J., 'Postcolonialism: The Emperor's New Clothes', *Social and Legal Studies*, vol. 5, no. 3, 1996, pp. 405–26.

Queensland, Parliament, *Report of the Select Committee on Prison Discipline*, Queensland Parliamentary Papers, Brisbane, 1868.

—— *Report from the Board of Inquiry Appointed to Inquire into the General Management of the Gaols, Penal Establishments, and Lockups of the Colony of Queensland*, Queensland Parliamentary Papers, Brisbane, 1887.

—— *Report of Committee of Inquiry Regarding Sex Offences*, Queensland Parliamentary Papers, Brisbane, 1944.

Radzinowicz, L. & Hood, R. G., *The Emergence of Penal Policy in Victorian and Edwardian England,* Clarendon Press, Oxford, 1990.

Ramsland, J., *Children of the Backlanes*, NSW University Press, Sydney, 1986.

—— 'The Agricultural Colony at Mettray: A 19th Century Approach to the Institutionalisation of Delinquent Boys', *Melbourne Studies in Education*, vol. 29, 1987–88.

Ramsland, J. & Cartan, G. A., 'The Gosford Farm Home for Boys, Mt Penang, 1912–1940', *Journal of the Royal Australian Historical Society*, vol. 75, no. 1, June 1989, pp. 65–82.

'Reformer', *Crime and Criminals: Study of Defects in our Prison System*, [1923], a pamphlet derived from a series of articles first published in the *Sunday Times*, (Mitchell Library, Sydney).

Reynolds, H., 'That Hated Stain: The Aftermath of Transportation in Tasmania', *Historical Studies*, no. 53, 1969, pp. 19–31.

Ritchie, J., *Punishment and Profit*, Heinemann, Melbourne, 1970.

—— 'Towards Ending an Unclean Thing: The Molesworth Committee and the Abolition of Transportation to New South Wales, 1837–40', *Historical Studies*, no. 67, October 1976, pp. 144–64.

—— *Lachlan Macquarie: A Biography,* Melbourne University Press, Melbourne, 1986.

Robinson, P., *The Women of Botany Bay*, Macquarie Library, Sydney, 1988.

Robson, L., *The Convict Settlers of Australia: An Enquiry into the Origin and Character of the Convicts Transported to New South Wales and Van Diemen's Land 1787–1852,* Melbourne University Press, Melbourne, 1965.

—— *A History of Tasmania*, vol. 1, Oxford University Press, Melbourne, 1983.

Roe, M., *Nine Australian Progressives*, University of Queensland Press, St Lucia, 1984.

—— *Quest for Authority in Eastern Australia, 1835–1851*, Melbourne University Press, Melbourne, 1965

Ross, R., *Gaol Life: Prison Administration in NSW — The 'Humane' System Criticized*, self-published pamphlet, Sydney, 1908 (Mitchell Library, Sydney).

Rothman, D., 'Perfecting the Prison', in N. Morris & D. J. Rothman (eds), *The Oxford History of the Prison: The Practice of Punishment in Western Society*, Oxford University Press, Oxford, 1995.

Rowse, T., 'Strehlow's Strap: Functionalism and Historicism in Colonial Ethnography', in B. Attwood & J. Arnold (eds), *Power, Knowledge and Aborigines*, La Trobe University Press, Melbourne, 1992.

Royal Commission into Aboriginal Deaths in Custody, *National Report*, AGPS, Canberra, 1991.

—— *Report of the Inquiry into the Death of the Young Man who Died at Wujal Wujal on 29 March 1987*, AGPS, Canberra, 1991.

Royal Commission on Escapes from Hobart Gaol, Report, typescript in Tasmanian State Library, Hobart, 1935.

Rudé, G., *Protest and Punishment: The Story of the Social and Political Protesters Transported to Australia, 1788–1868*, Clarendon Press, Oxford, 1978.

Ryan, L., 'From Stridency to Silence: The Policing of Convict Women, 1803–1853', in D. Kirkby (ed.), *Sex, Power and Justice: Historical Perspectives on Law in Australia*, Oxford University Press, Melbourne, 1995.

Saleilles, R., *The Individualisation of Punishment*, Heinemann, London, 1911.

Salt, A., *These Outcast Women: The Parramatta Female Factory, 1821–1848*, Hale & Iremonger, Sydney, 1984.

Saunders, K., 'The Study of Domestic Violence in Colonial Queensland', *Australian Historical Studies*, no. 82, 1984, pp. 68–85.

Sernack, M., Penal Reform in New South Wales: Frederick William Neitenstein, 1896–1909, PhD thesis, University of Sydney, 1979.

Shaw, A. G. L., *Convicts and the Colonies*, Melbourne University Press, Melbourne, 1977 (1966).

Smith, B., *A Cargo of Women: Susannah Watson and the Convicts of the Princess Royal*, Sun Australia, Sydney, 1992 (1988).

Smith, G. T., 'Civilized People Don't Want to See That Kind of Thing: The Decline of Physical Punishment in London, 1760–1840', in C. Strange (ed.), *Qualities of Mercy: Justice, Punishment and Discretion*, UBC Press, Vancouver, 1996.

Snow, F. (ed.), *Forgotten Men* (pamphlet), Prison Reform Council of New South Wales, Sydney, 1947 (Mitchell Library, Sydney).

South Australia, Parliament, *Report of Stockade Inquiry Board*, South Australian Parliamentary Papers, Adelaide, 1869, no. 55.

—— *Report of Rev. John Pearce on Prison Reform, Great Britain and America*, South Australian Parliamentary Papers, Adelaide, 1912, no. 62.

Spierenburg, P., *The Prison Experience: Disciplinary Institutions and their Inmates in Early Modern Europe*, Rutgers University Press, New Brunswick, 1991.

Statham, P., 'Why Convicts I: An Economic Analysis of Colonial Attitudes to the Introduction of Convicts', *Studies in Western Australian History*, vol. 4, December 1981, pp. 1–10.

Strange, C., 'Discretionary Justice: Political Culture and the Death Penalty in New South Wales and Ontario, 1890–1920, in C. Strange (ed.), *Qualities of Mercy: Justice, Punishment and Discretion*, UBC Press, Vancouver, 1996.

—— (ed.), *Qualities of Mercy: Justice, Punishment and Discretion*, UBC Press, Vancouver, 1996.

Strong, C., *Prison Reform* (pamphlet), n.d. (reprinted from *Review of Reviews*), in the possession of the Mitchell Library, Sydney.

Sturma, M., 'Eye of the Beholder: The Stereotype of Women Convicts, 1788–1852', *Labour History*, no. 34, May 1978, pp. 3–10.

—— *Vice in a Vicious Society: Crime and Convicts in Mid-Nineteenth-Century New South Wales*, University of Queensland Press, St Lucia, 1983.

Summers, A., *Damned Whores and God's Police: The Colonization of Women in Australia*, Penguin Books, Melbourne, 1975.

Tasmania, Parliament, *Report on Criminality and Levels of Intelligence: Being Report of a Mental Survey of the Hobart Gaol*, Tasmanian Parliamentary Papers, Hobart, 1925–26.

—— *Report of the Parliamentary Standing Committee on Public Works (Tasmania): New Gaol Proposal*, Tasmanian Parliamentary Papers, Hobart, 1935.

—— *Report of Board of Inquiry on Riot at Hobart Gaol*, Tasmanian Parliamentary Papers, Hobart, 1939.

—— *Report of the Royal Commission into Hobart Gaol*, Tasmanian Parliamentary Papers, Hobart, 1943.

Thomas, J. E. & Stewart, A., *Imprisonment in Western Australia: Evolution, Theory and Practice*, University of Western Australia Press, Perth, 1978.

Trollope, A., *Australia*, eds P. D. Edwards & R. B. Joyce, University of Queensland Press, St Lucia, 1967 (1873).

Turner, G., *National Fictions*, Allen & Unwin, Sydney, 1986.

Tyler, B., 'Penology on an Australian Frontier', *Journal of Northern Territory History*, vol. 4, 1993, pp. 23–35.

United Kingdom, Parliament, *Report from Select Committee on Transportation (1837–38)* (Molesworth Committee), British Parliamentary Papers, London, 1837–38, xxii.

—— *Report from the Select Committee on Prison Discipline*, British Parliamentary Papers, London, 1850, xvii.

—— *Report from Select Committee on Transportation*, British Parliamentary Papers, London, 1861, xiii

Victoria, Parliament, *Report from the Select Committee upon Penal Discipline*, Victorian Parliamentary Papers, Melbourne, 1856–7.

—— *Progress Report of the Royal Commission on Penal and Prison Discipline (Pentridge Penal Establishment)*, Victorian Parliamentary Papers, Melbourne, 1870, 2nd session.

—— *Report from the Royal Commission on Penal and Prison Discipline (No. 2) (Penal and Prison Discipline)*, Victorian Parliamentary Papers, Melbourne, 1871.

—— *Report of the Board Appointed to Enquire into the Outbreak of the Inmates . . . at Jika, on the 13th of March 1878*, Victorian Parliamentary Papers, Melbourne, 1878.

—— *Report of the Inspector-General on the New York State Reformatory at Elmira*, Victorian Parliamentary Papers, Melbourne, 1901, vol. 2.

—— *Report of the Inspector-General on Prison Systems of Europe and America*, Victorian Parliamentary Papers, Melbourne, 1901, vol. 2.

—— *Report of the Chairman, Indeterminate Sentences Board on Reformatory Prisons and Institutions in Europe and America*, Victorian Parliamentary Papers, Melbourne, 1910, vol. 3.

Vinson, T., *Wilful Obstruction: The Frustration of Prison Reform*, Methuen, Sydney, 1982.

Waite, W. G., 'From Penitentiary to Reformatory: Alexander Maconochie, Walter Crofton, Zebulon Brockway, and the Road to Prison Reform — New South Wales, Ireland, and Elmira, New York, 1840–70', *Criminal Justice History*, vol. 12, 1991, pp. 85–105.

Walker, D., 'Youth on Trial: The Mt Rennie Case', *Labour History*, no. 50, 1986, pp. 28–42.

Weidenhofer, M., *Port Arthur: A Place of Misery*, Oxford University Press, Melbourne, 1981.

Western Australia, Parliament, *Report of a Commission . . . to Inquire into the Treatment of Aboriginal Native Prisoners of the Crown in the Colony*, Western Australian Parliamentary Papers, Perth, 1884.

—— *Final Report of the Royal Commission on Fremantle Prison*, Western Australian Parliamentary Papers, Perth, 1899.

—— *Report from the Commission Appointed to Inquire into the Penal System in the Colony*, Western Australian Parliamentary Papers, Perth, 1899.

—— *Report of the Royal Commission on the Condition of the Natives* (W. E. Roth, Commissioner), Western Australian Parliamentary Papers, Perth, 1905, 2nd Session.

'Whipping as a Penal Sanction: Its Consideration in a Recent Case', *Australian and New Zealand Journal of Criminology*, vol. 1, no. 1, March 1968, pp. 10–25.

Wiener, M. J., *Reconstructing the Criminal: Culture, Law, and Policy in England, 1830–1914*, Cambridge University Press, Cambridge, 1990.

Wilkes, G., *A Dictionary of Australian Colloquialisms*, Sydney University Press, Sydney, 1978.

Wood, G. A., 'Convicts', *Journal of the Royal Australian Historical Society*, vol. 8, no. 4, 1922, pp. 177–208.

Zdenkowski, G., 'Judicial Intervention in Prisons', *Monash University Law Review*, vol. 6, 1980, pp. 294–330

—— 'Review of Disciplinary Proceedings in Australian Prisons', *Criminal Law Journal*, vol. 7, 1983, pp. 3–43.

Zdenkowski, G. & Brown, D., *The Prison Struggle: Changing Australia's Penal System*, Penguin Books, Melbourne, 1982.

Zedner, L., *Women, Crime and Custody in Victorian England*, Clarendon Press, Oxford, 1991.

—— 'Wayward Sisters', in N. Morris & D. J. Rothman (eds), *The Oxford History of the Prison: The Practice of Punishment in Western Society*, Oxford University Press, Oxford, 1995.

INDEX